CONSPIRACY THEORY AND AMERICAN FOREIGN POLICY

MANCHESTER
1824

Manchester University Press

New Approaches to Conflict Analysis

Series editors: Peter Lawler and Emmanuel Pierre Guittet, School of Social Sciences, University of Manchester

Until recently, the study of conflict and conflict resolution remained comparatively immune to broad developments in social and political theory. When the changing nature and locus of large-scale conflict in the post-Cold War era is also taken into account, the case for a reconsideration of the fundamentals of conflict analysis and conflict resolution becomes all the more stark.

New Approaches to Conflict Analysis promotes the development of new theoretical insights and their application to concrete cases of large-scale conflict, broadly defined. The series intends not to ignore established approaches to conflict analysis and conflict resolution, but to contribute to the reconstruction of the field through a dialogue between orthodoxy and its contemporary critics. Equally, the series reflects the contemporary porosity of intellectual borderlines rather than simply perpetuating rigid boundaries around the study of conflict and peace. *New Approaches to Conflict Analysis* seeks to uphold the normative commitment of the field's founders yet also recognises that the moral impulse to research is properly part of its subject matter. To these ends, the series is comprised of the highest quality work of scholars drawn from throughout the international academic community, and from a wide range of disciplines within the social sciences.

Conspiracy theory and American foreign policy

Tim Aistrope

Manchester University Press

The right of Tim Aistrope to be identified as the author of this work has been asserted by him in accordance with the Copyright, Designs and Patents Act 1988.

Published by Manchester University Press
Altrincham Street, Manchester M1 7JA

www.manchesteruniversitypress.co.uk

British Library Cataloguing-in-Publication Data
A catalogue record for this book is available from the British Library

Library of Congress Cataloging-in-Publication Data applied for

ISBN   978 0 7190 9919 9   hardback

First published 2016

The publisher has no responsibility for the persistence or accuracy of URLs for any external or third-party internet websites referred to in this book, and does not guarantee that any content on such websites is, or will remain, accurate or appropriate.

Typeset
by Toppan Best-set Premedia Limited
Printed in Great Britain
by CPI Group (UK) Ltd, Croydon CR0 4YY

For Camille

CONTENTS

LIST OF ILLUSTRATIONS

ACKNOWLEDGEMENTS

This book has benefited from the wisdom and generosity of many fine people. First, it would never have been written without the guidance of Roland Bleiker. An outstanding mentor and scholar, I owe him a great debt of gratitude for his dedication to this project. I also want to thank Martin Weber for his many hours of provocative conversation, which pushed me out of my comfort zone and into new territory. More broadly, Jim George gave me the confidence to engage with international politics in the way I have, and his influence is everywhere in the pages that follow.

Special thanks go to the numerous scholars and friends who have read drafts and added their perspective. In particular, I want to thank Rob Cameron, Mark Chou, Luke Hennessy, Emma Hutchison, Nico Taylor, Jan Fadnes, Mike Spann, Ben Walter, Connie Duncombe, George Karavas, Ange Setterland, Jess Gifkins, Caitlin Sparks, Samid Suliman, John De Bhal, Shannon Brincat, Emily Tannock, Kamil Shah, Seb Kempf, Andrew Philips, Tim Dunne and Richard Devetak. I am grateful to the School of Political Science and International Studies at the University of Queensland for its support and for the vibrant intellectual atmosphere that it facilitates, not least through the visiting scholar programme and weekly seminar series. Visits from David Campbell, Siba Grovogui, James Der Derian and Nita Crawford were all important for the development of this work.

I also want to acknowledge valuable reviews from Richard Jackson and Anthony Burke on the doctoral thesis the book is based on, as well as the direction of three anonymous reviewers at later stages of manuscript development. I am also grateful for the valuable guidance provided by Tony Mason at Manchester University Press.

Finally, I want to thank my family. Mum and Dad have been an enduring source of encouragement across my unlikely transition from professional rugby player to international relations scholar. The Serisier clan have welcomed me in and made my causes their own. Most important of all, I want to thank my wonderful wife, Camille, without whose love and inspiration none of this would have been possible.

Introduction

Conspiracy theories exist in a world of myth, where imaginations run wild, fears trump facts, and evidence is ignored. As a superpower, the United States is often cast as a villain in these dramas. (United States State Department)[1]

In times of terror, when everyone is something of a conspirator, everyone will be in a situation where he has to play detective. (Walter Benjamin, 1938)[2]

Conspiracies abound. States plot in secret, together and against each other. Intelligence agencies operate covert programs of surveillance, rendition and assassination on a global scale. Terrorist organisations are, by their very nature, conspiratorial. This is one reason why the threat of conspiracies has often loomed large in foreign policy discourses. Yet allegations about the secret operation of international political power are regularly thought of as paranoid. Of all the ways an idea can be discredited, the label 'conspiracy' ranks among the most effective. Images of delusion and irrationality come thick and fast. Which conspiracies are real? Which allegations are paranoid? And who decides? These questions are particularly acute since the opaque, covert, self-interested conditions of international politics make conspiracies highly conceivable – a dynamic amplified in recent times by revelations from Wikileaks and Edward Snowden about the machinations of America's national security state.

This book examines the relationship between secrecy, power and interpretation around international political controversy, where foreign policy orthodoxies come up hard against alternative interpretations. It does so in the context of American foreign policy during the War on Terror, a conflict characterised by shadowy networks, secret plots and ambiguous motives.[3] Its political context was the subterranean world of CIA operations, the murky history of the mujahideen, and the realpolitik imperatives of American power in the Middle East.[4] The terrifying spectacle of terrorist attacks implied unseen causal logics that would explain the seemingly inexplicable, if only they could be uncovered. Secrecy, as Guy Debord has noted, is intrinsic to the spectacular, and the spectacular is itself a central site where the secrecy all around us comes in to view.[5] Spectacular events draw attention and demand explanation – they focus the mind on cause and effect, on the deeper forces behind the scene.

1

How did 9/11 happen? Who was responsible? For many people, the answers to these questions lay below the surface – in unfamiliar beliefs, experiences and histories. Under these circumstances, a range of scholars from disciplines as varied as neuroscience and cultural studies have examined the apparent prolif-eration of paranoia around 9/11, focusing mainly on the activism of organisa-tions like the 9/11 Truth Movement, a group who allege that elements of the United States (US) government organised or were complicit in the terrorist attacks.[6]

This book adds a new dimension to the debate by examining what I coin the 'Arab-Muslim paranoia narrative': the view that Arab-Muslim resentment towards America was provoked by a conspiratorial perception of American power in the Middle East. In the wake of 9/11, the problem of Arab-Muslim conspiracy theories was initially identified by prominent foreign policy commen-tators, who pointed to an Arab-Muslim culture of blame as an important cul-tural driver of terrorism. Conspiracy theories about American power were said to be fuelling Arab-Muslim anger towards America; that this anger had moti-vated Al-Qaeda's attacks; and that it continued to provide Al-Qaeda with moral support and a ready stream of recruits. Here is Thomas Friedman in the *New York Times*:

> I'm glad that the FBI agents are banging away at all the missed signals that might have tipped us off to 9/11, but we need to remember something: not all signals for 9/11 were hidden. Many were out there in public, in the form of hate speech and conspiracy theories directed at America and preached in mosques and religious schools throughout the Muslim world. If we are intent on preventing the next 9/11, we need to do more than just spy on our enemies better in secret. We need to take on their ideals in public.[7]

Framed like this, the connection between Arab-Muslim anti-Americanism and conspiracy theory became a matter of national security. According to the US National Security Strategy (NSS) 2006,

> terrorism springs from ... subcultures of conspiracy and misinformation. Terrorists recruit most effectively from populations whose information about the world is con-taminated by falsehoods and corrupted by conspiracy theories. The distortions keep alive grievances and filter out facts that would challenge popular prejudices and self-serving propaganda.[8]

This Arab-Muslim paranoia narrative subsequently made its way into numerous US government policy documents and initiatives advancing a War of Ideas strat-egy aimed at winning the 'hearts and minds' of Arab-Muslims.[9]

The post-9/11 concern about the national security implications of Arab-Muslim conspiracy theories is particularly interesting since the conceptual form and character of 'conspiracy theory' is so contested. A common-sense understanding does pervade American political discourse: a conspiracy theory is usually defined as 'a belief that an unpleasant event or situation is the result of a secret plan made by powerful people'.[10] This definition exists within a broader set of associations about the improbability of this kind of explanation. First set out by Richard Hofstadter in his paradigmatic essay 'The Paranoid Style in American Politics', here conspiracy theories are understood to be delusional beliefs produced by irrational individuals on the political fringe.[11]

Yet conceptual ambiguity around conspiracy theory is suggested by the fact that actual conspiracies are alleged quite regularly by figures of political authority. For instance, there are strong similarities – in terms of narrative structure and logic – between the claim that 9/11 was planned and carried out through a terrorist conspiracy and the claim that 9/11 was carried out by elements of the US government.[12] Indeed, David Ray Griffin, a key proponent of the later claim, points out that there are at least two conspiracy theories about 9/11: the official and the unofficial one.[13] While the comparison is no doubt presumptuous, it highlights the key tension that attends conspiracy theory as a category of analysis: what are the definitive properties that render one conspiracy allegation plausible and another paranoid?

This definitional problem is captured in Daniel Pipes's assertion that Arab-Muslim conspiracy theories are just 'fears of non-existent conspiracies'.[14] But Pipes never sets out a systematic schema for distinguishing *actual* conspiracies from *non-existent* conspiracies, which leaves open the possibility of prejudgement and inconsistency. Recent work in the field of applied philosophy has made a more rigorous effort to make this differentiation.[15] Brian Keeley, for instance, provides that 'unwarranted conspiracy theories run counter to the official account, present conspiracies as nefarious, tie together apparently unrelated events, and make use of "errant data"'.[16] Whatever the intuitive appeal of this definition, on reflection, Keeley's first three clauses ignore the many historical examples of *actual* conspiracies that seemed unlikely, contradicted the official account, and were illegal or otherwise unsupportable – for instance the many cases of American involvement in the covert overthrow of foreign governments;[17] the Watergate Scandal;[18] or the Tuskegee syphilis experiments.[19] Moreover, taken in isolation, the 'errant data' clause tends to undermine 'conspiracy theory' as a special category, since the validity of evidence is the main criteria for judging any claim at all.[20] Ultimately, Keeley concludes that there is nothing analytical that can help distinguish between conspiracy theories we should write off and conspiracy theories we should take seriously.[21]

The point here is that explaining precisely what counts as a conspiracy theory is a contentious moment in scholarly debates.[22] Indeed, a growing literature calls into question the conceptual usefulness of the term, pointing to the power relations implicit in the identification of conspiracy theories, which often manifests in the intimation of psycho-pathological paranoia, or insisting that conspiracy narratives be judged alongside any other claim.[23] At the very least, there is much to suggest that, in the common-sense view, conspiracy theory is like pornography in Justice Porter Stewart's notorious definition: 'You know it when you see it.'[24] In this sense, the identification of conspiracy theories can be thought of as both intuitive and contextual. My own description of post-9/11 concerns about the problem of Arab-Muslim conspiracy theories as the 'Arab-Muslim paranoia narrative' deliberately highlights the casual interchange between terms like conspiracy theory, paranoia, misinformation, irrationality and delusion made possible by this definitional ambiguity.

It is especially curious, then, that a concern with conspiracy theory, a term with such contentious definitional parameters and loaded with connotations of illegitimacy, should appear in key national security documents such as the NSS 2006 or in US State Department public diplomacy programs aimed at quelling anti-Americanism. This is particularly the case since the endemic secrecy, suspicion and self-interest often associated with international politics seems to set up a dynamic whereby actual conspiracies are eminently plausible.[25]

Conspiracy and legitimacy

Instead of taking 'conspiracy theory' at face value, as a neutral description of a pre-existing phenomenon with identifiable properties, I take seriously the ambiguity, intuition and political context animating the identification of conspiracy theories.[26] One way to think about this shift in focus is to consider conspiracy theory as a *label* that does political work on the subjects and claims it is applied to. It is obvious enough that referring to a claim as a conspiracy theory situates it as somehow problematic.[27] Moreover, this categorisation often entails an *ad hominem* effect, intimating a social-psychological failure in conspiracy theorists that places their views beyond consideration. But language is not a free-floating rhetoric that is simply deployed instrumentally by actors for strategic ends. Language provides the field of possibility in which actors emerge, make decisions and give meaning to the world they encounter. Understood like this, the term 'conspiracy theory' is inseparable from, and indicative of, power relations between specific actors in a particular political landscape – relations that are both delegitimising and productive. For instance, 'conspiracy theory' can be delegitimising of views that do not fall within an acceptable range of political positions or legitimate modes of inquiry, and productive of a political space where normal politics can occur, secured by contrast with the irrational views of conspiracy theorists. As Jack Bratich explains incisively,

> They [conspiracy theories] are portals into the contexts that problematise them. The panics surrounding conspiracy theories demonstrate that trust, truth, and rationality are at the heart of the current political context. In their prominence as objects

of public concern, conspiracy theories provide insights into the current configuration of political rationality.[28]

The point here is that conspiracy theories are more than a category of claims about the secret operation of political power: they indicate something about the political institutions and actors that worry about them and the political landscape in which they emerge as subjects of concern.

Why study the link between Arab-Muslim conspiracy theories and anti-Americanism after 9/11? It is important to recognise at the outset that the study of the Arab-Muslim paranoia narrative is illustrative of a particular sort of foreign policy language that tends to place the legitimacy of subjects or claims in question. Connotations of illegitimacy attend terms like 'radical', 'extremist' or 'terrorist'. More broadly, such connotations are embedded in entire frames of reference, like the prevailing Western development discourse that contrasts a modern Western world with a pre-modern 'third world', full of backwards traditions and attitudes, which are thought to stand in the way of modernisation.[29] This book takes the post-9/11 concern with Arab-Muslim conspiracy theories as an opportunity to examine the way some foreign policy actors and orthodoxies are secured and other actors and views rendered incredible.

The War on Terror serves this purpose well. Secrecy, intrigue and controversy were inescapably implicated in its production. From its opening day, back to its origins, and on through its prosecution, this conflict was both controversial and conspiratorial to the core.[30] The status of 9/11 as an 'event' is also important.[31] Events stand out from the normal course of history; they exceed existing frames of reference and change the world irrevocably.[32] If history is the tale of momentous events, then 9/11 is the event of our time.[33] Like all events, its meaning emerged in and through narratives: cultural, political and moral, drawn together into a meaningful story of terrorism, its origins and implications.[34] Analysing this formation process provides a portal into the power and influence of particular discourses and dispositions as they were brought to bear on the confusion and ambiguity of 9/11.[35]

The peculiarity of the connection between the Arab-Muslim paranoia narrative and US national security makes this portal all the more useful. The contention and negative connotations surrounding conspiracy theory stand in contrast with the apparently sober practices of 'high politics'. The language of foreign policy is carefully crafted.[36] Rarely a word is uttered that is unintentional. Under these circumstances, examining the Arab-Muslim paranoia narrative provides an opportunity to disclose the unarticulated, unthinking, latent meanings that circulated in America's War on Terror discourse around the issue of Arab-Muslim anti-Americanism.

The book asks: 'What role did the Arab-Muslim paranoia narrative play in American foreign policy after 9/11?' I answer this question by analysing two areas of foreign policy discourse. In the first case study I analyse expert foreign policy commentary on terrorism over the year after 9/11. In the second case study I analyse Bush Administration counter-terrorism policy, laid out in speeches and strategic documents like NSS 2006, as well as the implementation of that policy in State Department public diplomacy programs focused on 'debunking' anti-American misinformation.

The book's central argument is that the Arab-Muslim paranoia narrative enacted a potent delegitimising effect that deterred criticism of American foreign policy and secured an image of America as benign and misunderstood in its international political interactions. Its power and significance was rooted in deep cultural scripts embedded in American political culture around populism and dissent, folded together with a historically pervasive orientalist narrative framing the American encounter with the Middle East. I show that this understanding of Arab-Muslim resentment towards America was inseparable from an unreflective reaffirmation of a particular American identity. Rather than rational policy analysis, careful calculation and the logic of consequences, the resurgence of powerful identity markers underpinned the production of legitimacy in the heartland of national security. Yet, while the Arab-Muslim paranoia narrative was delegitimising and self-affirming, in the practical context of the Bush Administration's War of Ideas it also had the capacity to provoke the destabilising conditions it sought to address, including resentful subjects, emerging again as paranoid Arab-Muslims through the same discursive framing. In this sense, the War of Ideas reproduced itself – sanctifying both a particular American foreign policy identity and a specific understanding of its Arab-Muslim other.

In the year after 9/11, concerns about the problem of Arab-Muslim conspiracy theories appeared in the writings of prominent foreign policy commentators, where they addressed the link between terrorism and anti-Americanism. I show that this Arab-Muslim paranoia narrative was part of a broader post-9/11 political landscape that contained multiple conspiracy narratives, including blowback accounts of US foreign policy in the Middle East that dwelt on covert operations and secret connections, and identitarian perspectives that emphasised the threat of diabolical terrorist masterminds with vast networks spanning the world's major cities. In doing so I elucidate what I refer to as a *conspiracy discourse*, consisting of competing conspiracy narratives that each made claims about the origins and implications of 9/11. Following Foucault's understanding of the way discourses are structured by unwritten rules and regularities that designate legitimacy/illegitimacy, my focus here is on the processes through which some narratives achieve standing and authority, while others are excluded from consideration.[37]

As explained, 'conspiracy theory' can be understood in this context as a potent discursive position, attaching associations of paranoia and irrationality to particular interpretations. Specifically, when foreign policy commentators identified the problem of Arab-Muslim conspiracy theories, readers were pointed away from the substance of claims and towards the deeper cognitive or social-psychological pathologies of the people making them. The political effect was to disqualify criticism of American foreign policy – both at home and abroad – and mark out the ground for legitimate interpretation of 9/11.

The same conspiracy discourse had moved to the heart of the Bush Administration's counter-terrorism strategy by 2005, where it fitted neatly with an approach that situated ideas as the instruments of more fundamental strategic objectives. Here the Arab-Muslim paranoia narrative became a *weapon* in a so-called War of Ideas between American liberal democracy and terrorist ideology, with the 'hearts and minds' of Arab-Muslim people the field of battle and the ultimate prize. My analysis indicates that the gap opened up between the language of liberal idealism and the conduct of the War on Terror produced the dynamic of hypocrisy and double-dealing often regarded as a major source of resentment towards America. I suggest that it should be no surprise if, in these circumstances of empty rhetoric and ulterior motives, Arab-Muslim people, and people generally, became suspicious of America's foreign policy, to the extent that they speculated about its actual aims. Here the suspicion of secret plots and plans is not some social-psychological or cognitive condition, but just the ordinary consequences of structural hypocrisy.

None of this is to deny that many interpretations of 9/11 forwarded by Arab-Muslim people were demonstrably false. Like interpretations of political events the world over, there was clearly a range of views. But the Arab-Muslim paranoia narrative was concerned with much more than the validity of specific claims. It was focused on the dysfunctional characteristics of undifferentiated Arab-Muslims, which were said to produce endemic paranoia. The point of my analysis is to examine the circumstances in which Arab-Muslim political culture came to be understood in these terms and to identify the political dynamics therein. I do not seek excuse acts of violence committed in the name of particular ideas: Al-Qaeda's terrorism was and remains unquestionably abhorrent. Instead, my aim is to open up space for a more self-reflective understanding of American foreign policy and a more subtle account of the resentment it has often engendered in the Arab-Muslim world.

More broadly, this book contributes a cultural perspective on the dynamics through which legitimacy and illegitimacy are produced in foreign policy discourse. This issue has often been approached in international relations from an identity politics perspective, which explains how group identity is secured and difference suppressed or demonised.[38] Terrorism scholars have also focused on the power dynamics at play in the production of academic and policy orthodoxy during the War on Terror.[39] My research builds on this work. But by examining conspiracy theory I capture the interaction between secrecy, power and interpretation in foreign policy, an area often overlooked in the existing literature.

The focus on conspiracy theory draws my analysis towards the 'strategies of deterrence and frames of containment' that congregate around foreign policy controversy, which provide powerful disincentives against critical engagement with elite power or dissent from a narrow range of acceptable views.[40] These dynamics were highly relevant in the wake of 9/11, when explaining the origins and motivations of the terrorist attacks was a crucial task for foreign policy commentators, government officials and everyday people the world over.

The book also contributes to a critical appraisal of US public diplomacy, the policy area dedicated to influencing the attitudes and opinions of foreign publics towards America. My analysis of the Bush administration's War of Ideas draws to the surface a broader set of issues, centred on the tension between the image of America projected by the US government and the substance of US foreign policy. Understanding this tension is particularly important as the US State Department continues to address online audiences through a range of new media technologies. My analysis points to some of the pitfalls and challenges that may accompany this ongoing e-diplomacy effort, particularly in the area of counter-radicalisation.

Finally, I add a new perspective to the literature on conspiracy theory. Scholarly interest in this issue has increased since the late 1990s, yet only a handful of book-length enquiries have looked at the international political dimension of this issue, despite the global proportions of many conspiracy narratives.[41] Moreover, whereas these few studies attempt to explain why conspiracy theories are endemic in particular cultures or extremist individuals, along with the consequences of this mode of thinking, I take seriously the ideological function of the Arab-Muslim paranoia narrative in American foreign policy discourse. At the same time, a larger body of research deals with conspiracy theory in American political culture and I draw many of the themes developed here into my foreign policy analysis. But my approach is grounded in the discipline of international relations and engages explicitly with its key concepts – for instance, sovereignty, national security, counter-terrorism and public diplomacy. The target of my examination is also more specific. Where the literature on conspiracy theory in American culture tends to provide a general account of the phenomenon, my analysis traces the Arab-Muslim paranoia narrative back to its cultural and conceptual roots in a post-war liberal understanding of populism and forward through foreign policy debates about the origins of 9/11 to the strategic heart of the Bush administration's War of Ideas. In doing so it provides a window into the ideological commitments of America's War on Terror discourse.

Chapter outline

The book is divided into two parts. Part I lays out the intellectual context and conceptual framework. The opening chapter examines the origins of the Arab-

Muslim paranoia narrative in American political culture. The historian Richard Hofstadter first established conspiracy theory as a subject of political concern in his account of the paranoid style, which I use as an entry point into the key themes animating the contemporary view. I then show how this view has been used to think about conspiracy culture abroad, and specifically in relation to the issue of Arab-Muslim conspiracy theories. Chapter 2 develops a framework for thinking about Arab-Muslim conspiracy theories after 9/11, drawing on post-colonial theory and a Foucauldian reading of the relationship between power and knowledge.

Part II uses a series of case studies to examine the Arab-Muslim paranoia narrative as it manifested during the War on Terror decade. Chapter 3 focuses on the way the paranoia narrative emerged in foreign policy commentary around the connection between terrorism and anti-Americanism. It shows how this narrative emerged in a broader political landscape woven through with conspiracy narratives, all vying for legitimacy and standing. I then use discourse analysis to examine excerpts from articles in *Foreign Affairs* and the *New York Times* (both prominent forums for expert foreign policy opinion) that are repre-sentative of this common paranoia/anti-Americanism association. I show how these texts work and the consequences of this for the way terrorism was understood.

The focus then moves from foreign policy commentary to actual policy making. Chapter 4 focuses on the role played by the Arab-Muslim paranoia narrative in the Bush Administration's War on Terror strategy as it shifted to address the ideological roots of terrorism. Termed the 'War of Ideas', this approach tied long-run success against Islamist terrorism to winning the 'hearts and minds' of Arab-Muslim populations. I examine the ideological function of the Arab-Muslim paranoia narrative in key strategic documents like the NSS 2006 and the National Strategy for Combating Terrorism 2006, as well as national security speeches from the US President and his National Security Advisors.

Chapter 5 traces the Arab-Muslim paranoia narrative into US State Depart-ment public diplomacy efforts that enacted the War of Ideas strategy. It focuses on the work of two State Department programs aimed at quelling anti-American misinformation online: the Counter-Misinformation Team, which 'debunked' conspiracy theories and misinformation through reports published on the State Department's website and distributed to US embassies; and the Digital Outreach Team, which employed a team of bloggers to engage directly with anti-American views expressed online in an attempt to set the record straight. My examination of the Digital Outreach Team shows how this counter-radicalisation effort has continued on into the Obama administration, which expanded and evolved US digital diplomacy efforts significantly. I begin now by introducing the prevailing view of conspiracy theory in foreign policy.

NOTES

1   Bureau of International Information Programs, US Department of State, 'Conspiracy Theories and Misinformation', Washington, DC. Available at www.america.gov/conspiracy_theories.html (accessed 5 January 2015).

2   W. Benjamin, cited in J. Der Derian, 'The War of Networks', *Theory & Event*, 5:4 (2002). Available at http://muse.jhu.edu/journals/theory_and_event/v005/5.4derderian.html (accessed 5 January 2015).

3   J. Bratich, 'Public Secrecy and Immanent Security', *Cultural Studies*, 20:4–5 (2006), pp. 494–499; and J. Der Derian, 'The War of Networks', *Theory & Event*, 5:4 (2002). Available at http://muse.jhu.edu/journals/theory_and_event/v005/5.4derderian.html (accessed 5 January 2015).

4   See for instance, J. Burke, *Al Qaeda: The True Story of Radical Islam* (London: Penguin, 2004); L. Wright, *The Looming Towers: Al Qaeda's Road to 9/11* (London: Penguin, 2006); M. Beardon, 'Afghanistan, Graveyard of Empires', *Foreign* Affairs, 80:6 (2001), pp. 17–30; P. Todd, J. Bloch and P. Fitzgerald, *Spies, Lies and the War on Terror* (London: Zed Books, 2009).

5   See G. Debord, *Comments of the Society of the Spectacle* (London: Verso, 2002), p. 12. See also, J. Bratich's insightful discussion of this theme in Bratich, 'Public Secrecy and Immanent Security', pp. 494–495.

6   J. Bratich gives a good summary of this fascination with 9/11 conspiracy theories in J. Bratich, *Conspiracy Panics: Political Rationality and Popular Culture* (New York: State University of New York Press, 2008), pp. 123–157. M. Fenster's analysis of the 9/11 Truth Movement is among the most incisive. See M. Fenster, *Conspiracy Theories: Secrecy and Power in American Culture* (Minneapolis: University of Minnesota Press, 2008), pp. 233–278.

7   T. Friedman, 'War of Ideas', *New York Times* (2 June 2002), p. 19.

8   The White House, *The National Security Strategy of the United States of America* (Washington DC: Government Printing Office, 2006), p. 10.

9   It is important to acknowledge that 'Arab-Muslim' and 'anti-Americanism' are exceptionally general terms. They reduce complexity and diversity into catch-all categories. I use such language with reference to a specific American foreign policy discourse that operated on these grounds. My mode of engagement is first and foremost immanent, so I retain this foreign policy terminology while showing at various points just how limiting it can be.

10 *Cambridge Dictionary Online*, available at http://dictionary.cambridge.org/dictionary/english-chinese-simplified/conspiracy-theory (accessed 24 February 2015).

11 The full version appears in R. Hofstadter, *The Paranoid Style and other Essays* (Cambridge: Harvard University Press), pp. 3–40. An abridged version appeared in *Harper's Magazine* in 1964. See R. Hofstadter, 'The Paranoid Style in American Politics', *Harper's Magazine* (November 1964), pp. 77–86.

12 Bratich, *Conspiracy Panics*, pp. 1–2.

13 D. R. Griffin, *Debunking 9/11 Debunking: An Answer to Popular Mechanics and Other Defenders of the Official Conspiracy Theory* (Petaluma, CA: Olive Branch Press, 2007).

14 D. Pipes, *The Hidden Hand: Middle East Fears of Conspiracy* (London: Macmillan, 1998), p. 1.

15 This work was undertaken by philosophers in the analytic tradition – a discipline noted for its attention to logic and precision in language. For a survey of the debate around conspiracy theory in philosophy see D. Coady, *Conspiracy Theories: The Philosophical Debate* (Aldershot, Hampshire: Ashgate, 2006).

16 C. Birchall, 'Conspiracy Theories and Academic Discourses: The Necessary Possibility of Popular (Over)Interpretation', *Continuum: Journal of Media & Cultural Studies*, 15:1 (2001), p. 68.

17 For a comprehensive account of covert US action abroad, see W. Blum, *Killing Hope: US Military and CIA Interventions Since WWII* (London: Zed Books, 2003).

18 See B. Woodward and K. Bernstein, *All the President's Men* (New York: Simon & Schuster, 1974).

19 V. Gamble, 'Under the Shadows of Tuskegee: African American Health Care', *American Journal of Public Health*, 87 (1997), pp. 1773–1778; and F. Gray, *The Tuskegee Syphilis Study* (Montgomery, AL: Newsouth Books, 1998).

20 G. Hustings and M. Orr, 'Dangerous Machinery: 'Conspiracy Theorist' as a Transpersonal Strategy of Exclusion', *Symbolic Interaction*, 30:2 (2007), p. 141.

21 B. Keeley, 'Of Conspiracy Theories', *The Journal of Philosophy*, 96:3 (1999), pp. 109–126. Lance De Haven-Smith provides a helpful summary and incisive discussion of contemporary definitions that attempt to deal with this issue while retaining conspiracy theory as a category of misguided belief. See L. De Haven Smith, *Conspiracy Theory in America* (Austin: University of Texas Press, 2013), pp. 36–41.

22 J. Dean, 'Declarations of Independence', in J. Dean (ed.), *Cultural Studies as Political Theory* (Ithaca: Cornell University Press, 2000), pp. 299–302; L. Jones, 'How do the American People Know? Embodying Post-9/11 Conspiracy Discourse', *GeoJournal*, 75 (2010), pp. 359–371; and D. Coady, 'Introduction: Conspiracy Theories', *Episteme: A Journal of Social Epistemology*, 4:2 (2007), pp. 131–134.

23 *Ibid.* Several scholars suggest that the conventional wisdom that conspiracy theories should be dismissed rather than investigated is misguided and limiting for democratic politics. See K. Goshorn, 'Strategies of Deterrence and frames of containment: On Critical Paranoia and Anti-conspiracy Discourse', *Theory & Event*, 4:3 (2000). Available at http://muse.jhu.edu/journals/theory_and_event/v004/4.3r_goshorn.html (accessed 5 January 2015); and C. Pidgen, 'Conspiracy Theories and the Conventional Wisdom', *The Journal of Philosophy*, 96:3 (1999), pp. 219–232.

24 J. Bratich uses the same reference to Stewart's view on pornography to great effect in his earlier problematisation of conspiracy theory. I reproduce it here because it captures evocatively the intuitive dimension of the common sense account. See Bratich, *Conspiracy Panics*, p. 2.

25 J. Der Derian, 'The CIA, Hollywood, and the Sovereign Conspiracy', in J. Der Derian (ed.), *Critical Practices in International Theory: Selected Essays* (New York: Routledge, 2009), pp. 167–189.

26 As Bratich notes, 'when it comes to conspiracy theory, many semiotically savvy analysts adhere to a reflectionist model of language. While other terms are afforded a deconstructive analysis, this one somehow escapes the linguistic turn, circulating in a world where language simply refers to already existing objects.' See Bratich, *Conspiracy Panics*, p. 2.

27 Kathryn Olmsted overcomes the definitional difficulties identified above by expanding conspiracy theory out to 'a proposal about a conspiracy that may or may not be true; it has yet to be proven'. While this approach is consistent and cogent – and Olmsted writes incisively about the relationship between power and interpretation in her wider study – it tends to downplay the power relations that circulate around the *term* 'conspiracy theory' as it operates in American political culture. See K. Olmsted, *Real Enemies: Conspiracy Theories and American Democracy, World War I to 9/11* (Oxford: Oxford University Press, 2009), p. 3.

28 Bratich, *Conspiracy Panics*, p. 19.

29 See R. Higgott, *Political Development Theory: The Contemporary Debate* (London, Taylor & Francis, 2005); and B. Hindess, 'The Past is Another Culture', *International Political Sociology*, 1:4 (2007), pp. 325–338.

30 Bratich, 'Public Secrecy and Immanent Security', pp. 493–511.

31 M. Fenster, *Conspiracy Theories*, pp. 233–278.
32 R. Devatak, 'After the Event: Don Dellilo's White Noise and September 11 Narratives', *Review of International Studies*, 35:4 (2009), pp. 791–198.
33 *Ibid.*, p. 791.
34 *Ibid.* On this issue see also D. Campbell, 'Time is Broken: The Return of the Past in Response to September 11', *Theory & Event*, 5:4 (2001). Available at http://muse.jhu.edu/journals/theory_and_event/v005/5.4campbell.html (accessed 5 January 2015); and R. Bleiker, 'Retracing and Redrawing the Boundaries of Events: Postmodern Interferences with International Theory', *Alternatives*, 23:4 (1998), pp. 471–497.
35 For comprehensive studies of the War on Terror discourse that do precisely this see: R. Jackson, *Writing the War on Terror: Language, Politics and Counterterrorism* (Manchester: Manchester University Press, 2005); S. Silberstein, *War of World: Language and Politics After 9/11* (London: Routledge, 2002); R. Jackson, 'Constructing Enemies: 'Islamic Terrorism' in Political and Academic Discourse', *Government and Opposition*, 42:3 (2007), pp. 394–426; R. Jackson, 'Knowledge, Power and Politics in the Study of Political Terrorism', in R. Jackson, M. B. Smyth and J. Gunning, *Critical Terrorism Studies: A New Agenda* (Hoboken: Taylor & Francis, 2009); and S. Croft, *Culture, Crisis and America's War on Terror* (Cambridge: Cambridge University Press, 2006).
36 Many scholars have shown that sites of peculiarity, disjunction and change can provide a window into the underlying preoccupations of institutions and discursive regimes. See, for instance, I. Shapiro, 'Problems, Methods, Theories: What's Wrong with Political Science and What to do about it', in S. K. White and J. D. Moon (eds), *What is Political Theory* (London: SAGE, 2004), pp. 193–216.
37 M. Foucault, *The Archeology of Knowledge* (New York: Routledge, 2002). I draw a distinction between narrative and discourse, which turns on the knowledge producing function of the latter. While a discourse can include many narratives – stories that connect facts, events and circumstances in a coherent and meaningful way – some narratives are legitimised and others marginalised across a spectrum of discursive positions that collectively constitute a discourse. Claire Birchall's work on popular culture (including conspiracy theory) as a knowledge producing discourse is an excellent example of the Foucauldian inspired approach I have in mind. See C. Birchall, *Knowledge Goes Pop: From Conspiracy Theory To Gossip* (London: Berg Publishers, 2006).
38 See, for instance, D. Campbell, *Writing Security: United States Foreign Policy and the Politics of Identity* (Manchester: Manchester University Press, 1998); and A. Burke, *Fear of Security: Australia's Invasion Anxiety* (Melbourne: Cambridge University Press, 2008). For a good summary of identity politics in international relations see I. Neumann, 'Self and Other in International Relations', *European Journal of International Relations*, 2:2 (1996), pp. 138–174.
39 See, for instance, R. Jackson, 'The Ghosts of State Terror: Knowledge, Politics and Terrorism Studies', *Critical Studies on Terrorism*, 1:3 (2009), p. 388; Jackson, 'The Ghosts of State Terror', pp. 72–29; and Jackson, 'Constructing Enemies', pp. 421–422.
40 This phrase is the title of Keith Goshorn's incisive review of the literature on conspiracy theory. See Goshorn, 'Strategies of Deterrence and Frames of Containment'.
41 These are R. S. Robins and J. M. Post, *Political Paranoia: The Psychopolitics of Hatred* (New Haven: Yale University Press: 1997); D. Pipes, *The Hidden Hand: Middle East Fears of Conspiracy* (New York: St Martin's Press, 1996); and M. Gray, *Conspiracy Theories in the Arab Muslim World* (London: Routledge, 2010).

Part I

Conceptualising conspiracy theory

The paranoid style in international politics

WHILE PARANOID politics has received significant attention as a characteristic of American popular culture, only a handful of scholars have examined its international political dimensions. This gap is particularly notable since the paranoid psychology of enemy leaders and the conspiracy mindedness of regional cultures are regular subjects of foreign policy commentary in the American media. In these accounts irrational views feed into political instability and stoke anti-Western sentiment. This excerpt from a *New York Times* forum about the possibility of democracy in the Middle East gives a sense of the view:

> When Americans visit the Middle East, or the broader Islamic world, they are often struck by the vitality of the public interest and discussion about world affairs. Less comfortably, they often find the public to be cynical about Western interests, and quick to believe that shadowy groups control the world: that a cabal of Jews was responsible for 9/11 or that the CIA instigated the Arab Spring for oil access.[1]

While Arab-Muslim paranoia gained prominence after 9/11 as an explanation for resentment towards America, it is important to recognise that the identification of the same social-psychological tendencies in other cultures is a recurring theme in the American political imaginary and media landscape. Take, for instance, an account of popular paranoia in Pakistan about bombings that followed the death of Osama bin Laden:

> Lawmakers, media pundits, retired generals, and even government officials often hint at suspicions of a 'foreign hand' in the violence ... Aired on television talk shows and in the newspapers, conspiracy theories are everywhere underscoring the challenge facing the United States as it seeks to convince Pakistan's overwhelmingly anti-American population that it faces a shared enemy in the Taliban.[2]

This excerpt fits comfortably within a genre of foreign affairs commentary that situates conspiracy thinking as endemic not just in Pakistan or the Arab-Muslim world, but also in a range of different cultural settings like, for instance, Iran,[3] Turkey[4] and Russia.[5]

This chapter aims to situate the Arab-Muslim paranoia narrative in relation to a common-sense understanding of conspiracy theory pervasive in American culture. A crucial starting point here is Richard Hofstadter's paradigmatic account of 'The Paranoid Style in American Politics', which locates conspiracy theories on the periphery of pluralistic American democracy as the irrational pathology of angry extremists, and contrasts it with a rational political centre where sensible politics occurs. Although Hofstadter wrote this seminal piece in 1964, it is difficult to overestimate its traction and influence on both popular and scholarly perspectives. Indeed, the 'paranoid style' is still deployed by political commentators of all stripes to frame, for instance, the 9/11 Truth Movement,[6] Tea Party Republicans,[7] resurgent right-wing extremists,[8] the Occupy Wall Street movement[9] and the anti-war left.[10] Similarly, in political science Hofstadter has regularly provided the key conceptual materials for considerations of the issue.[11]

This resonance is in large part due to the fact that Hofstadter's account taps into, and deploys, many of the most common conceptual features of post-war liberal pluralism, the pervasive ideology of America's political class, which abhorred populism and focused on the mediation of competing interests through bargain and compromise.[12] Indeed, it is important to understand that post-war liberalism was involved in the production of a particular political order and the management of dissent in that context. In this same vein, post-war liberals situated America as a moderate democracy – pragmatic, centrist and non-ideological – in contrast to the radical politics sweeping the post-war world. The crucial point here is that the paranoid style can be understood as part of a broader liberal discourse involved in dampening down populism and buttressing the political status quo.

When foreign affairs commentators identify paranoid conspiracy theories in the international context, they regularly locate them not just on the political fringes of liberal democracies, but also on the periphery of international power and legitimacy in a western geopolitical world-view. Paranoia moves to the heart of political life in the mentality of rogue leaders, as well as the everyday political cultures of unstable regions. This reflects the extrapolation of Hofstadter's framework on to the world at large. Like populism on the margins of Western democracy, conspiracy theory is thought to be a potent force on the international periphery from the point of view of these commentators.

This underlying structure, I argue, indicates a powerful dynamic of ideological reproduction embedded in the Arab-Muslim paranoia narrative, which delegitimises Arab-Muslims and affirms a particular Western liberal identity. I show how the paranoid style framework is reinforced by an influential orientalist narrative prominently forwarded by Bernard Lewis and likeminded Arabist scholars, which situates Arab-Muslim culture as fundamentally anti-modernist and points to a culture of bitterness, self-denial and blame as an explanation for resentment towards the West. Like post-war liberal orthodoxy secured by contrast with the irrational views of alienated extremists, here the image of liberal modernity is secured by contrast with the irrational views of backwards Arab-Muslims. The Arab-Muslim paranoia narrative, then, can be understood in terms of a powerful liberal discourse in American political culture, rather than a simple description of the way Arab-Muslim people think about the world.

The chapter begins by examining the intellectual origins and cultural resonance of paranoia in American political culture. It focuses on Hofstadter's paranoid style paradigm, connecting it with a specific historical and intellectual context, then pointing to its ideological function in that setting.[13] The second section shows how this common-sense account has been extrapolated in interpretations of international politics, emphasising the persistence of a centre/periphery structure. The third section connects the paranoid style paradigm to an orientalist narrative, showing how together they draw out and reinforce negative connotations around populism embedded in the liberal imaginary. The chapter ends by focusing on the way this narrative carries connotations of psychological dysfunction that overlap and work in tandem with the broader themes of alienation and cultural malaise at play in the Arab-Muslim paranoia narrative.

The 'paranoid style' and political culture

Richard Hofstadter's account of political paranoia is a crucial starting point for any examination of this issue in American political discourse. Though he had relatively little to say about international politics, the academic and popular understanding of paranoia pervasive in America is heavily indebted to his conceptualisation.[14] Hofstadter's analysis exceeded the narrow disciplinary confines of academic history, capturing the imagination of scholars and commentators operating within a similar conceptual framework and a broader public confronted by radicalism abroad and extremism on the far right of American politics.[15] In order to understand the intellectual and cultural connotation evoked by the Arab-Muslim paranoia narrative, it is important to situate Hofstadter's work in a wider political and historical setting – in a particular account of populism and in the cultural imperatives of post-war America.

Hofstadter's account of political paranoia was penned in response to the rise of radical right-wing politics in the post-war decades, epitomised by McCarthyism and, later, the Goldwater presidential campaign.[16] Hofstadter related the rise of the radical right to a broader tradition of political extremism recurring throughout American history. His wide-ranging historical analysis drew together notable instances of populist conspiracy fears about freemasons, the Illuminati, the Catholic church, international bankers and communism, not to mention the apocalyptic 'end of days' fervour that had accompanied the turn of the millennium, and situated them as manifestations of what he coined the 'paranoid style'.[17] In this conceptualisation, conspiracy theory emanates from extremist minorities disconnected from the political mainstream – prejudiced, frustrated, alienated and, in the end, *pathological*.[18] According to Hofstadter, this mode of understanding – a form of status anxiety – is first and foremost a defensive mechanism that, in the past, had been deployed to ward off threats to a particular way of life thought to be under attack.[19] In its more modern manifestations a similar dynamic was obvious, though proponents were less defensive of a way of life than angry about its loss.[20] In the case of the right-wing movement of his day, Hofstadter thought that this anxiety arose from a sense that traditional America had been taken away: its virtues undermined by cosmopolitan intellectuals, its independence ruined by the welfare state and communist subversives.[21] The 'paranoid style', then, offers an explanation for such circumstances and a way of exerting some cognitive control over them by allocating blame to clearly defined enemies, charting the lines of causal power, and setting out concrete targets for opposition.[22] And this occurs in epic terms:

> The enemy is clearly delineated: he is the perfect model of malice, a kind of amoral superman – sinister, ubiquitous, powerful, cruel, sensual, luxury loving. Unlike the rest of us, the enemy is not caught in the toils of the vast mechanisms of history, himself a victim of the past, his desires, his limitations. He wills, indeed he manufactures, the very mechanisms of history, or tries to deflect the normal course of history in an evil way. He makes crises, he starts runs on banks, causes depressions, manufactures disasters, and then enjoys and profits from the misery he has produced. The paranoid's interpretation is distinctly personal: decisive events are not taken as part of the stream of history, but as the consequence of someone's will.[23]

The significance of this phenomenon for Hofstadter lay in the danger it posed for a stable political community.[24] While the truly paranoid operate on the margins, their pathology could be infectious for the body politic in times of economic or social hardship.[25] Indeed, the phenomenon was only worth studying because, when populist movements were seduced by, and swept up with, the paranoid delusions of the few, conspiratorial fantasy might force its way into the public square, undermining democratic politics centred on the mediation of competing interests through rational deliberation.[26]

But it was not simply that delusional and wrongheaded views would taint sober political discourse. The real danger of the paranoid mass movement lay in its absolutist outlook. Since, for those under the sway of the 'paranoid style', the conspiracy they oppose is vast and all-encompassing, and politics is explicable in these terms alone, the only viable alternative is to defeat the conspiracy and its villainous perpetrators and restore an idealised vision of society.[27] There is little room in this kind of dualistic view for differing perspectives, particularly since contrary accounts can be easily subsumed into the conspiracy as well. The important point here is that, for Hofstadter, the 'paranoid style' entails 'not the usual methods of political give and take, but an all out crusade'.[28] Hofstadter captures this stark oppositional mindset vividly:

The paranoid spokesman sees the fate of conspiracy in apocalyptic terms – he traffics in the birth and death of whole worlds, whole political orders, whole systems of human value. He is always manning the barricades of civilization ... He does not see social conflict as something to be mediated and compromised, in the manner of the working politician. Since what is at stake is always a conflict between absolute good and absolute evil, what is necessary is not compromise but the will to fight things out to a finish. Since the enemy is thought of as being totally evil and totally unappeasable he must be totally eliminated – if not from the world, at least from the theatre of operation to which the paranoid turns his attention.[29]

Understood like this, it was difficult for Hofstadter to see how a political movement infused with the 'paranoid style' could effectively participate in, or even be reconciled with the pragmatic process of bargain and compromise, which he thought characterised stable liberal democracy.[30] Politics would become intractably partisan – irreconcilable, vindictive and illiberal.

The relationship between normal politics and this account of political paranoia makes more sense in the context of the Cold War liberal understanding of populism.[31] Although liberalism had historically been a force for radical and reformist agendas, by the early 1950s it was very much the ideological status quo of the American political class.[32] Roosevelt's New Deal had been taken up and institutionalised in the federal bureaucracy and liberal elites were largely content to manage and defend these gains.[33] The basic groundwork of liberal ideology was taken for granted: the consent to be governed; the equality of individuals; and freedom of expression and belief.[34] But layered on top of this was an institutional mindset that sought above all to reconcile the competing interests of individuals, represented through interest groups.[35] The primary issue in this institutional mode of politics was the tension between difference and order in mass democracy. How was government to respond to the differing interests of the community without causing conflict or alienation? On the one side, the marketplace of vote competition would allow groups to trade votes for the satisfaction of their members' interests. On the other side, governing parties and pertinent interests could engage in bargain and compromise until a mutually appropriate accommodation was reached. Reason and pragmatism were the watchwords here.[36]

Less explicitly, the answer for this political class was to narrow the terrain on which individuals and groups conducted their political engagements. This narrowing made particular kinds of difference problematic. As Jodi Dean argues, 'although pluralists premise politics on diversity, they do not include an endless variety of positions'.[37] Populism, with its emotive, activist idealism fell outside this range. But more than that, populism was framed in this discourse as almost antithetical to liberal centrism. William Connolly explains incisively:

Outside the warm, protected spaces of the normal individual and the territorial state, conventional pluralists project a lot of abnormality, anarchy and cruelty in need of exclusion and regulation ... Stark definitions outside contain the range and reach of diversity inside, and vice versa.[38]

The point here is not just that a particular conceptualisation animated the post-war liberal understanding of populism. It is that populism was understood as explicitly problematic and this served to, at once, marginalise challenges to the consensus of the political class and position that consensus as a bulwark against radical politics.[39]

This post-war intellectual framework furnished Hofstadter – and indeed, those writing in the liberal pluralist tradition – with a set of conceptual reference points with which to think about paranoia. Understood in this way, it could never be anything but the populist radicalism of the irrational fringe. It could never be anything but a threat to the stability of the political status quo. The opposition between normal politics and an unstable periphery, between the cosmopolitan city and alienated small town America, rested comfortably with a more general political orthodoxy. Established as part of this broader paradigm and politics, paranoia has continued to be understood, from the inside out, as a threat to America's centrist politics and a confirmation of the political norm.

Indeed, more than impartial observers of politics and history, post-war liberals were writing with the production of a particular political norm in mind.[40] Hofstadter was acutely aware of his broader social and political responsibilities, and articulated this awareness with some eloquence.[41] Consensus history, wrote Hofstadter, is analogous to the relationship of

> an appropriate frame ... to a painting: it sets the boundaries of the scene and enables us to see where the picture breaks of and the alien environment begins. Consensus is, in other words, the limited field within and upon which any (thus limited) conflict takes place; it does not play the role of a general theory that functions outside of historical context and circumstance, but instead works best as a measure of the degree of legitimacy and acceptance a political system or specific system, or specific issue achieves among 'the politically active public'.[42]

Mark Fenster situates this consensus approach as part of a historically specific political hegemony that entrenched a particular set of priorities and assumptions as the common sense of politics.[43] While it would be simplistic to claim that Hofstadter's analysis was no more than a delegitimising strategy, the emergence of political paranoia as a matter of intellectual and public concern inevitably positioned political dissent, especially populism, as illegitimate, beyond consideration, and outside the 'frame' of public discourse.[44] The 'paranoid style' paradigm did this by 'offering a well-crafted, palatable means for elites to understand the threatening political movements that arose from outside mainstream political parties and the academic and media institutions that built and shared post-War liberal consensus'.[45] Indeed, the main thrust of Hofstadter's scholarly project was to expose the significant and often destabilising effects of social-psychological forces on American political history – and it was in this context that he advanced a pragmatic model of liberal democracy as the best chance of keeping irrational impulses at bay.[46]

More broadly, Jack Bratich has highlighted the way paranoia became a subject of scholarly concern as part of a discourse of social betterment and normalisation espoused by a raft of experts in the emerging post-war liberal order.[47] Chief among these experts was Harold Lasswell, the father of personality type analysis and an important influence on Hofstadter's thinking about the 'paranoid style'.[48] Indeed, Hofstadter credited Lasswell with his own discovery that 'the significance of political opinions was not to be grasped apart from the private motivations they symbolise' – an insight particularly significant for his understanding of extremism.[49] Lasswell had made much of the *pathological* tendencies, first, of 'agitators' and later, of 'non-democratic' personalities.[50] Agitators, in Lasswell's view, are characterised by their 'high value on public emotional response, narcissism, and suspicion'.[51] These 'hyper-suspicious' types reflected a broader deterioration of public reason, which could only be dealt with by identifying and preventing the psychological dynamics that lay behind the irrational behaviour of the agitators.[52]

At the same time, Lasswell contrasted these dissenters with a more appropriate leader, with a personality structure sufficient for managing elite power.[53] The origins of these personalities could be understood by looking at personal biographies, and particularly an individual's early experiences.[54] Returning to the liberal discourse of social betterment, Lasswell specifically advocated that experts in government and the academy should attempt to foster the democratic leader personality and eliminate the circumstances that give rise to pathological dissent.[55]

The point for Bratich is that these experts and others like them had the improvement of society in mind. They provided reasonable standards of right conduct and said with authority what was abnormal.[56] Individuals were encouraged to guard their thoughts against unreasonable ideas or impulses and to monitor the behaviour of others, enacting a new mode of liberal government as self-regulation.[57] In this regard, paranoia emerged as a problem to be at once solved and avoided. The point here, then, is that this emerging concern with paranoid politics was inseparable from the production of a particular kind of political order. It helped set the limits on acceptable political discourse and affirmed the propriety of the political status quo in contrast to these unruly forces.

Given this conceptual affinity with post-war political orthodoxy it is perhaps unsurprising that the 'paranoid style' paradigm remains pervasive in scholarly and popular characterisations of paranoia and conspiracy since that time. Different renditions emphasise particular aspects of his framework – some accentuate the psychological while others remain more attuned to the socio-cultural trajectory – but all remain firmly fixed within the liberal pluralist context. In political science this is evidenced in the numerous publications dealing with the subject matter that mobilises the same centre/periphery dynamic, where populism threatens to overwhelm sensible liberal democratic politics.[58] As Fenster explains,

> Hofstadter at once created and cleared the field, establishing both that extremist political movements and thoughts were important objects of research and that a researcher's normative position should be that of a detached, centrist critic who explains and admonishes extremism's marginal role in the unfolding American historical and political narrative.[59]

Likewise, the 'paranoid style' remains the pervasive account in political commentary around these issues.[60] Typical of this influence is a report from the Department of Homeland Security released in 2009, which found that rightwing extremism, fuelled by paranoid conspiracy theories, is resurgent across middle America.[61] The report argues that violence from the radical right poses the greatest threat of domestic terrorism. In this view, the global financial crisis, restrictions on gun ownership, and the election of the first black president have led to a growing sense of frustration and detachment from the political process in some segments of the population, and this has aided the recruitment and radicalisation of right-wing extremists.[62] Hofstadter's basic assumptions are clear enough in this analysis: an alienated few, disconnected from the pluralistic consensus of mainstream politics by socio-economic stress and their own prejudices, find an easy explanation for their troubles in a paranoid understanding of the world. More broadly, this same narrative commonly appears in descriptions of, for instance, the 9/11 Truthers;[63] Occupy Wall Street;[64] climate-change scepticism;[65] and hyper-partisans at both ends of the political spectrum.[66]

The discussion so far has identified some initial intellectual and cultural connotations evoked in American political culture by the Arab-Muslim paranoia narrative. Here the emergence of political paranoia as a subject of concern was inseparable from the production of a particular liberal political order and the management of dissent in that context. Significantly, the management of dissent involved identifying particular thoughts and behaviours as pathological and abnormal. A raft of identity markers entrenched in liberal pluralist politics – centre/periphery, inside/outside, pragmatic/emotive, rational/irrational, and so on – located paranoid conspiracy theories on the cultural fringe, as a threat to the rational orthodoxy and the normally functioning liberal subject, which were all the more stable by contrast. The important point here is that these negative connotations have been embedded in the common-sense view of paranoia in American political culture right up to the present day, where the 'paranoid style' remains a common trope.

Conspiracy culture abroad

This section connects the 'paranoid style' paradigm with the Arab-Muslim paranoia narrative by showing how its centre/periphery structure and broader understanding of populism are drawn into interpretations of conspiracy culture abroad. Daniel Pipes's *Conspiracy! How the Paranoid Style Flourishes and Where it Comes From* provides a useful starting point.[67] According to Pipes, Western conspiracy culture was mainstream throughout the nineteenth and early twentieth centuries, but was forced to the margins in reaction to the mass paranoia of Hitler's Germany and Stalin's Soviet Union.[68] Yet for Pipes the 'paranoid style' remained prevalent and mainstream right through the Cold War in the communist states:

> The soviets created the mould, and other communist movements and regimes followed. Virtually without exception, all made the paranoid style central to their message. In Kim's Korea, Mao's China, Pol Pot's Cambodia, Hoxha's Albania, and Castro's Cuba, an inordinate fear of conspiracies characterised the system itself, not just individuals at the apex of power.[69]

Although conspiracy theory has moved from the political fringe to the heart of political culture in these states, Pipes nevertheless retains the core elements of the 'paranoid style' paradigm. Here the paranoid style exists on the margins of Western democracies, but remains pervasive in populist politics of communist polities at the margins of international power and legitimacy in a Western geopolitical world-view. A reasonable West is juxtaposed with paranoid and ideologically radical pariah states. This structure is perhaps unsurprising since the wider context for post-war liberalism was always communism and fascism, which had swept across Europe and East Asia.[70] Fear of populist ideologies that had uprooted societies abroad amplified the concern with populism on the fringe of American liberal democracy.

This dimension is drawn to the fore when the 'paranoid style' paradigm is brought into the international context. Indeed, in the post-Cold War world it is the resurgence of these populist forces that is often the focus of international affairs commentary on political paranoia. According to Daniel Drezner, for instance, 'the paranoid style has gone global' and is 'spreading into the body politic of advanced industrialised democracies in new and profound ways'.[71] Here extremists at both ends of the political spectrum, fuelled by the social impacts of the recent global economic crisis, threaten to overwhelm normally functioning democracies with their irrational views. Likewise, Mark Strauss has explored the international political dimension of anti-Semitic conspiracy theories through the same 'paranoid style' frame, tracing their resurgence in the new millennium, which he links with the destabilising forces of globalisation.[72] He argues that the left critique of global capitalism and of the Israeli occupation of Palestinian territories feed into right-wing neo-fascist conspiracy theories.[73] In

Western democracies conspiracy theories exist in activist groups critical of the political orthodoxy. At the same time, conspiracy theories are pervasive in the rhetoric of political leaders from non-Western countries and in mainstream political cultures across the Muslim world.[74] The important point here is the conceptual structure underpinning all these accounts: paranoid conspiracy theories are an extremist threat to normal politics in the modern West, while they flourishes in populist political cultures at the margins of international power and legitimacy.

Pipes brings this paranoid style framework to bear on Arab-Muslim political culture in *The Hidden Hand: Middle East Fears of Conspiracy*, which is emblematic of the Arab-Muslim paranoia narrative and provides a useful entry point.[75] *The Hidden Hand* examines Arab-Muslim conspiracy theories about foreign powers and their own governments.[76] For Pipes, conspiracy theory is endemic in Middle Eastern culture, propagated by everyday people, the mainstream media and political leaders, and espoused by 'most of the outstanding Muslim thinkers of the twentieth century'.[77] Indeed, according to Pipes,

> Whoever hopes to understand the Middle East must recognise the distorting lens of conspiracy theories, understand them, make allowances for them, and perhaps even plan around them ... It spawns its own discourse, complete in itself and almost immune to rational argument. It suffuses life from the most private family conversations to the highest and most public levels of politics. It helps explain much of what would otherwise be illogical or implausible, including the region's record of political extremism and volatility, its culture of violence and its poor record of modernisation.[78]

This conspiracy culture, according to Pipes, erects a 'strange and many mirrored world' where Zionists and imperialists lurk nefariously behind every political event.[79] Traumatised by the disparity between the golden era of Islamic civilisation and its modern-day reality, and conditioned to the intervention of foreign forces by Western colonial domination, in this account Middle Easterners find a convenient explanation for their unsatisfactory circumstances in far-fetched delusions of hidden power.[80] In turn, wherever conspiracy culture flourishes so too does absolutism and extremism.[81]

The fuller conceptual implications of Pipes's framework become explicit in a section titled 'The Paranoid Style', where he compares the American experience of political paranoia to the contemporary Middle East.[82] Here the Middle Eastern phenomenon is roughly equated with a historical American political culture, saturated with irrational populism and rife with conspiracy theory, which would later be dispelled by the triumph of liberal democratic values.[83] But this analysis does not simply take Middle Eastern political culture on its own terms; it situates it in relation to the West, and specifically America. This relational analysis implicitly extrapolates the 'paranoid style' schema onto the world at large by situating a broadly defined West at the centre of international affairs and locating the Middle East on the periphery – a sober, pragmatic international core distinguished from an irrational, populist fringe.

This constellation is clear in Pipes's remedy for a Middle Eastern political culture apparently 'lagging behind the West in all important ways'.[84] First and foremost among his proposals is 'a thoroughgoing commitment to learn from the outside world, to set up strong structures, and to implement policies conducive to economic growth'. But Westerners have a part to play too – they can teach:

> [for] while Arabs and Iranians first encountered such concepts as democracy, freedom of speech, freedom of religion, civil rights, and the rule of law almost two centuries ago, these principles remain alien to all but a small minority of them. Not comprehending these doctrines, Middle Easterners cannot make out the motives of Western governments.[85]

Here the modern West is situated as an exemplar for backward, pre-modern Arabs, who need to learn from and replicate the enlightened practices of 'the outside world' if they are to advance out of their conspiracy minded malaise. Accordingly, exposure to the *real* operation of power in more modern states will go some way towards replacing Middle Eastern conspiracy theories about foreign powers with an understanding of how the world actually works. Here the paranoid Middle East is relegated to the periphery of international affairs, while the West appears as the very heart of modernity, rationality and right-minded behaviour. Thus, Pipes is able to move conspiracy theory to the centre of Middle Eastern politics while retaining the 'paranoid style' as a fringe phenomenon in international politics.

This same narrative is evident in the work of prominent foreign policy commentators seeking to explain the origins of 9/11. For instance, here is Fareed Zakaria's in his *Newsweek* cover story 'The Politics of Rage: Why do they Hate us?', still cited today as a debate shaping account of the origins of 9/11:

> The disproportionate feelings of grievance directed at America have to be placed in the overall context of the sense of humiliation, decline and despair that sweeps the Arab world ... Arabs ... feel that they are under siege from the modern world and that the United States symbolises this world. Thus every action America takes gets magnified a thousand-fold. And even when we do not act, the rumours of our gigantic powers and nefarious deeds still spread. Most Americans would not believe how common the rumour is throughout the Arab world that either the CIA or Israel's Mossad blew up the World Trade Center to justify attacks on Arabs and Muslims. This is the culture from which the suicide bombers have come.[86]

Like the narrative in *The Hidden Hand*, there is a clear parallel here in the liberal imaginary between the way Arab-Muslim alienation and Western modernity are opposed, and the way emotive populism and liberal pragmatism are contrasted.

A more recent example is Roger Cohen's reflections on 'The Captive Arab Mind', which appeared in the *New York Times* in late 2010:

> I say 'thinking', but that's generous. What we are dealing with here is a paltry harvest of captive minds. Such minds resort to conspiracy theory because it is the ultimate refuge of the powerless. If you cannot change your own life, it must be that some greater force controls the world ... Milosz wrote powerfully of the 'solace of reverie' in worlds of oppression. I found much solace in Lebanon but little evidence that the Middle East is ready to exchange conspiratorial victimhood for self-empowerment – and so move forward.[87]

Although Western modernity is not mentioned explicitly here, an implicit contrast is drawn between the 'paltry minds' of Arab Muslims and Cohen's sensible interpretations of Middle Eastern politics, as well as the normal political culture he takes as a reference point. Likewise, alienation and victimhood are contrasted with self-empowerment, replicating Pipes's narrative about backwardness and blame.

Of course, this centre/periphery structure has often characterised liberal political culture in the international context, outside of the identification of cultures of conspiracy abroad. Take, for instance, the quintessential liberal development model, modernisation theory, which focuses on accelerating supposedly pre-modern societies along an economic trajectory towards the modern industrial state.[88] This approach had its intellectual impetus in the Cold War attempt to offer 'developing' economies an alternative to communism. In this account 'traditional societies' with apparently pre-modern cultures could be seduced by populist socialism and turned against liberal democracy.[89] To prevent this, the liberal project needed to be exported and 'traditional societies' set on the path to modernity. This concern shared similar narrative and ideational properties with a domestic discourse in American political culture, which was preoccupied with populism as the breeding ground of radical ideology at both ends of the political spectrum.[90]

Linking back to the Arab-Muslim paranoia narrative, this section has identified the extrapolation of the 'paranoid style' discourse onto the Middle East, which can be situated as an iteration of a particular liberal understanding of 'development' – as a purely Western abstraction based in a specific reading of the historical rise of liberalism and the vanquishing of traditional society.[91] The post-war liberal understanding of populism is particularly significant here, since it provides the broad and largely negative scripts that inform the characterisation of these supposedly backward peoples.

Orientalism and anti-modernism

This section establishes affinities between the post-war liberal view of populism that informs the paranoid style paradigm and a historically powerful orientalist narrative that has often framed the American encounter with the Middle East. The negative connotations around populism embedded in the paranoid style framework are reinforced by this orientalist narrative, which situates Arab-Muslim culture as fundamentally anti-modernist and points to a culture of bitterness, self-denial and blame as an explanation for resentment towards the West.

One entry point here is to note that Fareed Zakaria's diagnosis of post-9/11 Arab-Muslim conspiracy culture was clearly influenced by Bernard Lewis's classic orientalist account, 'The Roots of Muslim Rage'. Often regarded as America's most politically influential Arabist scholar, Lewis explains the 'crisis of Islam' in terms of an endemic anti-modernism at the core of Muslim civilisation.[92] Put simply, it is the tension between the modern West and pre-modern Islam that is the key to understanding contemporary anti-Americanism in the region. For Lewis, this tension arises out of the disparity between a historic conviction that Islam is the last, best revelation of God, such that Muslims can learn nothing from the outside world, and the fact that Western modernity has come to dominate the world technologically, economically and politically.[93] This tension manifests in envy and frustration at the decline and deprivation of a once powerful civilisation, forced to bend and accede in the face of the modern West.[94] More fundamentally, it is present in the incompatibility of secularism and Islam, a faith that regulates not just spiritual life, but politics, economics and law.[95] According to Lewis, the only time modern ideas have ever succeeded in an Islamic country is when they displaced Islam from the top down – as Kemal Atatürk had done in his modernisation of Turkey.[96] In this view, Islam stands in the way of modernisation. It is a fundamentally anti-modernist force.

For the purposes of this analysis it is the political conclusions drawn from this narrative that are most telling: by blaming their problems on the West and modernity, by playing the victim and pointing to historical wrongs, Arab-Muslims are merely avoiding the root causes of their problems, which are primarily self-inflicted. This emphasis on a culture of blame and denial was at the heart of Lewis's own explanation of 9/11.[97] 'What Went Wrong?' explains that for Arab-Muslims 'the question 'who did this to us?' has only lead to neurotic fantasies and conspiracy theories. The other question – 'what did we do wrong?' – has led naturally to a second question 'how do we put it right?'[98]

Of course, the apposition of a dysfunctional Arab-Muslim culture full of blame and denial with a self-reflective modernity folds together neatly with the liberal modernisation discourse flagged above. Here is Thomas Friedman making this connection plain in his assessment of the so-called 'war of ideas' apparently underway in the Middle East after 9/11:

> It is a war between the future and the past, between development and underdevelopment, between authors of crazy conspiracy theories versus those espousing

rationality, between advocates of suicide bombing and those who know that you can't build a society out of gravestones. Only Arabs and Muslims can win this war within but we can openly encourage that progress.[99]

What stands out is the series of dichotomies that structure the paragraph: underdevelopment/development, extremist/progress, and craziness/rationality. Here Western modernity is the consistent counterpoint to the problems of Arab-Muslims. Even where no explicit reference is made to rationality, modernity and progress this contrast remains the latent structuring principle. For instance, here is Friedman once again connecting paranoia to Arab-Muslim cultural dysfunction:

> At the same time, there does seem to be a certain strain of self-loathing at work in parts of the Arab-Muslim world today. What else can one think when someone tells you that Arabs or Muslims could never have been clever enough to pull off Sept. 11 – only Mossad or the C.I.A.? It is a sad fact that Arab self-esteem is very low these days, because of the lagging state of Arab political systems and economies, and that feeds the free-floating anger that bin Laden has been surfing on.[100]

It is the 'lagging state' of their economies and politics that is the underlying source of Arab-Muslim paranoia – implying a disparity between their circumstances and a Western world they 'lag' behind.[101] The ideational markers between rational/irrational, reason/emotion, normal/abnormal, adjusted/alienated, modern/backwards, centre/periphery, and so on, set off a formidable array of negative valences that attach seamlessly. But these valences cannot be separated from their broader frame of reference: a modernisation theory narrative entwined with an orientalist perspective, which both contrast liberal modernity with pre-modern peoples, mired in backwards traditions and attitudes, which are thought to stand in the way of progress.[102] In this sense, the Arab-Muslim paranoia narrative after 9/11 emanated from a particular political culture engaged in a long-running encounter with the world 'outside the warm, protected spaces' of liberal modernity, as Connolly had it.

It was in precisely this context that Edward Said co-opted and inverted the term 'orientalism' as a way of capturing the endemic stereotyping of Arab-Muslim cultures, and the 'orient' at large, which emerged in train with the colonial penetration of these societies.[103] Here the conception of a romanticised Middle East, full of passionate and unruly people, helped affirm the superiority of Western civilisation and legitimise the colonial enterprise. Although Said focused mainly on nineteenth and early twentieth century scholarship about the 'orient', for our purposes it is interesting to note that he singled out the work of Bernard Lewis as a key contemporary example of this mindset – a point he continued to make as Lewis, along with Zakaria and a raft of other scholars advancing this narrative, became a key intellectual guarantor of the Bush administration's War on Terror strategy.[104] The important point for now is that the Arab-Muslim paranoia narrative blended easily with long-run intellectual currents, which are inseparable, as Said suggests, from the *self-understanding* of particular Western communities. Moreover, this hybrid narrative accentuated the negative connotations around populism embedded in the paranoid style discourse, tying them to a narrative about Arab-Muslim cultural dysfunction characterised by bitterness, self-denial and blame.

The chapter so far has shown that the Arab-Muslim paranoia narrative had significant cultural and ideational depth in American political culture, which was at once highly delegitimising in its portrayal of Arab-Muslims and productive of a particular liberal identity. This narrative had roots in a pervasive account of populism that connected with historically powerful perspectives framing the Western encounter with the Middle East. Here the latent negative connotations around populism embedded in the paranoid style are accentuated. It is these cultural materials that the Arab-Muslim paranoia narrative draws on when it appears in foreign affairs commentary.

Paranoid psychology abroad

The Arab-Muslim paranoia narrative and the paranoid style paradigm generally, tend to imply psychological pathology as much as cultural dysfunction. Indeed, the paranoid style paradigm always contained a psychological dimension, most obviously through the influence of Harold Lasswell on Hofstadter's thinking. Although cultural and psychological connotations are often present simultaneously, the paranoid psychology theme is worth considering in its own right. This section shows how references to the irrationality and paranoia connect with a well-established academic discourse that has often informed foreign affairs commentary.

Robins and Post's path-breaking work *Political Paranoia: The Psychopolitics of Hatred* is a good place to start, particularly since both authors have been important contributors to media commentary about conspiracy theory.[105] The main international targets of their book-length analysis are dictators and despots – for instance, Stalin, Hitler, Pol Pot, Idi Amin and the Ayatollah Khomeini.[106] Instead of focusing on dysfunctional culture as the driver of a 'paranoid style', the emphasis here is on the way an explicitly pathological psychology produces paranoia and thus conspiracy theory. The authors concede that paranoia operates on a sliding scale – from the mild paranoia or suspiciousness that manifest from time to time in most normal people, to the extremes of paranoid personality disorder – yet they end up centring their analysis on a clinical definition of paranoia. This definition and the key characteristics of paranoid psychology are demonstrated by drawing on case examples from Post's professional career as a clinical psychologist.[107]

From this point of view, the leaders of pariah states are prone to suspiciousness, the personalisation of threat, grandiosity, hostility, agency panic, delusional thinking and projection.[108] According to Robins and Post, it is projection that supplies the underlying pathological dynamic, which is established in early childhood and then carried out in the adult lives of conspiracy theorists. Drawing on the psychoanalytical theory of 'object relations' proposed by Melanie Klein, Robins and Post trace paranoia to the primitive ego defence mechanism, which young children use to deal with intense feelings of anger and fear.[109] One way they do this is by projecting it onto their mother, who becomes not just the source of comfort and sustenance, but also the cause of frustration and pain.[110] The child also internalises this dualistic view as part of an emerging self-identity – using the good parts as the base of an idealised self and projecting the bad parts onto others.[111] Klein labels this initial childhood phase the 'paranoid schizoid position', and argues that it is an underlying psychological dynamic that is embedded in all of us, a defensive mechanism we sometimes return to in times of stress, and a position that the clinically paranoid never actually depart from.[112] When it is dominant, the paranoid mindset accentuates the projection mechanism established in early childhood: negative internal traits are projected onto external objects, which are then situated in opposition to an idealised self.[113]

The upshot of this dynamic is that when something goes wrong the reason for it is located in the outside world and in the actions of other people. Here responsibility is shifted:

> Instead of being guilt ridden over his own inner rage, the paranoid is now indignant over his enemies' unjust persecution of him and must defend himself against them. The aggression is required by them. It is defensive aggression. His aggression is, quite literally, self defence. How much better to be all powerful than to be powerless; how much better to be the center of a world conspiracy than to be insignificant and ignored.[114]

Thus, for Robins and Post, it is largely the psychological patterns established in early childhood that are the crucial driver of conspiracy theory in the political figures they diagnose. For instance, Adolf Hitler, in purifying the German body politic of Jews, 'was projecting the reviled hated parts of himself onto the Jews and then aggressively attacking them'.[115] Similarly, the Soviet purges were not simply a ruthless consolidation of power – it was 'Stalin's desire to purge his own psychological demons that was being expressed'.[116] Terrorists, as a general category, are also framed as the product of the paranoid schizoid position, where 'the zeal of the torturer, the alacrity of the killer, represents his eagerness to destroy the devalued and disowned part of the self'.[117] Post has gone on to write extensively on both the motivations of terrorism and the personalities of foreign leaders in his capacity as a long-time profiler for the CIA.[118]

In all these cases, it is personal biography, particularly focused on early child-hood, which provides the central evidence for the psychological profiles developed.

This kind of approach also informs one of the more widely cited analyses of conspiracy theory in the Middle East, penned by Zonis and Joseph in 1994.[119] This work examines conspiracy theory in 'Arab-Iranian-Muslim' culture by looking at common childrearing practices.[120] Although the authors go to some length to caveat themselves against accusations of reading an endemic psychological condition into all Middle Easterners, they fall back on a clinical definition of paranoia as a starting point, which they then attempts to use as an analogy for their analysis of political culture. This inevitably leads to heavy connotations of psychological abnormality.[121] Freud's infantile fantasy stages underwrite the analysis – young boys, raised in a 'women's world', are ripped away from this safe space into a tightly demarcated 'man's world', leaving men with a wounded self and a yearning to recover an idealised past. Thus,

> Middle Eastern culture, as reflected in common childrearing practices, is particularly likely to foster patterns of perception and expectations in individuals which constitute a tendency towards conspiracy thinking as a response to chronic psycho-social stressors.[122]

The sources of psychological stress are the same as those identified by Pipes and Lewis as causal factors: despondence over the decline of the Muslim world; dominance by colonial powers; and general social frustration over economic and political failures. But instead of being the primary source of conspiracy theory, Zonis and Joseph argue that these conditions 'induce regression in mental processes and facilitate the eruption of more primitive ideation, including conspiracy theory'.[123] In this way, abnormal individual psychology is broadened out into abnormal cultural psychology. Robins and Post perform a similar move in the last sections of their book. In order to explain how a paranoid leader mobilises a following, they propose that individuals can appeal to the latent paranoia of vulnerable groups, accentuating their underlying insecurities and playing on a widely held ego defence mechanism.[124]

It is important to note that these academic accounts have had a wider influence. For instance, Jerrold Post has had a public presence in American foreign policy debates, assessing the personality types of key US adversaries for the US government and offering his expert opinion through the media.[125] During the first Gulf War he gave evidence to the House Armed Services Committee, classifying Saddam Hussein as a malignant narcissist, which was the result of a traumatic childhood that produced a wounded self.[126] This had resulted in a messianic ambition for unlimited power, 'absence of conscience, unconstrained aggression, and a paranoid outlook'.[127] In this context, Post brings in conspiracy theory as one of Saddam's signal traits:

> The conspiracies he spins are not merely for popular consumption in the Arab world, but genuinely reflect his paranoid mindset. He is convinced that the United States and Iran have been in league for the purposes of eliminating him, and finds a pervasive chain of evidence for this conclusion.[128]

More recently, Post has redeployed his analysis of the Iraqi leader in the wake of operation Iraqi Freedom, as well as profiling other rogue leaders such as Osama bin Laden, who was also identified as a malignant narcissist with tendencies towards paranoia, self-absorption, ruthlessness and a lack of empathy.[129]

Whatever the impact of expert opinion about paranoid psychology, this kind of explanation remains an influential theme in foreign affairs commentary.[130] For instance, a 2010 report from the think tank Demos, *The Power of Unreason: Conspiracy Theories, Extremism and Counter-Terrorism*, highlights a psycho-social dynamic linking paranoia and radicalisation.[131] Although the psychological mechanism underpinning conspiracy beliefs are not addressed head on, it is implied when the authors explain that one of the effects of conspiracy theory in the extremist context is 'demonology'.[132] Here the in-group opposes an external other, which is demonised, thus providing a sense of cohesion and a ready target for attack.[133] But this demonology is explained as a product of 'sinister attribution syndrome' and 'paranoid cognition'.[134]

The broader point is that this psychological dimension reinforces the centre/periphery dynamic that I have identified in the paranoid style paradigm and the Arab-Muslim paranoia narrative. Psychological dysfunction is regularly implied or intimated as part of the broader narrative highlighting a conspiracy-ridden culture of blame and victimhood. Terms like irrational, delusional, fantasy, deranged and crazy are often woven in, pointing the reader towards the psychological deficiencies of extremists and communities thought vulnerable to radicalisation. Here the beliefs of Arab-Muslims are framed as psychologically abnormal, by comparison with the stable psyches of the people they oppose. Indeed, the contrast between foreign policy commentators and their pathological subjects, between normal behaviour and paranoid irrationality, sits comfortably within a geopolitical imagination where unstable minds emerge from unstable regions. Of course, the approach of political psychologists like Robins and Post parallels the diagnostic model underpinning the Arab-Muslim paranoia narrative generally: resentment towards America in the Arab-Muslim world is said to be provoked by paranoid conspiracy thinking, which is explained as a symptom of deeper social-psychological dysfunction in political cultures on the periphery of international power and legitimacy in a Western geopolitical world-view.

I have argued across the chapter that this underlying ideational structure indicates a powerful form of ideological reproduction at play in the Arab-Muslim paranoia narrative, which both delegitimises Arab-Muslim culture and affirms a specific Western liberal identity. This is particularly the case where the paranoid style paradigm overlaps with the influential orientalist account of Arab-Muslim anti-modernism that highlights an apparent culture of bitterness, self-denial and blame as an explanation for resentment towards the West. This narrative accentuates the negative connotations around populism embedded in the paranoid style paradigm and the liberal imaginary more broadly. Like the post-war liberal status quo opposed to the irrational views of ideological demagogues, here the image of liberal modernity is secured by contrast with the irrational views of backwards Arab-Muslims. With these dynamics in mind, the Arab-Muslim paranoia narrative can be understood in terms of a particular liberal imaginary and a specific account of populism in that context.

NOTES

1 J. Bartlett, 'Conspiracy Theories Fuel Anti-Western Sentiment in the Middle East', *New York Times* (13 September 2012). Available at www.nytimes.com/roomfordebate/2012/09/12/does-mideast-democracy-complicate-diplomacy/conspiracy-theories-fuel-anti-Western-sentiment-in-the-middle-east (accessed 5 January 2015).
2 C. Brummit, 'Amid Bombings, Pakistan Turns Towards Conspiracy Theories', *Huffington Post* (29 May 2011). Available at www.huffingtonpost.com/2011/05/29/pakistan-bombing-conspiracy-theories_n_868604.html (accessed 5 January 2015).
3 A. Baker, 'Why Iran thinks the Militant Group ISIS is an American Plot', *Time* (19 July 2014). Available at www.time.com/2992269/isis-is-an-american-plot-says-iran (accessed 5 January 2015).
4 'The Paranoid Style in Turkish Politics', *Wall Street Journal* (11 March 2014), p. 12.
5 E. Borenstein, 'Why Conspiracies Take Hold in Russia', *Huffington Post* (27 September 2014). Available at www.huffingtonpost.com/eliot-borenstein/why-conspiracy-theories_b_5626149.html (accessed 5 January 2015).
6 L. Grossman, 'Why Conspiracy Theories won't go Away', *Time Magazine* (3 September 2006); C. Haynes, '9/11: The Roots of Paranoia', *The Nation* (8 December 2006); and Lexington, 'Still Crazy After all These Years', *The Economist* (20 August 2009).
7 Jonathan Kay, 'Black Helicopters over Nashville', *Newsweek* (10 February 2010). Available at www.freerepublic.com/focus/news/2447957/posts (accessed 7 August 2015); D. Barshaw, 'Tea Party Lights Fuse for Rebellion on Right', *New York Times* (15 February 2010). Available at www.nytimes.com/2010/02/16/us/politics/16teaparty.html?adxnnl=1&pagewanted=all&adxnnlx=1352178761–/mnOVioRX86lKIl0Yuv NKg (accessed 5 January 2015).
8 P. Krugman, 'The Paranoid Style', *New York Times* (9 October 2006). Available at www.nytimes.com/2006/10/09/opinion/09krugman.html?_r=0 (accessed 5 January 2015); G. Greenwald, 'Dick Cheney's Warped Vision of the World', *Salon* (13 March 2007); and Department of Homeland Security, 'Right Wing Extremism: Current Economic and Political Environment Fuelling Resurgence in Radicalization and Recruitment' (Washington, DC: Government Printing Office, April 2009).
9 M. Seaton, 'Naomi Wolf: Receptions, Responses, Critics', *Guardian* (28 November 2011). Available at www.guardian.co.uk/commentisfree/cifamerica/2011/nov/28/naomi-wolf-reception-responses-critics (accessed 5 January 2015); and T. Hayden, 'Why Naomi Wolf's Occupy Conspiracy can't Explain Occupy L.A.', *The Nation* 29

November 2011). Available at www.thenation.com/article/164851/why-naomi-wolfs-occupy-conspiracy-theory-cant-explain-occupy-la# (accessed 5 January 2015).

10 M. Strauss, 'Globalization's Jewish Problem', *Foreign Policy*, 130 (2003), pp. 58–67.

11 The best account of this link is M. Fenster, *Conspiracy Theories: Secrecy and Power in American Culture* (Minneapolis: University of Minnesota Press, 2008).

12 It is important to distinguish here from other sorts of liberalism – such as liberal internationalism or neo-liberalism – common in discussions about international politics. I refer here to the specific American domestic political ideology synonymous with the centre-left policies of Franklin Roosevelt's 'New Deal', which dominated the political landscape of post-war America. Likewise, the account of populism I set out here is a product of this same liberal discourse.

13 See R. Hofstadter, *The Paranoid Style and other Essays* (Cambridge, MA: Harvard University Press), pp. 3–40. An abridged version appeared in *Harper's Magazine* in 1964. See R. Hofstadter, 'The Paranoid Style in American Politics', *Harper's Magazine* (November 1964), pp. 77–86.

14 See Fenster, *Conspiracy Theories*, pp. 1–51; and J. Bratich, *Conspiracy Panics: Political Rationality and Popular Culture* (New York: State University of New York Press, 2008), pp. 1–50.

15 *Ibid.*

16 *Ibid.* See also D. S. Brown, *Richard Hofstadter: An Intellectual History* (Chicago: Chicago University Press, 2006), pp. 154–176.

17 Hofstadter, 'The Paranoid Style in American Politics', pp. 77–81.

18 *Ibid.*, p. 82.

19 *Ibid.*, pp. 82–85.

20 *Ibid.*

21 *Ibid.*

22 *Ibid.*, p. 85.

23 *Ibid.*

24 *Ibid.*, p. 86.

25 *Ibid.*, pp. 82–86.

26 *Ibid.*

27 *Ibid.*

28 Hofstdadter, 'The Paranoid Style and other Essays', p. 29.

29 Hofstadter, 'The Paranoid Style in American Politics', p. 82.

30 *Ibid.*, pp. 82–86.

31 It is important to emphasise that I am describing a particular version of populism that emerged along with post-war liberal pluralism. Mark Fenster's work on the historical and intellectual context of Hofstadter's approach is instructive here, particularly in his account of consensus history and liberal pluralism. See Fenster, *Conspiracy Theories*, pp. 24–36.

32 For a critical perspective on the ideological convergence of Cold War liberals see, C. Wright Mills, *The Power Elite* (Oxford: Oxford University Press, 2000).

33 Fenster, *Conspiracy Theories*, pp. 25–31.

34 W. Connolly, 'The Challenge to Pluralist Theory', in W. Connolly (ed.), *The Bias of Pluralism* (New York: Atherton Press, 1969), pp. 3–34; A. Heywood, *Political Ideologies: An Introduction* (New York: Palgrave Macmillan, 2007), pp. 53–61.

35 *Ibid.* For a seminal account of this institutional approach see R. Dahl, *Democracy in the United States* (Boston: Houghton Mifflin, 1981). For a collection of critical engagements with pluralism see Connolly (ed.), *The Bias of Pluralism*. Connolly has gone on to reformulate pluralist theories of democracy into what he calls a bicarmal attitude of open-

ness towards difference. See W. Connolly, *Pluralism* (Durham: Duke University Press, 2005).

36 See Fenster, *Conspiracy Theories*, pp. 25–31.

37 J. Dean, 'Declarations of Independence', in J. Dean (ed.), *Cultural Studies and Political Theory* (Ithaca: Cornell University Press, 2000), p. 292.

38 Connolly, cited in *ibid.*, p. 292.

39 This point also resonates with a more general critique of Cold War pluralism, which emphasises the institutionalised exclusion of dissent. In this argument an established set of interests and values are embedded and perpetuated by the liberal pluralist system and alternative approaches positioned beyond the bounds of legitimate political consideration. Dissent then emerged as a problem, in itself, for pluralist politics. See Connolly, 'The Challenge to Pluralist Theory', pp. 3–34.

40 See Bratich, *Conspiracy Panics*, pp. 25–33.

41 Hofstadter was much more than a liberal ideologue – his thinking was influenced by Freudian psychoanalysis through Lasswell and a broader conception of ideology rooted in the Frankfurt School tradition, which he accessed via the work of Karl Manheim, as well as a sophisticated reading of American historiography. See D. Walker Howe and P. E. Finn, 'Richard Hofstadter: The Ironies of an American Historian', *Pacific Historical Review*, 43:1 (1974), p. 6.

42 Hofstadter cited in Fenster, *Conspiracy Theories*, p. 28.

43 *Ibid.*, p. 29.

44 Indeed, rather than providing a critique of Hofstadter on his own terms, the point of highlighting these broader dynamics is to show how a particular historico-ideological formation informed the Arab-Muslim paranoia narrative – a connection I draw extensively in the next section. Hofstadter had many valuable insights to offer on the rise of the far right in American politics and on that peculiar strain of anti-intellectualism that runs through the American political culture.

45 *Ibid.*, p. 25.

46 D. Geary, 'Richard Hofstadter Reconsidered', *Reviews in American History*, 353 (2007), pp. 425–431; D. Brown, 'Redefining American History: Ethnicity, Progressive Historiography and the Making of Richard Hofstadter', *The History Teacher*, 36:4 (2003), pp. 527–548.

47 Bratich, *Conspiracy Panics*, pp. 25–46.

48 *Ibid.*, pp. 26–31.

49 *Ibid.*, p. 8.

50 H. Lasswell, *Psychopathology and Politics* (New York: Viking Press, 1930); and H. Lasswell, *Power and Personality* (New York: Viking Press, 1948).

51 Bratich, *Conspiracy Panics*, p. 27.

52 *Ibid.*, pp. 26–31.

53 *Ibid.*

54 *Ibid.*

55 *Ibid.*, p. 29.

56 *Ibid.*

57 This way of thinking is, in the liberal context, the mode through which individuals are made to govern themselves, stepping away from their personal behaviours, communities and institutions and making them an object of thought, self-critique and thus self-regulation. See B. Hindess, *Discourses of Power: From Hobbes to Foucault* (Oxford: Blackwell, 1996), pp. 105–136.

58 See, for instance, D. B. James, *The Fear of Conspiracy: Images of Un-American from the Revolution to the Present* (Ithaca: Cornell University Press, 1971); J. H. Bunzel,

Anti-politics in America: Reflections on the Anti-political Temper and its Distortion of the Democratic Process (New York: Alfred A Knopf, 1967); S. M. Lipset and E. Raab, *The Politics of Unreason: Right Wing Extremism in America, 1790–1977* (New York: Harper & Row, 1970); R. O. Curry and T. M. Brown (eds), *Conspiracy: The Fear of Subversion in American History* (New York: Holt, Reinhart and Winston, 1972); J. M. Roberts, *The Mythology of Secret Societies* (London: Secker & Warburg, 1972); J. George and L. Wilcox, *American Extremism* (Amherst, NY: Prometheus Books, 1996); L. Sargent (ed.), *Extremism in America: A Reader* (New York: New York University Press, 1996); D. Pipes, *Conspiracy! How the Paranoid Style Flourishes and Where it Comes From* (New York: Simon & Schuster, 1997); D. Pipes, *The Hidden Hand: Middle East Fears of Conspiracy* (London: Macmillan Press 1998); and M. Barkin, *A Culture of Conspiracy: Apocalyptic Visions in Contemporary America* (Berkeley: University of California Press, 2003).

59 Fenster, *Conspiracy Theories*, p. 24.

60 The term 'paranoid style' is regularly used in political commentary. See, for instance, N. Lemann, 'Paranoid Style', *The New Yorker* (6 October 2006); P. Krugman, 'The Paranoid Style', *New York Times* (9 October 2006); Lexington, 'The Paranoid Style in American Politics' *The Economist* (7 January 2006); W. Kristol, 'The Paranoid Style in American Liberalism', *The Weekly Standard* (1 February 2006); and D. Brooks, 'Paranoid Style', *New York Times* (4 May 2006).

61 Department of Homeland Security, 'Right Wing Extremism: Current Economic and Political Environment Fuelling Resurgence in Radicalization and Recruitment' (Washington, DC: Government Printing Office, April 2009).

62 *Ibid.*

63 See, for instance, J. Norman, '9/11 Conspiracy Theories Won't Stop', *CBS News* (11 September 2011). Available at www.cbsnews.com/news/9-11-conspiracy-theories-wont-stop/ (accessed 5 January 2015).

64 See, for instance, 'Conspiracy Envy', *The Economist* (29 November 2011); M. Jessup, 'Spotted at Occupy Wall Street: Tin Foil Hats!', *The Blaze* (21 October 2011); and A. Greenwald, 'Occupy Wall Street has an Anti-Semitism Problem', *Commentary* (11 October 2011).

65 L. Kaufman and K. Zernike, 'Activists Fight Green Projects, Seeing U.N. Plot', *New York Times* (3 February 2012).

66 J. Avalon, 'A Brief History of Wingnuts: From George Washington to Woodstock', *Daily Beast* (17 August 2014). Available at www.thedailybeast.com/articles/2014/08/17/a-brief-history-of-wingnuts-in-america-from-george-washington-to-woodstock.html (accessed 5 January 2015).

67 D. Pipes, *Conspiracy!*.

68 *Ibid.*, pp. 109–128.

69 *Ibid.*, p. 109.

70 See K. A. Cuordileone, 'Politics in an "Age of Anxiety" ': Cold War Political Culture and the Crisis in American Masculinity, 1949–60', *The Journal of American History*, 87:2 (2000), pp. 515–545.

71 D. W. Drezner, 'The Paranoid Style in World Politics', *The Spectator* (5 May 2010). Available at www.spectator.co.uk/features/5972613/the-paranoid-style-in-world-politics (accessed 5 January 2015).

72 M. Strauss, 'Anti-globalism's Jewish Problem', *Foreign Policy*, 139 (2003), pp. 58–67.

73 *Ibid.*

74 It is important to recognise here that anti-Semitism is abhorrent and unacceptable in any and all contexts. The archetypal anti-Semitic conspiracy narrative is the 'Protocols of the Elders of Zion', a product of nineteenth-century Tsarist propaganda,

which has been reproduced in various guises ever since. Often cited in neo-Nazi literature, the Protocols have found their way into the populist rhetoric of the Iranian leadership and the founding documents of the Palestinian group Hamas. For a comprehensive account of this issue see N. Cohen, *Warrant for Genocide: The Myth of the Jewish World Conspiracy and the Protocols of the Elders of Zion* (New York: Harper & Row, 1967).

75 Pipes, *The Hidden Hand*. Interestingly, Pipes participated in the post-9/11 Arab Muslim paranoia narrative too. See, for instance, E. Goode, 'The World; Finding Answers in Secret Plots', *New York Times* (10 March 2002).
76 Pipes, *The Hidden Hand*.
77 *Ibid.*, pp. 1–3.
78 *Ibid.*, pp. 1–2.
79 *Ibid.*, p. 1.
80 *Ibid.*, pp. 1–32.
81 *Ibid.*
82 *Ibid.*, pp. 8–9, 225, 374–380.
83 *Ibid.*, pp. 8–9, 374–380.
84 *Ibid.*, p. 375.
85 *Ibid.*, p. 376.
86 F. Zakaria, 'The Politics of Rage', *Newsweek Magazine* (14 October 2001).
87 R. Cohen, 'The Captive Arab Mind', *New York Times* (20 December 2010). Available at www.nytimes.com/2010/12/21/opinion/21iht-edcohen21.html?_r=0 (accessed 5 January 2015).
88 See R. Higgott, *Political Development Theory: The Contemporary Debate* (London, Taylor & Francis, 2005); and B. Hindess, 'The Past is Another Culture', *International Political Sociology*, 1:4 (2007), pp. 325–338.
89 *Ibid.*
90 See, for instance, T. A. McCarthy, 'From Modernism to Messianism: Liberal Developmentalism and American Exceptionalism', *Constellations*, 14:1 (2007), pp. 3–30.
91 Of course, the understanding of America as a 'city on the hill' and 'humanity's last, best hope' is a powerful theme in America's foreign policy tradition, which explicitly position American liberal democracy as the exemplar model for humanity. For an incisive account of the way liberal democracy has operated normatively in US foreign policy see, J. Moten, 'The Roots of the Bush Doctrine: Power, Nationalism, and Democracy Promotion in US Strategy', *International Security*, 29:4 (2005), pp. 112–156. For the broader contexts, see C. Coker, *Reflections on American Foreign Policy Since 1945* (New York: St Martin's Press, 1989); and W. R. Mead, 'The American Foreign Policy Tradition', *Foreign Affairs*, 81 (2002), pp. 163–176.
92 See, for instance, B. Lewis, 'The Roots of Muslim Rage', *The Atlantic* (September 1990), pp. 1–8. For the updated post-9/11 version of this see, B. Lewis, 'What Went Wrong', *The Atlantic* (January 2002), pp. 43–45. Jackson notes the prevalence of this narrative about dysfunctional Islamic culture in the academic and policy accounts of terrorism in the wake of 9/11. See R. Jackson, 'Constructing Enemies: 'Islamic Terrorism' in Political and Academic Discourse', *Government and Opposition*, 42:3 (2007), pp. 399–400, 406–407.
93 Lewis, 'The Roots of Muslim Rage' and Lewis, 'What Went Wrong'.
94 *Ibid.*
95 *Ibid.*
96 *Ibid.*
97 Lewis, 'What Went Wrong'.

98   *Ibid*. Jackson makes this connection in his analysis of the way the terrorist enemy was constructed by terrorism studies scholars and policy experts. See Jackson, 'Constructing Enemies', pp. 399–400.

99   T. Friedman, 'War of Ideas', *New York Times* (2 June 2002), p. 19.

100 *Ibid*.

101 *Ibid*.

102 Hindess, 'The Past is Another Culture', pp. 325–338.

103 E. Said, *Orientalism* (London: Penguin, 1977).

104 See, for instance, the explosive debate between Said and Lewis recorded in the *New York Review of Books* in 1982. 'Orientalism: An Exchange', *New York Review of Books* (12 August 1982). For an indication of Said's engagement with Lewis after 9/11 see E. Said, 'The Academy of Lagado', *London Review of Books* (April 2003). For an indication of the influence that commentators advancing the Arab-Muslim paranoia narrative had on the Bush administration, see B. Woodward, *State of Denial: Bush at War, Part III* (New York: Simon & Schuster, 2006), p. 84; and also E. Said, *Power, Politics and Culture: Interviews with Edward Said* (New York: Vintage Books, 2002), p. 359.

105 R. S. Robins and J. M. Post, *Political Paranoia: The Psychopolitics of Hatred* (New Haven, CT: Yale University Press: 1998). On contributions to media debates see, for instance, S. Kershaw, 'The Terrorist Mind: An Update', *New York Times* (9 January 2010). Available at www.nytimes.com/2010/01/10/weekinreview/10kershaw.html?pagewanted=all&_r=0 (accessed 5 January 2015); E. Goode, 'The World: Finding Answers in Secret Plots', *New York Times* (10 March 2002). Available at www.nytimes.com/2002/03/10/weekinreview/the-world-finding-answers-in-secret-plots.html (accessed 5 January 2015); 'Academic Says "Cult of Secrecy" Feeds Conspiracies on Kennedy', *Baltimore Sun* (21 November 2003). Available at http://articles.baltimoresun.com/2003-11-21/news/0311210366_1_conspiracy-assassination-jfk (accessed 5 January 2015); 'The Long Road to War: The Mind of Hussein', *PBS*. Available at www.pbs.org/wgbh/pages/frontline/shows/longroad/etc/mind.html (accessed 5 January 2015).

106 Robins and Post, *Political Paranoia*. Robins and Post do look at Nixon and McCarthy, but these are very much fall from grace-style post-mortems. McCarthy fits neatly with the paranoid style framework – and was actually one prominent provocation for Hofstadter's original essay.

107 *Ibid*.

108 *Ibid*.

109 *Ibid*., pp. 76–83.

110 *Ibid*.

111 *Ibid*.

112 *Ibid*. This is particularly the case in circumstances of uncertainty, or where a susceptible individual feels a loss of control.

113 *Ibid*.

114 *Ibid*., p. 82.

115 *Ibid*., p. 17. This references evidence that Hitler was himself part Jewish.

116 *Ibid*., p. 25.

117 *Ibid*., p. 146. See also, J. Victoroff, 'The Mind of the Terrorist: A Review and Critique of Psychological Approaches', *The Journal of Conflict Resolution*, 49:1 (2005), p. 24.

118 See J. M. Post, *Leaders and Their Followers in a Dangerous World: The Psychology of Political Behavior* (Ithaca, NY: Cornell University Press, 2004), p. xi.

119 M. Zonis and C. M. Joseph, 'Conspiracy Thinking in the Middle East', *Political Psychology*, 15:3 (1994), pp. 433–459.

120 *Ibid*.

121 *Ibid.*
122 *Ibid.*, p. 545.
123 *Ibid.*, p. 545.
124 Robins and Post, *Political Paranoia*, pp. 200–275.
125 See Post, *Leaders and Their Followers*.
126 J. M. Post, 'Explaining Saddam: A Psychological Profile', *House Armed Services Committee* (December 1990).
127 *Ibid.*, p. 4.
128 *Ibid.*
129 *Ibid.*
130 S. Kershaw, 'The Terrorist Mind: An Update'.
131 J. Bartlett and C. Miller, *The Power of Unreason: Conspiracy Theories, Extremism and Counter-Terrorism* (London: Demos, 2010).
132 *Ibid.*
133 *Ibid.*
134 *Ibid.*

2

Conspiracy culture

WHILE CONSPIRACY theories have usually been understood as fringe beliefs, commentators and scholars increasingly note their prevalence in mainstream American culture – in the activist left and movement conservatism, in foreign policy rhetoric about looming threats, and in popular narratives from the spy thriller novel through to gamer culture. According to recent research, large portions of the general public believe at least one conspiracy theory.[1] Take, for instance, the Zogby Poll published in 2007, which found that 51 per cent of Americans want Congress to investigate the Bush administration's actions before, during and after the 9/11 attacks.[2]

Such observations pose a significant challenge to the paranoid style tradition described in Chapter 1. They suggest that conspiracy theories are integral to the American experience; that conspiracy theories are embedded in the ostensibly rational practices of liberal democracy; that a rational centre cannot be cleanly separated from an irrational fringe.[3] Of course, the existence of a demarcation between rationality and irrationality is the cornerstone of the paranoid style account. It is this ideal rationality that conspiracy theories inevitably fall short of, and it is this deficiency that is understood to be the hallmark of abnormality. Put simply, an acknowledgment of conspiracy thinking in mainstream culture points to the way 'normal' politics, with its purported rationality and pragmatism, is shot through with the same kinds of irrationality and emotion often situated on the margins as a pathological danger to liberal democracy.[4] These issues are also a problem for the Arab-Muslim paranoia narrative, involved as it is in the production of a particular ideological imaginary, where the irrational periphery is held at bay and liberal modernity remains coherent. This division is likewise challenged by the apparent proliferation of conspiracy theories at the rational core of modernity's apex state.

This chapter engages with approaches that move away from the paranoid style paradigm, using these resources to rethink the issue of Arab-Muslim conspiracy theory.[5] A central theme advanced in what I call the conspiracy culture literature is that conspiracy theories are more common than was previously thought because the underlying sociological and psychological dynamics that produce them are actually widespread. The dynamics identified here include the sense that supposedly democratic institutions actually serve the ends of a powerful few; the feeling that vital knowledge is being concealed by an ever-expanding national security state; anxiety about the way opaque processes, systems and organisations now seem to shape social reality and individual subjectivity; an unquenchable psychic desire for a total account of reality or a stable subjectivity in a postmodern circumstance lacking these very things; or a pervasive suspicion of every authority, every claim to truth and every official account, when there is always another angle and a new connection.

Many of the themes identified in this literature resonate across cultural horizons, highlighting important commonalities and potential points of connection with Arab-Muslim political culture. Yet extrapolating these theories remains a fraught enterprise. The problem is suggested by the reticence of postcolonial scholars about the usefulness of Eurocentric frameworks for radically dissimilar regions. Indeed, as shown earlier, Edward Said set off a powerful line of critique against such enterprises by pointing to the self-justifying identity politics embedded in European accounts of the 'Orient', which took root in consonance with the colonial subjugation of the region. The point here is to recognise that the 'Orient' did not exist as a pre-discursive object in the world, with a set of fundamental properties and essences, which were simply uncovered and documented by disinterested scholars. It emerged as a subject of concern in a specific context, where the relationship between power and knowledge was decisive.

I argue that conspiracy theory should be similarly understood – as a discursive position as much as a category describing a specific type of claim. Much of the conspiracy culture literature exhibits a comparable concern with the power/knowledge nexus, noting for instance that conspiracy theory is entwined with well-established discourses mediating between legitimate and illegitimate knowledge.[6] For scholars pursuing this line of analysis, the 'conspiracy panics' of media commentators, public intellectuals and political leaders, rather than conspiracy theories per se, can provide an insight into the dominant forms of political rationality and the underlying power dynamics of an interpretive community.[7] This inversion parallels Said's analytical mode of operation, which was concerned not with uncovering a more accurate account of the 'Orient', but with understanding the origins and consequences of the culturally pervasive discourse of orientalism. Both perspectives suggest that important insights can be garnered by examining the way Arab-Muslim conspiracy theories emerged as a subject of concern in the writings of foreign policy commentators, in key strategic documents such as the National Security Strategy 2006, in US State Department public diplomacy programmes, and in wider modes of orientalist cultural reproduction, on which this foreign policy discourse draws.

Conspiracy culture in America

I begin my rethinking of Arab-Muslim conspiracy theory by engaging with works that consider conspiracy theories as mainstream rather than pathological. A useful entry point is Fredrick Jameson's influential account of the relationship between conspiracy theory and the postmodern condition, which provided much of the early impetus for a departure from the 'paranoid style' paradigm.[8] Jameson positions conspiracy theory as the 'poor person's cognitive mapping',[9] drawing on Kevin Lynch's famous study of urban living, where the inability to hold a coherent image of the cityscape in one's mind was linked to the alienation of the modern city.[10] Taking this dynamic as a metaphor for a postmodern culture where lived experience can no longer be easily associated with the global networks and international political arrangements that produce it, Jameson suggests that conspiracy theory is an attempt to produce a cognitive map of late capitalism and situate the subject in relation to it.[11] It is a geopolitical aesthetic that produces a comprehensible world from the incomprehensible fragments and pastiches of the postmodern experience.[12]

The broader issue for Jameson is that capitalism has grown so complex and all-encompassing, and late capitalist culture so disconnected from its base, that it is no longer possible to understand the underlying economic and political conditions that produce social reality, let alone plan for revolution.[13] In this context, conspiracy theory is identified as a mode of thinking that attempts to express the, by now, inaccessible, imperceptible base of late capitalism.[14] While Jameson's understanding of conspiracy theory is not paradigmatic, it brings together several trajectories running through the conspiracy culture literature: the way conspiracy theories help make sense of complex and opaque circumstances; the role of conspiracy theories as a popular critique of dominant social formations; and the unsettling effect of contemporary social structures on individual cognition. But the unifying theme running through both Jameson and the conspiracy culture literature is the way individuals or groups make sense of the forces that shape the world around them and their personal prospects. Put simply, conspiracy theory is consistently framed in terms of the relationship between power and knowledge.

One manifestation of this theme is the claim that conspiracy theories are implicit in the political institutions at the heart of American life. Conspiracy theories are often thought to express legitimate concerns about disjunctions between America's purported ideals and the reality of its political and economic systems. According to Mark Fenster, for instance, 'conspiracy theory does not pose a threat from outside some healthy centre of political engagement; rather, it is a historical and perhaps even necessary part of capitalism and democracy'.[15] Fenster shifts populism away from the negative account outlined in Chapter 1, where alienated mass movements threaten to overwhelm liberal democracy, towards a more positive and productive role, where populism acts as a force for progressive change and a check on the infidelity of fundamental institutions.[16] This is perhaps why conspiracy theories have often been associated with social movements confronting systems of structural prejudices that seem to amount to an unspoken conspiracy against particular groups – for instance, around issues of class, race, gender and sexuality.[17] Here conspiracy theory is said to expresses deep scepticism of the status quo and of attempts to explain away the silent yet intending source of inequality.

Jodi Dean takes up the relationship between democracy and conspiracy in a slightly different way.[18] Rather than a rough populist critique of democratic shortcomings, Dean positions conspiracy theory as an attempt to come to grips with an increasingly complicated world.[19] The confrontation between anxious subjects and overwhelming circumstances is a recurring theme in the conspiracy culture literature, but Dean cleverly draws it into the institutional context of American democracy by linking it to the relationship between secrecy and the idea of the public. She points out that the constitution of the public relies on disclosure: 'the compulsion to reveal is at the very core of the notion of the public ... publicity depends on the notion of secrecy. The power of the public is the power to unmask and reveal.'[20] This act of revealing brings the public into being. For Dean, conspiracy theory can be understood as a contemporary adaptation of democratic politics to the uncertainties and complexities of the information age.[21]

Of course, the relationship between secrecy and publicity still resonates with the idea of conspiracy theory as a populist critique of democracy gone wrong. It is for this reason that several scholars have pointed towards increasing levels of secrecy in American government as an important cause of conspiracy theories. Peter Knight, for instance, argues that since the early years of the Cold War ever more information has been classified as sensitive to national security, making it inaccessible to the general public.[22] This has produced what Knight calls a 'spectacle of secrecy', a perception that large organisations that occupy centre stage in American politics have and hold deeper truths, which they are not telling us about.[23] Kathryn Olmsted points towards the interrelationship between actual conspiracies, carried out (though kept secret) by the US government against foreign enemies and its own people, and the culture of suspicion and conspiracy theory that has proliferated in the American context.[24]

Robert Goldberg makes a similar point about the way intelligence failures around the 9/11 terrorist attacks provoked existing suspicions about the national security apparatus, which were then fuelled by an underwhelming investigation of the events in question, the unfolding of a neoconservative foreign policy agenda that took advantage of the circumstances, expanded powers of surveillance and interrogation under the Patriot Act, and controversial War on Terror programmes, including extraordinary rendition and torture.[25] Here, the expansion of state secrecy, the covert operation of state power, the historical awareness of elite malfeasance, all amplified by an international political circumstance characterised by secrecy and suspicion, imply that conspiracies do exist and are currently underway.

All of these perspectives recognise a move away from conspiracy theories centred on shadowy figures in smoky rooms and towards a concern about large organisations like the Federal Emergency Management Agency (FEMA), The World Bank, transnational corporations or the United Nations. For Timothy Melley, the location of sinister conspiracies in large organisations rather than individuals reflects an underlying tension between a liberal conception of the self as autonomous, rational and contained – an image that has dominated American identity since federation and liberal theory, since Hobbes and Locke – and a growing sense that the individual is shaped by social environmental forces.[26] This 'agency panic' manifests in the fear and rejection of structural forces, and the reassertion of a stable liberal model of the individual. In the words of R. D. Laing, 'we defend ourselves violently ... with terror, confusion and "defences", against ego-loss experiences'.[27] Instead of complex flows and structures, purposeful actors are substituted as the source of the problem. The move charted here points once again to the impact of contemporary circumstances on the way individuals interpret the world. It also taps into a wider recognition throughout the conspiracy culture literature that subjectivity is less stable than it once appeared and that conspiracy theories might have something to do with this unsettling and anxiety inducing circumstance.[28]

But is it a striving for a total account of reality that conspiracy theories really represent? The radical contingency of contemporary circumstances may also induce an endemic doubt about every authority and truth claim. As Jodi Dean writes:

> We're all linked into a world of uncertainties, where more information is always available, and hence, a word where we face daily the fact that our own truths, diagnoses, and understandings are incomplete.[29]

Under these circumstances conspiracy theories might instead be positioned as radical scepticism rather than a drive for absolute certainty. This conclusion is suggested by the quintessential collision of postmodernity and conspiracy theory, the assassination of President John F. Kennedy, which Don DeLillo famously characterised as an 'aberration in the heartland of the real'.[30] Here the multiple narratives, the endless speculation, the very unresolvability of the event, reflected the 'unmanageable reality' of the postmodern condition. For Knight this moment is a marker for the onset of a 'not entirely unfounded suspicion that the normal order of things itself amounts to a conspiracy'.[31]

This is no doubt one reason why conspiracy narratives are so present in popular culture, providing compelling plot lines for the full range of cultural forms. Several scholars identify an ironic or playful disposition at work here, which involves less the belief in a specific theory, than an ambivalence or even cynicism about the socio-political status quo.[32] The best account of this dynamic comes from Claire Birchall, who points out that conspiracy theories run alongside rumour as a form of popular knowledge that can oscillate between social critique and mischievous affectation.[33] She notes incisively the way commoditising tendencies of global capitalism impact on conspiracy theories, making them both folk knowledge and internationally circulating mass production, an expression of serious scepticism and a mode of popular entertainment.[34]

All these approaches, then, are centred on the relationship between power and knowledge: on the way everyday people make sense of powerful institutions and organisations, global processes and world historic events, as well as their own feelings of powerlessness in the face of these things. At the same time, we need to pay attention to the way power and authority are implicated in the identification of particular claims as conspiracy theories. Indeed, the most common opening move in the conspiracy culture literature is to note the powerful negative connotations that come with the label 'conspiracy theory', which has often worked to delegitimise particular interpretations and demonise the people making them. Hofstadter's use of psycho-medical terminology like 'delusion' and 'irrationality' is often criticised here for pathologising conspiracy theory rather than explaining it. Chapter 1 pushed this critique further by situating the paranoid style discourse as part of a broader post-war liberal imaginary, intimately involved with the management of populist forces thought to threaten the sober pragmatism at the heart of liberal politics.[35]

Jodi Dean makes a similar connection in her analysis of elite disquiet about the effects of the Internet on liberal democratic institutions. If political and media elites are anxious about the spread of unmediated views via the Internet, it is through the identification of such views as irrational conspiracy theories that this liberal democratic order may be defended.[36] The point here is that the identification of worrying conspiracy theories can be both delegitimising and productive: delegitimising of unauthorised, unruly, dissenting views that do not conform to the orthodox account or the accepted mode of inquiry; productive of a political space in which acceptable politics can occur, secured by contrast to the problematic views of apparently irrational paranoiacs.

Of course, this kind of analysis evokes Michel Foucault's influential account of the power/knowledge nexus, and particularly the way bodies of knowledge are demarcated and sustained through rules and regularities that circulate in discursive regimes.[37] Birchall deploys precisely this mode of analysis to examine the relationship between popular knowledge and official knowledge, drawing out the power dynamics that produce and mediate these positions and pointing towards the way legitimacy and illegitimacy are mutually constitutive.[38] Her approach parallels Foucault's persistent concern with subjugated knowledge and the messy processes through which intellectual orthodoxies emerge. Significantly, Foucault based his genealogies of knowledge, his histories of the present, in the study of non-canonical, non-traditional texts. It was the relationship between the canon and what was left out that Foucault found so provocative.[39] For now it is enough to say that the conspiracy culture literature implies an awareness of power relations, which necessarily pushes the analysis of conspiracy theory into a critical engagement with the social production of knowledge.

The point of the discussion so far has been to highlight the key contours of the conspiracy culture literature and look for potential resources for thinking about Arab-Muslim conspiracy theories. My concern has been less the differences that distinguish each approach and more the themes the literature is organised around. Here conspiracy theory is understood as a mode of populist critique; a way of making sense out of complex contemporary circumstances; a reaction to the expanding secrecy of the national security state; a form of popular knowledge spanning radical scepticism and everyday entertainment; and, underlying all these interpretations, a set of power relations. These themes are an advance on the Arab-Muslim paranoia narrative, to the extent that they identify conspiracy theory with widely experienced social, political and historical circumstances. But any extrapolation necessarily involves thinking through these themes in the context of international political dynamics, a task made all the more important by the fact that concerns about Arab-Muslim conspiracy theories in the wake of 9/11 were articulated mainly by foreign policy commentators and analysts.

Conspiracy culture in international politics

The mainstream view of conspiracy theory in international politics has relied on the 'paranoid style' paradigm. In this account, the domestic division between a rational pluralistic centre and an irrational paranoid periphery has been extrapolated so that conspiracy theory is located not just on the fringe of Western democracies, but also on the margins of international power and legitimacy from the point of view of American foreign policy commentators. As explained in Chapter 1, conspiracy theory is positioned as the province of dysfunctional regional cultures and the unhinged leaders of rogue states. The conspiracy culture perspectives outlined so far pose a critical challenge to this common-sense account, since they propose that conspiracy theory is not confined to the margins, is not the domain of pathological or irrational peoples, but, rather, is implicated in the institutions, practices and circumstances at the heart of mainstream America. The two scholars engaged with here – James Der Derian and

Laura Jones – draw on similar themes to provide critical readings of conspiracy theory in international politics.

Der Derian takes the Hollywood spy genre as his entry point, associating it with official US national security discourses to show how the positing of conspiratorial threats actually shores up sovereignty in the face of a complex and contingent world that always threatens to undermine it.[40] Initially, Der Derian links the spy genre to a broader socio-cultural circumstance familiar from the conspiracy culture literature:

> let us interpret the spy film as symptomatic of highly contingent, late modern times, when borders are increasingly porous, dangers ubiquitous, politics ambiguous; when the fear and suspicion spreads that there must be someone, the *anarchist* or *terrorist*, behind the danger; that there must be a panoptic system, *espionage*, to uncover or keep track of it; that there must be, if necessary, a violent strategy, *counter-terrorism*, to fight it; and finally, that there must be some way, *conspiracy theory*, to make sense of it.[41]

Considering conspiracy theory alongside the fear of terrorist plots and the suspicions of intelligence bureaucracies, Der Derian repositions these practices as forms of boundary maintenance for a sovereign identity always in danger of unravelling in the face of incoherency and contradiction. The search for perfect knowledge of the security environment, for the underlying logic of international actions, for the ultimate technology to penetrate the surface and uncover conspiratorial dealings – these are essential to the sovereignty discourse:

> If danger and high anxiety produce the categorical imperative, the moral 'must' behind the spy genre, it is the desire to secure a sovereign self-identity that sustains the conspiratorial narrative, and raises it to the power of theology ... 'ye shall know the truth and the truth shall set you free' reads the inscription on the entry to the CIA. Cinema and espionage share, mediate and magnify the constitutional power of the sovereign gaze: knowing the truth implies, indeed necessitates, seeing the other as alien, different, threatening.[42]

Here conspiracy narratives are drawn towards, and at the same time secure anxious subjects against, the ultimate arbitrariness of sovereignty, 'the "abnormality" of an unprotected territory and an unpredictable death', when the distinctions between an orderly inside and an anarchical outside are tenuous and increasingly blurred.[43] Put another way, 'the fictional sovereignty of the self and the state melds and materialises as a truth in such moments of high conspiracy and eventful contingency'.[44]

This awareness of sovereign instability resonates with concerns about the relationship between power and knowledge that run through the conspiracy culture literature. As much as a politico-legal identity, the sovereign presence sketched by Der Derian is also presented as the source of authoritative knowledge about the reality of opaque international politics. Reflecting on the unsettling effects of Oliver Stone's cinematic reconstruction of the JFK assassination, Der Derian suggest that the opprobrium directed towards Stone by the political establishment was not just the result of the challenge it posed to the official account laid out by the Warren Commission. It was also about the way Stone presented his alternative narrative using the stylistic devices of authenticity, deploying actual footage of the assassination, dramatic reconstructions of the alternative assassination scenario, and a docu-drama aesthetic, which seemed to challenge the normal procedures for establishing authoritative knowledge, particularly around issues of high politics and national significance. This challenge occurred at an epistemic level, and for Der Derian it shows that 'the authenticity of the truth is constructed through the technical production of reality – and it is through the over-representation of reality that Stone deconstructs any claims for an "original" version of the truth'.[45] Of course, this revelation disrupts and decentres established modes of knowledge production about international politics, closely guarded by political and media elites, and ultimately grounded in a pervasive discourse of sovereign control.

Der Derian continues on with this theme from a slightly different angle in his full-length examination of the confluence between intelligence, technology and security.[46] Of particular relevance is his focus on the connection between paranoia and the intelligence apparatus, a connection that flourished during the Cold War:

> One policy implication of the new surveillance regime is that the great powers created a cybernetic system that displayed the classic symptoms of advanced paranoia: hyper-vigilance, intense distrust, rigid and judgemental thought processes, and projection of one's own repressed beliefs and hostile impulses onto the other. The very nature of the surveillance/cybernetic system contributes to this condition: we see and hear the other, but imperfectly and partially – *below* our rising expectations.[47]

Der Derian points to the 'missile gaps' of the early Cold War as an instance where paranoia and 'partial seeing' produced heightened threat perception and national security policy.[48] This ties in with his earlier argument about the connection between sovereignty and conspiracy. The reason of state is reason based in suspicious, covert, and perhaps paranoid knowledge: 'this means that realpolitik rules, permanent vigilance is necessary, and the preparation for war is constant'.[49]

Der Derian's account helps us translate several important themes from the conspiracy culture literature into the idioms of international politics: the rational liberal centre becomes the sovereign state and irrational populism becomes anarchy 'out there'; the liberal subject is replaced with the sovereign individual, though still counterpoised with the forces or irrationality. Likewise, at the heart of Der Derian's thinking is what was described earlier as agency panic, or what has been understood by international relations scholars as the 'anarchy problematique',[50] which produces the impetus for conspiracy thinking in both the national security state and everyday individuals. Der Derian's key insight is to show how conspiracy *narratives* – variously conceived of as conspiracy theories, spy thriller plots and the hyper-vigilant paranoia of intelligence agencies – hang together in a complex set of interrelationships around this theme of sovereign anxiety and reproduction. He takes seriously Jameson's account of conspiracy theory as a geopolitical aesthetic, but expands this out to the interpretations of intelligence agencies and defence departments also involved in 'a degraded attempt – through the figuration of advanced technology – to think the impossible totality of the contemporary world system'.[51]

Laura Jones adds another dimension to this broadening move by focusing on the question of discursive power around the interpretation of 9/11.[52] This is done, for instance, by comparing a statement from the 9/11 Truth Movement alleging that 9/11 was an inside job with a statement from Zbigniew Brzezinski proposing a strategic scenario in which a domestic crisis of some kind is contrived or exploited as a trigger for the invasion of Iran.[53] Jones asks, 'why is Brzezinski reasonable and the 9/11 Truth Movement not?'[54] The term conspiracy theory, she argues, operates in relation to an inside/outside binary that divides off non-expert views unauthorised by establishment institutions or discourses.[55] From here Jones proposes that conspiracy narratives with similar structural properties reside on the outside *and* on the inside of authoritative spaces.[56] She points to the way conspiracy narratives have historically existed on the *inside* of American foreign policy discourse, often helping to constitute national identity in opposition to nefarious others.[57]

Of course, this insight links with a broader identity politics literature in international relations concerned with the relationship between self and other in the foreign policy context.[58] A helpful reference point here is David Campbell's path-breaking examination of the way American national identity has often emerged in relation to discourses of danger and radical otherness, for instance, in the puritan jeremiad, which located perceived threats, and even unfamiliar circumstances, as the work of Satan and his minions, out to bring down the 'new Jerusalem' – be it native Indians, hysteria, Catholicism, or simply the hostility of nature.[59] Campbell argues that, through this oppositional dynamic, ever-present indeterminacy, difference and dissent *within* the group is delegitimised, while characteristics thought antithetical to the dominant identity are abstracted out onto foreign entities as negative signifiers. Thus, confronting nefarious enemies abroad is contiguous with domesticating identity at home.[60] As Campbell has it, 'the differences within become the differences between' and the borders of national identity are secured.[61]

Yet this inside/outside binary can be understood as another manifestation of the sovereign anxiety dynamic, which produces both the impetus towards conspiracy thinking and the differentiation between legitimate and illegitimate conspiracy narratives. As Campbell explains:

> The paradigm of sovereignty operates on the basis of a simple dichotomy: sovereignty versus anarchy. Although these terms have a special significance within the discourse of international relations ... sovereignty and anarchy are replicable concepts that are pivotal for the construction of various mutually reinforcing dichotomies, such as subject/object, inside/outside, self/other, rational/irrational, true/false, order/disorder, and so on. In each instance the former is the higher, regulative ideal to which the latter is derivative and inferior, and a source of danger to the former's existence. In each instance 'sovereignty' (or its equivalent) signifies a center of decision presiding over a self that is to be valued and demarcated from an external domain that cannot or will not be assimilated to the identity of the sovereign domain.[62]

While conspiracy narratives may be motivated by the attempt to secure sovereignty against the vicissitudes of an uncertain world, at an individual level such narratives often simultaneously undermine the state and the political establishment as a source of legitimate knowledge. Thus, the designation of such narratives as conspiracy theories represents a transition to the position of 'other' – and the status of outside, irrational, false, disorderly – against which an authoritative 'self' might be defined and defended. In recognition of these dynamics Jones dispenses with the term conspiracy theory as an analytical frame and instead focus on what she calls 'conspiracy discourse'.[63] According to Jones, 'it is necessary, and more insightful, to recognise a broader discursive assemblage of statements, representations and practices that pivot around the possibility of the conspiracy act'.[64] The fact that some conspiracy narratives are 'called forth' as conspiracy theories points to the importance of the power relations that shape and order political knowledge.[65]

Having identified these power relations, Jones directs her attention towards the conspiracy narratives of the 9/11 Truth Movement. This engagement is informed by a broader critical geopolitics project that aims to 'de-centre the geopolitical gaze, away from elite and official visions of global space, in order to consider other ways of knowing'.[66] Like much of the conspiracy culture literature, the broader theme here is that this usually marginalised knowledge has a positive part to play in engaging powerful geopolitical orthodoxies, and as such deserves consideration not condescension. Jones makes this case through a series of interviews and auto-ethnographic encounters with 9/11 truthers. She finds that conspiracy discourse is intensely personal: it gives voice to deep anxieties; it gives a sense of purpose; it produces both solidarity and alienation.[67] It is shot through with the same imperfections and incoherencies that are present in the people that give it voice. These people are at once marginalised, empowered, alienated, idealistic, reactionary, sometimes anti-Semitic and much more.[68] Rather than presenting a unified category, 'conspiracy theory', with a set of common properties and motivating logics, Jones demonstrates the messiness and specificity of popular geopolitical interpretation in the wake of 9/11. Indeed, the diverse range of claims and political objectives that existed within the 9/11 Truth Movement indicates this. For instance, members of the group used the term 'conspiracy theory' to distinguishing between sensible conspiracy narratives and those that went too far. As Jones explains, this 'illustrates the importance of attending to conspiracy discourse as a range of positions within which different actors seek to make claims for legitimate "knowledge"'.[69] Clearly, some people are in a better position than others to do this – to mobilise the trappings of authority and credibility, and to dismiss the claims of others as unreasonable.[70]

Both Jones and Der Derian indicate the limitations of the paranoid style paradigm for understanding this situation, not to mention the issue of Arab-Muslim conspiracy theories. Both point to the way the centre/periphery, rational/irrational, inside/outside dichotomies implicit in that approach sustain existing structures of power and authority, manifested here in a dominant geopolitical imagination and its accompanying institutions. With these insights in hand, we can now situate conspiracy theory in terms of a broader identity politics dynamic in international politics, which produces zones of legitimacy and illegitimacy, self and other, sovereignty and anarchy. Conspiracy narratives driven by similar anxieties and interpretive impulses, and sharing similar narrative structures, are distributed across these spaces, such that *conspiracy discourse* appears a more appropriate frame for thinking through these relations. Although Jones goes on to examine the 9/11 Truth Movement, a group that has typically been studied as an example of conspiracy theory par excellence, her focus might have just as easily fallen on the conspiracy narratives of the powerful or on the discursive production of the post-9/11 conspiracy discourse. While many of these conclusions are suggested in the conspiracy culture literature, the international context reveals something new: the common drive towards conspiracy – as a covert act or a narrative of danger and deception – implicit in the culture of sovereignty.

Orientalism and the limits of theory

The natural next step in this rethinking of Arab-Muslim conspiracy theories is to supplant the Arab-Muslim paranoia narrative with a more sophisticated account drawn from the preceding discussion. Yet I remain reticent about the prospect of uprooting theories developed to explain the Anglo-American experience and applying them to vastly different circumstances. Even the foregoing international politics accounts were grounded in the specific context of the US national security state and American political culture. This hesitation is further provoked by the problematic relationship between power and knowledge around conspiracy theory, highlighted across the last two sections. While it may well be the case that some conspiracy culture themes resonate in the Arab-Muslim world, the significance of these resonances is not at all clear. For instance, theorising about the problematic nature of political interpretations in societies that have been the subject of colonial domination, from within the intellectual tradition of the colonising powers, risks the reproduction of historical power relations.[71] Indeed, as Siba Grovogui makes clear in the opening paragraph of his introduction to postcolonialism, these historical power relations are very much about distinguishing legitimate and illegitimate knowledge:

> Upon conquest and colonization, Europe had aspired to direct world affairs by first writing the history of 'Man' in its own self-image. It then degraded the markers of culture, arts and science for others to the status of folklore, myths, and shamanism. Academic subjects such as Literature, Philosophy, History and Anthropology – and now International Relations – contribute to this endeavour.[72]

It is easy to see how conspiracy theory could be added alongside folklore, myths and shamanism as another feature of 'traditional' society. This is particularly the case when we consider that postcolonial critiques marry together with the critical reading of sovereignty and anarchy, self and other described. For instance, postcolonialism is explicitly concerned with the historical and ongoing implications of the self/other relations set in motion by colonial domination of the non-European world, including, notably, Arab majority territories in the Middle East. Attempts by Western scholars to identify and explain Arab-Muslim conspiracy theories seem particularly fraught in this light.

Edward Said's account of orientalism is especially relevant for understanding these dynamics. Said argued that knowledge about the Orient in colonial Europe emerged alongside and was entwined with the subjugation of the region, providing moral and political resources that justified colonialism, via a seemingly factual account of its history and the character of its peoples.[73] According to Said,

> In a sense Orientalism was a library or archive of information commonly and, in some of its aspects, unanimously held. What bound the archive together was a family of ideas and a unifying set of values proven in various ways to be effective. These ideas explained the behavior of Orientals; they supplied Orientals with a mentality, a genealogy, an atmosphere; most important, they allowed Europeans to deal with and even to see Orientals as a phenomenon possessing regular characteristics.[74]

Said shows how a reservoir of stereotypes and associations based in these early taxonomies were drawn upon by colonial administrators, and later by American foreign policy thinkers. Crucially, for Said knowledge about the Orient always existed in relation to an idealised Western identity – a relationship that was at once self-defining and morally edifying, and which worked in tandem with the commercial and strategic motivations for empire. The contrast drawn up in this orientalist imaginary should be familiar already: 'On the one hand there are Westerners, and on the other there are Arab-Orientals; the former are (in no particular order) rational, peaceful, liberal, logical, capable of holding real values, without natural suspicion; the latter are none of these things.'[75] Particularly pertinent for our purposes, Said points to the contemporary significance of these identities for American foreign policy. Taking framing practices deployed by Henry Kissinger as emblematic of latter-day orientalism, Said writes

> Kissinger may not have known on what fund of pedigreed knowledge he was drawing when he cut the world up into pre-Newtonian and post-Newtonian conceptions of reality. But his distinction is identical with the orthodox one made by Orientalists, who separate Orientals from Westerners. And like Orientalism's distinction Kissinger's is not value-free, despite the apparent neutrality of his tone. Thus such words as 'prophetic,' 'accuracy,' 'internal,' 'empirical reality,' and 'order' are scattered throughout his description, and they characterize either attractive, familiar, desirable virtues or menacing, peculiar, disorderly defects. Both the traditional Orientalist ... and Kissinger conceive of the difference between cultures, first, as creating a battlefront that separates them, and second, as inviting the West to control, contain, and otherwise govern (through superior knowledge and accommodating power) the Other.[76]

Of course, these contrasting visions of Western and oriental knowledge are highly relevant to the issue of Arab-Muslim conspiracy theory, particularly when it is dealt with in the foreign policy context. The term 'conspiracy theory' is so heavily consonant with the worst stereotypes about Arab-Muslim irrationality, suspicion, deficits in logic, lack of accuracy and objectivity, and general pre-scientific backwardness that even more sophisticated and self-aware accounts risk reproducing latent orientalist tropes.[77]

Perhaps the best book on Arab-Muslim conspiracy theories comes from Matthew Gray, who goes out of his way to caveat against the orientalism he astutely identifies in the work of Daniel Pipes and others.[78] Writes Gray,

> this book seeks to discredit the reductionist, often Orientalist explanations for conspiracism in the region, especially the view that would argue for pathological explanations of conspiracy theories and their frequency in the Arab world. Instead, the aim is to analyse and understand it through the tools of political science, and to explain the sources and structures of conspiracy theories from that perspective.[79]

Gray acknowledges that the theories he brings to bear are largely drawn from the American context and can therefore only be used with extreme caution and in a piecemeal fashion, with an awareness of their limitations and biases.[80] No single theory, he argues, can be superimposed onto the Arab world.[81] Instead, he draws on three key explanatory trajectories very much rooted in the conspiracy culture literature: marginalisation, state–society relations and political-sociological structures. These causal dynamics are contextualised by Gray's awareness of the region's extensive history of foreign intervention and geopolitical machinations.[82] According to Gray:

> Conspiracism can often be a discourse by marginalized elements that seeks to popularly deconstruct official or state versions of events, and it is a response to the failures of governments and leaderships to develop effective models of economic development and popular political participation. It is also a sign of diminishing state legitimacy and of a breach between state and society. It can even be a source of entertainment for some people who take it less seriously than others. Concomitantly, as states have responded to the failure of earlier developmental orthodoxies and a diminished legitimacy, they have adopted their own conspiracist rhetoric in their discourse with and to their societies, making conspiracism also a tool of state symbolism, legitimacy-building and control.[83]

This analysis reflects several of the key themes highlighted in the conspiracy culture literature: the way conspiracy theories can act as a popular critique of political institutions, structural inequalities or elite malfeasance;[84] are often a response to wider social conditions, from the dynamics of late capitalist culture and globalisation, through to the spectacle of state secrecy; and can occupy a range of positions from earnest politics through to playfulness. Gray is at his best when he points to the complexity of political discourse – to the way conspiracy narratives sit alongside other sorts of language and serve multiple purposes interchangeably; are part of people's identity, while not defining them; and participate in living histories and cultural mythologies that are hitched to the ongoing structural dynamics of politics. He is particularly compelling, for instance, when he notes that entertainment and popular culture are suffused with conspiracy narratives, which simultaneously reflect concerns, suspicions, even cynicism about the status quo.[85]

However, despite an awareness of the problem of orientalism, one theme that is conspicuously underdeveloped is the relationship between power and knowledge. Said's analytical focus was directed towards the discourse established by colonising societies *about* the 'Orient' – which in his view constituted it as a category of analysis and a subject of concern – with a view to understanding the way power and identity are asserted through the production of knowledge. A similarly self-reflective analysis of the narrative produced by Western scholars and commentators *about* Arab-Muslim conspiracy theories is so far absent in the study of the Arab-Muslim conspiracy theory issue. An important starting point is to recognise that the 'Orient' and 'conspiracy theory' are discursive positions in a particular discourse, as much as analytical categories deployed by sober researchers. Said notably never attempted to uncover a more authentic or precise version of the 'Orient', a task he thought impossible from his standpoint, since 'words such as "Orient" and "Occident" correspond to no stable reality that exists as a natural fact'.[86] To boot, despite a sophisticated understanding of discourse on display elsewhere in their analysis, researchers often inexplicably retain a flat account of language when it comes to conspiracy theory.[87] Language describes a pre-existing object, 'conspiracy theory', which analysts simply discover in the world 'out there'.[88] This leads to a mode of analysis that skates over the political and historical context in which scholarly concerns about conspiracy theory in the Arab-Muslim world emerge, as well as the relationship between conspiracy theory, dominant forms of political rationality and the power relations involved in distinguishing legitimate and illegitimate knowledge.

One indication of the problem here is the widely acknowledged difficulty with defining conspiracy theory. For instance, its key characteristics often diverge in competing renditions, ranging from irrationality to excessively rationality, from false reasoning to pedantry, and from grandiosity to blinkered thinking.[89] As Gray admits:

> The terms 'conspiracy theory' and 'conspiracism' defy easy definition, perhaps because there is such a breadth of discourses from such a variety of individuals and groups, all with varying goals and emphases to their language. A further challenge is the epistemological opaqueness of many conspiracy theories: it is difficult to draw a clear and concise line between an idea that is conspiracist versus one that, for example, is derived from political paranoia or denial – or even one that, wittingly or not, has successfully identified an actual case of a conspiracy.[90]

Yet this excess of subjects, goals, styles and epistemologies never leads to the abandonment of the category, nor stands in the way of the proceeding analysis. Robert Irwin makes a complementary point when he suggests that the category 'conspiracy theory' carries unhelpful conceptual baggage that distorts analysis of political rhetoric in the Arab world.[91] Instead, he argues, the rich literature on rumour provides a better conceptual fit, particularly since the utterances cited as conspiracy theories are mostly colloquial in nature, rather than formal political explanation:

> I propose the use of Ockham's razor: Entities should not be multiplied unnecessarily. Why assume lasting effects of a nineteenth century European pattern of thinking on the thoughts of a shopkeeper in Amman in April 2003 if the explanation as an instance of rumor will do?[92]

What Irwin indicates is that the category 'conspiracy theory' is itself the product of a particular cultural setting. He also suggests that the way particular narratives emerge as conspiracy theories has something to do with the ability of analysts and commentators writing about Arab-Muslim culture to identify them in this way. Hustings and Orr make a similar point about research on conspiracy

theory in the American context, including much of the conspiracy culture
literature:

> Instead of questioning the coherency of 'conspiracy theory' as a category, or point-
> ing to the power of the phrase, these analyses come dangerously close to reifying it.
> Clumping together alien abductees, the *X Files*, and concerns about corporate cor-
> ruption erases distinctions between the various concerns of conspiracy, treating
> them all as part of the freak show of American culture in the postmodern moment.[93]

While these criticisms are telling, conspiracy, both the act and the suspicion
of it, remains an important feature of contemporary politics everywhere. And
it is well worth investigating the dynamics of secrecy, power and interpretation captured by the conspiracy theme. Even if one still believes in the analytical value of conspiracy theory as a discrete concept, an important part of any
such investigation must be to analyse the function of conspiracy theory as a
discursive position in a wider conspiracy discourse, encompassing multiple
conspiracy narratives and competing interpretations, all vying for legitimacy
and standing.[94] A crucial starting point in the Arab-Muslim context will be to
look at the intersection between contemporary orientalism and the way conspiracy theory emerges as a subject of concern for scholars, commentators and
analysts.

Conspiracy theory as discursive position

These critical interjections present an unavoidable challenge for a book focused
on Arab-Muslim conspiracy theories during the War on Terror. It would be easy
enough to follow the conspiracy culture literature and provide another, albeit
more sophisticated explanation of conspiracy narratives about American power.
Yet there are several important reasons to take a different approach. On the one
hand, any advance on Gray's explanation of conspiracy rhetoric in the Arab-
Muslim world would need to be based on detailed ethnographic research, situated in specific locations, and conducted from within the cultural and political
traditions in question. The emphasis here would have to be on taking political
language on its own terms, a process that might entail testing existing concepts
and schemas from the Anglo-American tradition for their usefulness and appli-
cability. It should be clear from the foregoing discussion that neither Gray nor I
are in a position to conduct this kind of research.

On the other hand, there are good reasons to think that the relationship
between power and knowledge, highlighted by postcolonial scholars and in critical readings of conspiracy discourse, is very relevant for understanding the way
Arab-Muslim conspiracy theories became a subject of concern for American
foreign policy commentators and policy makers after 9/11. It has been shown
that the common-sense view of conspiracy theory in foreign policy and media

renditions entails a potent delegitimising effect, where particular claims are associated with the backward irrationality of alienated regional cultures or the cognitive pathology of dictators and extremists. It is not too much to suggest that a concern about the problem of Arab-Muslim conspiracy theories delegitimised some perspectives and shut down space for alternative interpretations of 9/11. This process is worth examining since it is an important aspect of the way historical truth emerges, foreign policy orthodoxy is established and specific strategies legitimised. At the same time, as Said's analysis of orientalism indicates, studying power relations around the issue of Arab-Muslim conspiracy theory can provide an insight in to the underlying political rationality and identity politics at play in America's War on Terror. Set out in what follows are some key lines of analysis for the rest of the book via an engagement with several works that treat conspiracy theory as a discursive position.

A helpful way of introducing a discursive account of Arab-Muslim conspiracy theory is to identify clearly the way power works through language – a task that can be easily achieved by comparing the dictionary definitions of 'conspiracy' and 'conspiracy theory'. The everyday sense of 'conspiracy' is commonly defined as 'a secret plan by a group to do something unlawful or harmful',[95] while the legal definition expands this to 'an agreement between two or more people to commit an act prohibited by law or to commit a lawful act by means prohibited by law'.[96] The dictionary definition of 'conspiracy theory' is 'a belief that an unpleasant event or situation is the result of a secret plan made by powerful people'.[97] The most obvious difference here is that the definition of 'conspiracy theory' implies a definite power relationship. The 'powerful' are located at the centre of these theories – as the object – with the theorist implicitly situated in the pejorative as someone who merely believes. Why does this definition exclude the powerful from having conspiracy theories about the powerful or about the weak?

This is particularly curious since there have been many well-documented attempts to unseat the status quo through conspiracies – the Gunpowder Plot, the thwarting of which is still celebrated in England with firecrackers and the burning of Guy Fawkes dolls or 'guys', or the assassination by Serbian nationalists of Archduke Franz Ferdinand, which triggered World War I, are both notable examples.[98] The extreme manifestation of an anti-government conspiracy is a *coup d'état*, a term first used to describe Napoleon Bonaparte's successful overthrow of the French Directorate in 1799, though there are countless examples of deposed sovereigns across history.[99] In the early part of the sixteenth century, for instance, Niccolò Machiavelli, regarded by many as an early political realist, spent a section of his first book, *The Prince*, and the longest chapter of his second, *Discourses of Livy*, examining the prevalence of conspiracies against the state.[100] For Machiavelli conspiracies were common because 'few can venture to make open war upon their sovereign, whilst every one may engage in conspiracies against him', a point he illustrated with case studies of Roman emperors brought down by conspiracies.[101]

This definitional disjunction highlights the power dynamic implicit in the term. Why is there such slippage between the definition of 'conspiracy' and 'conspiracy theory'? On their own, each word, 'conspiracy' and 'theory', has a technical and precise meaning that is fairly impartial in its connotation, notwithstanding the dishonesty or illegality associated with conspiracy. But together they are a dismissal, a closure – an indication of personal belief not verifiable fact. While the distinctions between conspiracy and conspiracy theory may on closer examination seem ambiguous, they are not *arbitrary*. These categories position subjects and apportion authority. The conspiracy culture literature deepens this initial observation by identifying these power relations with the production of particular political orders. For Dean, Birchall, Der Derian and Jones, political authority and the illegitimate category of conspiracy theory are mutually constitutive. The delegitimising effect of conspiracy theory enacts a closure that is useful in the production of a particular orthodoxy.

The issue of delegitimising closure is at the heart of Gina Hustings and Martin Orr's analysis of 'conspiracy theory' as an exclusionary *label*, which operates by 'stripping claimants of the status of reasonable interlocutor'.[102] Encountering the conspiracy label prompts a reader to 'go meta', to pull back from the specific claims of the accused conspiracy theorist and instead assess their right to say anything at all.[103] It directs the reader to motive, character, personal history, associations, psychology and away from the content of a claim – 'no matter how true or false or conspiracy related [the] claim is'.[104] Hustings and Orr suggest that the move to 'go meta', while most explicit in the 'paranoid style' discourse, is still implicit in much of the ostensibly sympathetic conspiracy culture literature, such that these accounts tend to look less at the content or character of an allegation and more at the causes of them.[105] Rather than taking any claim on its own terms, conspiracy culture remains a problem to be solved. This problem-solving approach is filled out by explanations that tend to 'shift between words that denote certain kinds of truth claims and words that denote cognitive failures and psychological states'.[106] However mainstream conspiracy theory may seem to be, and whatever the redeeming features ascribed to the term, it still inscribes its contents as somehow problematic.

Keith Goshorn fills out the political dimension of this delegitimising effect by identifying what he terms 'anti-conspiracy discourse'.[107] The point for Goshorn is that the identification of conspiracy interpretation as a subject of study produces a strong deterrent against interrogating the operation of elite power.[108] And this is the case for academics as much as media commentators and everyday interpreters, when the personal and professional costs of studying some topics are extremely prohibitive.[109] Explaining the cause of conspiracy theory avoids these prohibitions since the actual claims that make up the category are epiphenomenal.[110] Indeed, there is hardly an example in all the literature engaged so far of a scholar attempting to determine the veracity of a specific claim. Goshorn pushes the issue further, pointing out that these scholars often lack the area-specific expertise necessary to usefully comment on the controversies they take for granted as conspiracy theories.[111] In Goshorn's view there is a clear alternative:

> serious scholarly research would better occupy itself with the study of 'anti-conspiracy' culture before returning to a terrain marked 'conspiracy culture' already exhausted and emptied of meaning by exploitative popular media. The collective problem of dissuasion from critical thought and deterrence from ideological dissent is far more important for maintaining democratic principles than concerns about false interpretations and the erosion of a longstanding similacral edifice of rationality and consensus now gradually passing from the historical stage of western culture.[112]

The point here is that studying conspiracy theories tends to produce and sustain frames of containment that quarter off critical engagements with the operation of elite power, particularly around matters of political controversy. More broadly, such studies contribute to a discourse of deterrence, which can prevent scholars, as much as the general public, from beginning this kind of inquiry in the first place, lest their meta-motivations be called into question. Instead, it is these 'strategies of deterrence and frames of containment' that need to be analysed.[113]

This anti-conspiracy discourse is the focus of Jack Bratich's book-length study of what he calls 'conspiracy panics'.[114] His organising question is 'how does a particular claim come to be characterised as a conspiracy theory?'[115] Here Bratich turns symptomology, a method popular in the conspiracy culture literature, back on commentary and scholarship *about* conspiracy theory.[116] This methodology situates a particular phenomenon as the product of some other process or circumstance to which it is a clue. For the bulk of scholars this means looking at the underlying circumstances that produce conspiracy theories, for instance, alienation, the complexity of a globalising world, or the instability of the postmodern subject. Bratitch takes a step back. Instead of analysing the causes of conspiracy theory per se, he focuses on the deployment of the term 'conspiracy theory' as a symptom of something else – of something about the interpretive community making this identification.[117] Conspiracy theory becomes not a window into the minds and lives of conspiracy theorists, but into the dominant forms of rationality that we all take for granted.[118]

Rather than the anxieties of conspiracy theorists, Bratich focuses on the conspiracy panics of the media, the academy and the 'informed public'.[119] He positions these as (paradoxically anxious) attempts to defend rationalist truth claims from the threat of counter-knowledge and to head off dissent of one sort or another.[120] Most obviously, the concept of conspiracy theory monitors and disciplines the thoughts and behaviours of others.[121] Individuals with dangerous views must be identified and discredited. They must feel the weight of public opprobrium and correct their behaviour. Conversely, each individual must self-monitor.[122] They must make their own modes of thought an object of thought, guarding against unreasonable ideas or impulses.[123]

The delegitimising and productive dynamics identified by Hustings and Orr, Goshorn and Bratich have much to offer an analysis of conspiracy discourse in the foreign policy context. For instance, as Der Derian makes clear, the opaque, covert, self-interested conditions of international politics present scholars, analysts and everyday people with obvious matters of controversy, but limited scope for conclusive interpretation.[124] Under these circumstances, strategies of deterrence and frames of containment clearly congregate around foreign policy controversies, among which we must surely include the 9/11 terrorist attacks and the subsequent foreign policy adventures launched in its wake. These critical accounts indicate that concerns about the conspiracy theories motivating Arab-Muslim anti-Americanism may well have played a delegitimising role in post-9/11 political landscape, marking out the boundaries of acceptable interpretation and dampening down dissenting views. At the same time, taking Bratich's discursive symptomology seriously, a close analysis of post-9/11 conspiracy discourse can provide a window into the dominant form of political rationality regulating America's War on Terror discourse. With this in mind, the case studies that follow take as their starting point an analysis of the context in which conspiracy theory emerged as a subject of concern in America's foreign policy discourse after 9/11. As Bratich explains: 'We need to examine where and when it appears, who speaks it, what else is linked with it, and what it opposes. In other words, the context is the regime of truth and broader political rationality. The context is not separate from conspiracy theories; it is constitutive of them.'[125]

A final word is necessary about what are sometimes assumed to be the inadvertently problematic epistemological implications of this discursive approach. None of what is said here should be taken to mean that there are no grounds for identifying erroneous claims at home or abroad. Plainly many interpretations of American foreign policy forwarded by Arab-Muslim people (and people everywhere else too) are wrong, and a straightforward assessment of empirical evidence will suffice to make that determination. But it should be clear from the treatment of the Arab-Muslim paranoia narrative in Chapter 1, as well as the engagement with orientalism above, that the issue of Arab-Muslim conspiracy theory moves well beyond the assessment of specific claims on their merits. One important marker here is the potential for the category 'conspiracy theory' to sweep together a whole raft of different and unexamined claims, and then connect them with tropes about the dysfunctional cultural characteristics of undifferentiated Arab-Muslims. A discursive account of conspiracy theory is uniquely suited to identifying and understanding the ideological valences and power relations that circulate around the issue of Arab-Muslim conspiracy theory. In this particular sense, it might be simultaneously true that a specific claim is wrong *and* that the way it is understood signifies a discourse worth critically investigating.[126]

Much of the concern about the consequences of a discursive approach is based in narrow caricatures, such as the opposition between relativism and objectivism.[127] The view that knowledge is socially produced, or that our identities and possibilities for action are constituted through socio-cultural and linguistic practices, need not undermine our ability to make decisions or engage in politics. Indeed, every day, in everything we do, all of us make practical and ethical determinations without reference to any theory of knowledge whatever – this is an inescapable fact of living.[128] The point is to think critically about the significance of historical, cultural and political context and thereby have a better understanding to inform our unavoidable decision-making. Sensitivity to these issues is crucial to a meaningful understanding of the War on Terror and the issue of Arab-Muslim resentment towards America. The discursive approach I take is attuned to these lines of inquiry because it interrogates dominant discursive formations, underlining their priorities and assumptions, as well as what is derided or left out.

NOTES

1   After conducting systematic survey work between 2006 and 2011, Oliver and Wood conclude that half of the American public believes in at least one conspiracy theory. See T. E. Oliver and T. J. Wood, 'Conspiracy Theories and the Paranoid Style(s) of Mass Opinion', *American Journal of Political Science*, 58:4 (2014), pp. 952–966.

2   See 'Zogby Poll: 51% of Americans want Congress to Probe Bush/Cheney regarding 9/11 attacks', *Zogby International*. Available at www.zogby.com/news/readnews .cfm?ID=1354 (accessed 5 January 2015). In 2006, a Scripps Howard/Ohio University Poll found that 36 per cent of Americans suspect that federal officials had some involvement in 9/11. See, 'Anti Government Anger Spurs 9/11 Conspiracy Belief', *Newspoll*. Available at www.newspolls.org/articles/19604 (accessed 5 January 2015).

3   See J. Dean's incisive account of this collapse in Dean, 'Declarations Of Independence', pp. 290–292.

4   For a good account of these influences see S. Ahmed, *The Cultural Politics of Emotion* (New York: Routledge, 2004); and R. Bleiker and E. Hutchison, 'Fear No More: Emotions and World Politics', *Review of International Studies*, 34:1 (2008), pp. 115–135.

5   See T. Melly, *Empire of Conspiracy: The Culture of Paranoia in Post-War America* (Ithaca: Cornell University Press, 2000), pp. 1–20; M. Fenster, *Conspiracy Theories: Secrecy and Power in American Culture* (Minneapolis: University of Minnesota Press, 2008); P. Knight, 'Everything is Connected: Underworld's Secret History of Paranoia', *Modern Fiction Studies*, 45:3 (1999), pp. 811–836; R. Goldberg, *Enemies Within: The Culture of Conspiracy in Modern America* (New Haven, CT: Yale University Press, 2001); G. Marcus (ed.),

Paranoia Within Reason: A Casebook on Conspiracy as Explanation (Chicago: University of Chicago Press, 1999); J. Dean, 'Theorizing Conspiracy Theory', *Theory and Event*, 4:3 (2000). Available at www.muse.jhu.edu/journals/theory_and_event/v004/4.3r_dean. html (accessed 5 January 2015); H. G. West and T. Sanders (eds), *Transparency and Conspiracy: Ethnographies of Suspicion in the New World Order* (Durham, NC: Duke University Press, 2003); M. Barkin, *A Culture of Conspiracy: Apocalyptic Visions in America* (Berkeley: University of California Press, 2003); K. Olmsted, *Real Enemies: Conspiracy Theories and American Democracy, World War I to 9/11* (Oxford: Oxford University Press, 2009); and R. Pratt, 'Theorizing Conspiracy Theory', *Theory and Society*, 32 (2003), pp. 255–271.

6   Dean, 'Declarations of Independence'; Birchall, *Knowledge Goes Pop: From Conspiracy Theory To Gossip* (London: Berg Publishers, 2006); Fenster, *Conspiracy Theories*.

7   Bratich, *Conspiracy Panics*; Goshorn, 'Strategies of Deterrence and Frames of Containment: On Critical Paranoia and Anti-conspiracy Discourse', *Theory & Event*, 4:3 (2000).

8   F. Jameson, *Postmodernism, or, the Cultural Logic of Late Capitalism* (Durham: Duke University Press, 1991) and Fredric Jameson, 'Cognitive Mapping', in Cary Nelson and Lawrence Grossberg (eds), *Marxism and the Interpretation of Culture* (Chicago: University of Illinois Press, 1988), pp. 347–360.

9   Jameson, *Postmodernism*, p. 80.

10 *Ibid.*, pp. 350–351.

11 *Ibid.*, p. 353.

12 *Ibid.*

13 A. Roberts, *Fredric Jameson* (London: Routledge, 2007), p. 50.

14 Jameson, 'Cognitive Mapping', pp. 350–351.

15 Fenster, *Conspiracy Theories*, p. 11.

16 *Ibid.* Fenster draws on the work of Ernesto Laclau in the reformulation.

17 Knight, *Conspiracy Culture*, pp. 117–157. See also the interesting collection of essays in West and Sanders (eds), *Transparency and Conspiracy*.

18 See Dean, 'Declarations of Independence'; Dean, 'Theorizing Conspiracy Theory', pp. 1–15; J. Dean, 'Virtual Fears', *Signs*, 24:4 (1999), pp. 1069–1078; J. Dean, 'Webs of Conspiracy', in A. Herman, *The Worldwide Web and Contemporary Cultural Theory: Magic, Metaphor, Power* (London: Routledge, 2000), pp. 61–76; J. Dean, *Aliens in America: Conspiracy Cultures from Outerspace to Cyberspace* (New York: Cornell University Press, 1998), pp. 8–9, 142–152.

19 Dean, 'Theorizing Conspiracy Theory', pp. 12–13.

20 Dean, 'Webs of Conspiracy', p. 69.

21 *Ibid.* See also Dean, 'Theorizing Conspiracy Theory', pp. 12–13.

22 P. Knight, *Conspiracy Culture: From Kennedy to the X-Files* (London: Duke University Press, 2000); and P. Knight, 'Everything in Connected: *Underworld's* Secret History of Paranoia', *Modern Fiction Studies*, 45:3 (1999), pp. 811–836.

23 *Ibid.*, p. 29.

24 Olmsted, *Real Enemies*.

25 R. A. Goldberg, ' "Who Profited from the Crime?" Intelligence Failure, Conspiracy Theories, and the Case of September 11', *Journal of Intelligence and National Security*, 19:2 (2004), pp. 249–261.

26 *Ibid.*

27 R. D. Laing cited in *ibid.*, p. 186.

28 Fran Mason gives a strong account of the precarious state of contemporary subjectivity in F. Mason, 'A Poor Person's Cognitive Mapping', in P. Knight (ed.), *Conspiracy Nation:*

The Politics of Paranoia in Post-War America (New York: New York University Press, 2002), pp. 40–56.

29   Dean, 'Theorizing Conspiracy', p. 1.
30   See D. DeLillo, 'American Blood: A Journey through the Labyrinth of Dallas and JFK', *Rolling Stone* (1983), pp. 21–28.
31   Knight, *Conspiracy Culture*, p. 4.
32   See, for instance, Knight, *Conspiracy Culture*, pp. 51–53; and Birchall, *Knowledge Goes Pop*, pp. 40–58.
33   See C. Birchall, 'Just Because You're Paranoid, Doesn't Mean They're Not Out to Get You', *Culture Machine*, 6 (2004), pp. 1–10; C. Birchall, 'Conspiracy Theories and Academic Discourses: The Necessary Possibility of Popular (Over)Interpretation', *Continuum: Journal of Media & Cultural Studies*, 15:1 (2001), pp. 67–76; and Birchall, *Knowledge Goes Pop*.
34   Birchall, *Knowledge Goes Pop*, pp. 23–28.
35   I draw heavily on Fenster, *Conspiracy Theories*, and J. Bratich, *Conspiracy Panics*, in my own account of the paranoid style discourse.
36   J. Dean, 'Declarations of Independence', pp. 299–304.
37   M. Foucault, *The Archeology of Knowledge* (New York: Routledge, 2002).
38   Birchall, *Knowledge Goes Pop*, p. 12.
39   *Ibid.* Birchall takes this as a starting point for her own analysis of popular knowledge.
40   J. Der Derian, 'The CIA, Hollywood, and the Sovereign Conspiracy', in James Der Derian (ed.), *Critical Practices in International Theory: Selected Essays* (New York: Routledge, 2009), pp. 167–189.
41   *Ibid.*, pp. 168–169.
42   *Ibid.*, p. 169.
43   *Ibid.*, p. 172.
44   *Ibid.*, p. 176.
45   *Ibid.*, p. 172.
46   J. Der Derian, *Anitdiplomacy: Spies, Terror, Speed, and War* (Cambridge, MA: Blackwell, 1992).
47   *Ibid.*, p. 34.
48   *Ibid.*
49   *Ibid.*, pp. 49–50.
50   See See R. Ashley, 'Untying the Sovereign State: A Double Reading of the Anarchy Problematique', *Millennium: Journal of International Studies*, 17:2 (1988), pp. 227–262; J. George, *Discourse of Global Politics: A Critical (Re)Introduction to International Relations* (Boulder, CO: Lynne Rienner, 1994), pp. 200–204; and D. Campbell, *Writing Security: United States Foreign Policy and the Politics of Identity* (Manchester: University of Manchester Press, 1998), pp. 53–90.
51   Jameson, *Postmodernism*, p. 80.
52   L. Jones, ' "How do the American People Know … ?": Embodying Post-9/11 Conspiracy Discourse', *GeoJournal*, 75:4 (2010), pp. 359–371.
53   *Ibid.*, pp. 359–360.
54   *Ibid.*
55   *Ibid.*, pp. 360–364.
56   *Ibid.*
57   *Ibid.*, pp. 363–364.
58   For a summary of the main approaches to identity politics see I. B. Neumann, 'Self and Other in International Relations', *European Journal of International Relations*, 2:2 (1996), pp. 139–174.

59 Campbell, *Writing Security*, pp. 91–132.
60 *Ibid.*, pp. 1–33.
61 *Ibid.*, pp. 9–13 and 65.
62 *Ibid.*, p. 65.
63 L. Jones, 'The Common Place Geopolitics of Conspiracy', *Geography Compass*, 6:1 (2012), pp. 44–59.
64 Jones, 'The Common Place Geopolitics of Conspiracy', p. 48.
65 *Ibid.*
66 *Ibid.*, p. 46.
67 *Ibid.*
68 *Ibid.*
69 Jones, 'The Common Place Geopolitics of Conspiracy', p. 52.
70 Jones makes the interesting point that the conspiracy narratives of both the Bush Administration and the 9/11 Truth Movement serve the same value system, to the extent that they both mobilise patriotic duty and ward against un-American practices. This parallel resonates with Der Derian's account of the way sovereign identity is secured through conspiracy narratives.
71 The critical rejection of this possibility is a bedrock principle of the postcolonial literature. For an introduction to these arguments see S. Grovogui, 'Postcolonialism', in Tim Dunne, Milja Kurki and Steve Smith (eds), *International Relations Theories: Discipline and Diversity* (Oxford: Oxford University Press), pp. 238–256; G. C. Spivak, 'Can the Subaltern Speak?' in Nelson and Grossberg (eds), *Marxism and the Interpretation of Culture*, pp. 267–305; and E. Said, *Orientalism* (London: Penguin, 2003).
72 Grovogui, 'Postcolonialism', 239.
73 Said's focus was on British and French orientalism during the colonial period, and, more recently, orientalism in post-war American foreign policy.
74 Said, *Orientalism*, p. 42.
75 *Ibid.*, p. 49.
76 *Ibid.*, p. 48.
77 On the difficulty of stepping away from dominant discourses and assumptions see, for instance, P. van der Veer, *Imperial Encounters: Religion and Modernity in India* (Princeton, NJ: Princeton University Press, 2001); N. B. Dirks, *Castes of Mind: Colonialism and the Making of Modern India* (Princeton, NJ: Princeton University Press, 2001); and Spivak, 'Can the Subaltern Speak?'.
78 M. Gray, *Conspiracy Theories in the Arab World: Sources and Politics* (New York: Routledge, 2010).
79 *Ibid.*, p. 3. He also notes that conspiracy discourse is prominent the world over and is not a specifically Arab issue.
80 *Ibid.*, pp. 42–43.
81 *Ibid.*, pp. 9–10.
82 *Ibid.*, p. 10.
83 *Ibid.*, p. 12.
84 For a similar approach see J. W. Anderson, 'Conspiracy Theories, Premature Entextualization, and Popular Political Analysis', *Arab Studies Journal*, 4:1 (1996), pp. 96–102; P. A. Silverstein, 'An Excess of Truth: Violence, Conspiracy Theorizing and the Algerian Civil War', *Anthropological Quarterly*, 75:4 (2002), pp. 643–674; P. A. Silverstein, 'Regimes of (Un)Truth: Conspiracy Theory and the Transnationalization of the Algerian Civil War', *Middle East Report*, 214 (2000), pp. 6–10.
85 Gray, *Conspiracy Theories in the Arab World*, pp. 27–30.
86 Said, 'Afterword', in *Orientalism* (London: Penguin, 2003), p. 337.

87 Bratich, *Conspiracy Panics*, pp. 17–19.

88 *Ibid.*, p. 18.

89 Bratich, *Conspiracy Panics*, pp. 4–6.

90 Gray, *Conspiracy Theories in the Arab World*, p. 4.

91 R. Irwin, 'An Orientalist Mythology of Secret Societies', in Arndt Graf, Schirin Fathi and Ludwig Paul (eds), *Orientalism and Conspiracy: Politics and Conspiracy Theory in the Islamic World* (London: I. B. Tauris & Co. Ltd, 2001), pp. 99–100.

92 *Ibid.*, pp. 99–100. Irwin goes on to point out that, in his simpler approach, the conceptual problem of conspiracy theories that turn out to be true dissolves, since there is no claim to right knowledge entailed in rumors.

93 G. Hustings and M. Orr, 'Dangerous Machinery: 'Conspiracy Theorist' as a Transpersonal Strategy of Exclusion', *Symbolic Interaction*, 30:2 (2007), p. 143.

94 This is an approach taken by both Dean and Birchall, who tend to engage with the discursive field rather than taking conspiracy theory as a discrete subject of analysis, though Dean, particularly, still provides explanations for a defined category of behaviour. Bratich takes the critique one step further, treating conspiracy theory as a discursive position with no analytical or descriptive value in itself. For a useful summary of the tension between these positions see the fascinating discussion between J. Bratich and M. Fenster. J. Bratich, M. Fenster, Hye-Jin Lee, 'When Theorists Conspire: An Inte(re)view Between Mark Fenster and Jack Bratich', *International Journal of Communications*, 3 (2009), pp. 961–972; and M. Fenster and J. Bratich, 'Dialogues in Communication Research', *Journal of Communication Enquiry*, 33:3 (2009), pp. 279–286.

95 *Oxford Dictionary Online*. Available at www.oed.com (accessed 6 January 2015).

96 *Merriam Webster Dictionary*. Available at www.merriam-webster.com (accessed 6 January 2015).

97 *Cambridge Dictionary Online*. Available at dictionary.cambridge.org (accessed 6 January 2015).

98 See J. Bale, 'Political Paranoia v. Political Realism: On Distinguishing Between Bogus Conspiracy Theories and Genuine Conspiratorial Politics', *Patterns of Prejudice*, 41:1 (2007), pp. 45–60.

99 See 'Coup d'état', *Encyclopedia Britanica*. Available at www.britannica.com/EBchecked/topic/140445/coup-detat (accessed 6 January 2015).

100 N. Machiavelli, *The Prince and the Discourses* (New York: The Modern Library, 1950).

101 *Ibid.*, p. 410.

102 Hustings and Orr, 'Dangerous Machinery', p. 127.

103 *Ibid.*, pp. 127–150.

104 *Ibid.*, p. 127.

105 *Ibid.*, pp. 127–150.

106 *Ibid.*, p. 143.

107 Goshorn, 'Strategies of Deterrence'.

108 *Ibid.*

109 *Ibid.*

110 *Ibid.*

111 *Ibid.*

112 *Ibid.*, p. 13.

113 *Ibid.*

114 Bratich, *Conspiracy Panics*, p. 18. The term 'conspiracy panic' is a direct reference to Cohen's idea of 'moral panics', the strong reaction of a population to a perceived threat to social order. See S. Cohen, *Folk Devils and Moral Panics* (St Albans: Paladin, 1973).

115 *Ibid.*, p. 4.

116 *Ibid.*, p. 16.
117 *Ibid.*
118 At first glance, this resort to symptomology may seem contradictory. How can Bratich criticise the conspiracy theory literature for treating claims as epiphenomenal and then approach those commentators who participate in conspiracy panics with his own diagnostic analysis? As Hustings and Orr might say, Bratich seems to 'go meta' and thus perform the same disqualifying function. However, this apparent contradiction does not amount to very much when the issue of power is taken into consideration. It is hardly a delegitimising move to inquire into the modes of discourse that enable the powerful to act and to propound.
119 *Ibid.*, p. 18.
120 *Ibid.*, pp. 1–23, 43–50.
121 *Ibid.*, pp. 25–50.
122 *Ibid.*
123 See B. Hindess, *Discourses of Power: From Hobbes to Foucault* (Oxford: Blackwell, 1996), pp. 105–136.
124 Der Derian, 'The CIA, Hollywood, and the Sovereign Conspiracy', pp. 167–189.
125 Bratich, *Conspiracy Panics*, p. 19.
126 This point is often made from the other direction in the conspiracy culture literature, where the significance of a conspiracy theory is not necessarily bound up with its veracity. See, for example, Fenster, *Conspiracy Theories*.
127 R. Bernstein, *Beyond Relativism and Objectivism* (Philadelphia: University of Pennsylvania Press, 1983).
128 Indeed, as Stanley Fish notes incisively, when the deconstruction stops we immediately take positions that must be advanced, defended and negotiated through the ordinary muddle of politics. See S. Fish, 'French Theory in America', *New York Times* (6 April 2008).

Part II

Conspiracy discourse in the War on Terror

Strategies of deterrence and
frames of containment

C HAPTER 2 CONCLUDED with the observation that 'anti-conspiracy discourse', the long-running public and intellectual concern about the problem of conspiracy theory, tends to deter and contain serious investigations of political controversy.[1] I proposed that disincentives against critical engagement with political power or ideological dissent from established orthodoxies are at least as important as concerns about allegedly poor standards of political interpretation. This is particularly the case in the American foreign policy context, where the actions and approaches of the US government are regularly thought controversial. I suggested that studying the way conspiracy theories emerge as subjects of concern can provide a window into the underlying commitments and rationalities of a political culture.

This chapter examines the widespread concern expressed by foreign policy commentators about the link between anti-Americanism and Arab-Muslim conspiracy theories in the wake of 9/11. I argue that this Arab-Muslim paranoia narrative helped disqualify criticism of American power and limit interpretations of 9/11. When 'anti-Americanism' was connected to 'conspiracy theory', readers were directed away from the substance of specific claims and towards the deeper pathologies of the people making them. This happened in two main ways. On the one hand, the individual cognitive functions of radicals and dissidents were called into question: they were paranoid and irrational; their violence was motivated by cognitive deviancy. On the other hand, general anti-Americanism was linked to an underlying social-psychological condition. In this account, Muslim societies, traumatised by the disparity between the golden age of Muslim civilisation and its present malaise, and embittered by a recent history of colonial domination, found a convenient explanation for their unsatisfactory circumstances in far-fetched delusions of hidden power. Here conspiracy theory was considered endemic in Arab-Muslim culture such that it informed Arab-Muslim interpretations of America's regional engagement.

However abhorrent terrorism might be, both these narratives disqualified the political grievances motivating resentment towards America. They made terrorism psychotic and populism pathological. They prevented a genuine understanding of resentment towards America, shut down space for critical engagement with American foreign policy, and secured an image of American power as benign and misunderstood. These dynamics were embedded in a broader modernist discourse organised around an opposition between Western modernity and an Arab-Muslim world bound by time and history. The Arab-Muslim paranoia narrative contributed to the production of this status quo, providing certainty and stability, rational politics and coherent identity, foreign policy orthodoxy in the face of critical and dissenting perspectives. In this sense, the Arab-Muslim paranoia narrative after 9/11 was involved in an ongoing process of boundary maintenance.

One way to grasp this boundary maintenance process is to consider the concerns of foreign policy commentators after 9/11 as part of a wider conspiracy discourse, where multiple conspiracy narratives vied for standing and significance. Most obviously, accepting the fact of an Al-Qaeda conspiracy to fly planes into the World Trade Center and the Pentagon was the minimum condition for reasonable comment on the terrorist attacks. Indeed, it was the widespread rejection of this premise in the Arab-Muslim world that caught the attention of many foreign policy commentators. At the same time, answering the 'why' question about the terrorist attacks necessarily required a consideration of the opaque and often self-interested history of US involvement in the Arab-Muslim world.[2] Conspiracy narratives were central both to blowback accounts of US foreign policy that dwelt on covert operations and secret connection, and identitarian accounts that emphasised the threat of diabolical terrorist masterminds with vast networks spanning the world's major cities. Thinking in terms of conspiracy discourse focuses attention on the way these conspiracy narratives were demarcated and their positions of authority or illegitimacy sustained through rules and regularities that circulated in discursive regimes.

In order to make this case I use discourse analysis to examine post-9/11 foreign policy commentary. This approach aims to expose how particular regimes of truth are produced and sustained through a set of power relations – through structures, logics and techniques that discipline subjects and police the boundaries between legitimate and illegitimate thoughts and actions, or through the powerful cultural mythologies in which elites articulate their world-views and justify particular policies.[3] It draws out the priorities and assumptions of a discourse and flags the silences, exclusions and closures that flow from them. I focus in on a snapshot of the Arab-Muslim paranoia narrative in the year after 9/11, as the War on Terror narrative took shape and competing interpretations struggled for authority and standing.[4] I do this by engaging with excerpts from key articles in *Foreign Affairs* and the *New York Times*, both important forums of expert foreign policy commentary.[5] I now begin by introducing a post-9/11 political landscape woven through with conspiracy narratives.

Why do they hate us?

The overwhelming reaction to 9/11 was that everything had changed. According to the 9/11 Commission, the moment the planes hit the World Trade Center 'the United States became a nation transformed'.[6] This was not just the tragic death of nearly 3,000 people. It was a devastating attack on the symbols of American economic and military power. As Michael Shapiro noted a few months later, like Don DeLillo's assessment of the JFK assassination, 9/11 was an 'aberration in the heartland of the real'.[7] I begin here by explaining the shape of the foreign policy discourse that unfolded in the weeks and months after 9/11, before highlighting the way the conspiracy theme was implicated in this political landscape.

For all the trauma and uncertainty that accompanied 9/11, the basic facts of the terrorist conspiracy were quickly established. Long before the FBI or the CIA had completed their investigations, politicians and pundits identified Osama bin Laden and his Al-Qaeda network as the most likely perpetrators. A clear plot emerged: nineteen terrorists, largely from Saudi Arabia and Egypt, had made their way from jihadist training camps in Afghanistan through US borders, taken basic pilot training in middle America, then used box cutters to hijack four passenger planes, turning them from vehicles to missiles. This narrative was situated in a wider history of Al-Qaeda's terrorism against America, including the bombing of US military personnel at Khobar Towers in 1996; the simultaneous bombing of US embassies in Nairobi and Dar es Salaam in 1998; the bombing of the USS *Cole* at the port of Aden in late 2000; and, more broadly, Osama bin Laden's two fatwas urging Muslims to kill Americans everywhere.[8] These facts became the givens of the event – the ground upon which every reasonable interlocutor made the incomprehensible sensible.

Debate about the *meaning* of these facts was organised around a central question, famously posed by George W. Bush in his post-9/11 address to the US Congress: 'Why do they hate us?' Two broad kinds of answer emerged. The first looked towards the impact of American foreign policy in the Middle East and thought about Al-Qaeda in this context. It emphasised the involvement of the CIA in a covert war against the Russian occupation of Afghanistan in the mid-1980s, which mobilised, supplied and trained the very Islamic mujahideen that would later turn against America in the post-Cold War years. It also noted the festering grievances generated by US support for oppressive regimes across the Middle East through the Cold War and on into the 1990s. A more sympathetic version defended the legitimacy of strategies forged in the crucible of Cold War geopolitics or aimed at long-run energy security for an American-led global economy, but rued the unintended consequences that had come home on 9/11. While still rejecting the violence of 9/11, less sanguine accounts pointed to the terrorist actions of an imperialist American state. For instance, according to Arundhati Roy, Osama bin Laden was sculpted from the spare rib of a world laid to waste by America's foreign policy: its gunboat diplomacy, its nuclear arsenal, its vulgarly stated policy of 'full spectrum dominance', its chilling disregard for non-American lives, its barbarous military interventions, its support for despotic and dictatorial regimes, its merciless economic agenda that has munched through the economies of poor countries like a cloud of locusts.[9]

Indeed, a common move here was to point to America's involvement in the overthrow of Salvador Allende's socialist government in Chile on 11 September 1973. On this view, Al-Qaeda's could be understood in relation to long-running anti-imperialist grievances held in many parts of the world, however abhorrent their violence may have been.

The second kind of answer focused on identity. Prominent here was Samuel Huntington's 'Clash of Civilizations' thesis, which, for some prophetically, argued that conflicts in the post-Cold War world would occur along the fault lines between civilisations.[10] From this perspective, 9/11 could be understood in terms of a macro-historical conflict between the West and Islam. Fleshing out this dichotomy, resentment towards the West was often said to represent a rejection of modernity itself by those unwilling or unable to keep pace with a fast-changing world. Less prosaic renditions emphasised the spread of fundamentalist Islam, which had produced heavily indoctrinated radicals, violently opposed to the secular liberalism of the West. But binding all these accounts together was a clear distinction between 'us' and 'them'. Al-Qaeda had attacked because of *who we are*. It was this line of thinking that drove the Bush administration's understanding of 9/11 and its origins. A clear us/them dichotomy pervaded official statements, positioning the American nation as the innocent victim in contrast with despicable terrorists who were the personification of evil.[11]

What is interesting about this emerging War on Terror discourse is the centrality of the conspiracy theme. Secret histories and unexpected connections seemed to point below the surface of events towards deeper truths. The starting point was a terrorist conspiracy on 9/11. The wider historical context for the blowback account was the covert operation of American power in the Middle East, including *coup d'états*, assassinations, secret arms trading and Faustian alliances with unsavoury regional dictators. Al-Qaeda's genesis was directly tied to a clandestine programme of recruitment and training, which was funded through the CIA and Saudi intelligence, and coordinated by Pakistan's Inter-service Intelligence Service. The events of 9/11 took place against a backdrop of a close US alliance with Saudi Arabia, a key funder of radical Islamism internationally and home to fifteen of the 9/11 terrorists, as well as the bin Laden family, still part of the ruling Saudi oligarchy. At a personal level the family of the US President had a long-standing business relationship with the house of Saud. Moreover, on the morning of 9/11 the President's father, former President George H. W. Bush, attended a Carlyle Group annual investors meeting in Washington, where Osama bin Laden's brother, Shafiq bin Laden, was a guest of honour.[12] Whatever the substance of these connections, they drew the blowback analysis of American foreign policy in the Middle East towards the covert, often controversial, operation of US political and economic power.

At the same time, the identity politics explanation of 9/11 often entailed a broader concern about a monolithic terrorist threat poised for apocalyptic violence, buttressed by a standing reserve of easily radicalised Muslims already hostile towards America. Richard Jackson, for instance, notes how the diabolical character of the terrorists was emphasised in Bush administration rhetoric in the wake of 9/11. In this account, 'terrorists are made out to be incredibly sophisticated, ruthless, and numerous ... they hide in communities – the perennial enemy within – where they plot evil'. Jackson refers to this as the 'terrorist mastermind' narrative and points to its resonance throughout American history with the fear of subversives, servants of foreign power or dark forces, plotting destruction from the inside.[13] Fear of a vast terrorist conspiracy justified an extensive counter-terrorism infrastructure and a raft of special legal provisions for the surveillance and detention of terrorist suspects. Likewise, a looming nuclear conspiracy between terrorists and rogue states provided the primary justification for pre-emptive war against Iraq in 2003.

These narratives of suspicion circulated in the context of a contentious struggle over the meaning of 9/11. Proponents of a blowback account often pointed to the hypocrisy of eliding the historical and ongoing role of US foreign policy in the violence of 9/11, along with the fearmongering entailed in exaggerated descriptions of an apocalyptic terrorist threat. Conversely, proponents of identity politics narratives were quick to accuse foreign policy critics of apologising for terrorism. According to Judith Butler, 'the cry that "there is no excuse for September 11th" ... [became] a means by which to stifle any serious discussion of how US foreign policy has helped to create a world where such acts of terror are possible'.[14] Such concerns were often framed as the slippery slope to moral relativism, or at least the kind of reticence about distinguishing right from wrong that helped make America vulnerable in the first place, and which would no doubt aid the enemy in the coming conflict.

The line between legitimate analysis and fanciful speculation was also precarious. Take, for instance, the competing conspiracy narratives around the case for war with Iraq. Pushing back against the Bush administration's assertion of a nefarious connection between Al-Qaeda and Saddam Hussein, critics pointed to a conspiracy by a neoconservative 'cabal' to take the country to war. The neoconservatives, it was said, had stoked public fears, manipulated intelligence and fixed the evidence around a pre-existing and ideological preference for regime change.[15] Others pointed to the relationship between the philosopher Leo Strauss and the allegedly imperial ambitions of neoconservative foreign policy. Strauss had apparently thought that a bellicose foreign policy based in stark

Manichean oppositions would produce strong national identity and a sense of moral virtue, crucial antidotes for a modern age where cultural relativism left societies open to totalitarianism. At the same time, leading neoconservatives characterised these claims as paranoid delusions: Max Boot situated them as the product of 'conspiracy aficionados'; Robert Lieber pointed out a connection with the 'sinister mythology' of anti-Semitic conspiracy theories; Charles Krautham-mer highlighted long-standing leftists' delusion about a 'vast right wing con-spiracy'; while Gerard Baker dubbed such allegations 'neo-conspiracy theories'.[16] From this perspective, then, conspiracy can be situated as an important site for the production of foreign policy knowledge. After 9/11 some conspiracies were taken for granted as the fact of the matter, some were struggled over in a highly politicised foreign policy landscape, and some were called forth as conspiracy theories.[17]

It was in this context of interpretive contention and ambiguity that foreign policy commentators became concerned about the problem of Arab-Muslim conspiracy theories. According to a Gallup poll conducted in 2003, a startling 61 per cent of people in Muslim majority countries believed Arabs were not involved in the 9/11 attacks.[18] Foreign policy commentators were quick to draw a connection between scepticism about the official account of 9/11 and a broader anti-Americanism sweeping the Muslim world. While by no means the only explanation for Arab-Muslim resentment towards America, the Arab-Mus-lim paranoia narrative was surprisingly common in the foreign policy commen-tariat.[19] For instance, of the twenty-two *Foreign Affairs* articles dealing with the link between terrorism and anti-Americanism published in the year after 9/11, twelve made reference to the paranoia theme.[20] This excerpt from Peter L. Ber-gen's review of three books about the origins of 9/11 gives a flavour:

> And then comes Hill's masterstroke: his conclusion that the deleterious impact of political disenfranchisement has been amplified by 'the deeply rooted conviction that virtually every significant occurrence is caused by some external conspiracy. Every societal shortcoming is attributed to a foreign plot.' The best example of this culture of conspiracy, of course, is the widely circulated – and widely believed – story that the attacks on the World Trade Center were the work of the Jews, as demonstrated by the supposed fact that 4,000 Jews did not show up for work on the day of the attacks. Accordingly, the lead hijacker's father – an apparently sane Egyptian lawyer – remains convinced that the attacks were the work of the Mossad, Israel's security service. And even the appearance of the bin Laden home video – in which Osama is seen chuckling over the hijackings – has done nothing to dissuade the undissuad-able. After all, as a commentator on Al Jazeera television opined, the tape may have been a fake.

Hill goes on to explain that 'conspiracy theories blight every society they touch. The people who hold them become impervious to evidence and reason.' Indeed, it was precisely this culture of conspiracy that enabled bin Laden to convince a transnational coalition of Arabs that, despite evidence to the contrary, the problems of their home countries were the fault of the United States – rather than the incompetence and corruption of their various domestic elites.[21]

The same narrative also appeared regularly in the *New York Times*. Of the 91 opinion articles linking terrorism with anti-Americanism, 37 referred to the problem of conspiracy theory.[22] Moreover, Thomas Friedman, the paper's foreign affairs correspondent and one of the most influential public intellectuals in America, contributed thirteen editorials that produced the Arab-Muslim paranoia narrative.[23] Elsewhere, Fareed Zakaria's *Newsweek* cover story 'The Politics of Rage: Why do they Hate Us?', widely cited as a debate-shaping articulation of the origins of 9/11, explained that political resentment towards America was the product of 'the sense of humiliation, decline and despair that sweeps the Arab world', and in this context 'every action America takes gets magnified a thousand-fold. And even when we do not act, the rumours of our gigantic powers and nefarious deeds still spread.'[24] Of course, the title 'The Roots of Muslim Rage' references Bernard Lewis's seminal work of the same name (published a decade earlier), which established this narrative of Arab-Muslim dysfunction and denial.[25] Lewis reproduced this diagnosis in a post-9/11 article titled 'What Went Wrong?', which noted that an inability to take responsibility for self-made problems had led inevitably towards 'neurotic fantasies and conspiracy theories'.[26]

Perhaps unsurprisingly, Daniel Pipes also renewed his examination of Arab-Muslim conspiracy theories, explaining in a co-authored opinion piece titled 'Denial is a River' that 'This pattern of avoiding unpleasant facts offers an insight into the problems of Muslim society. Turning defeat into victory, evidence into forgery, and terrorism into an "inside job" creates an alternate and more hospitable world.'[27] But the important point for now is to recognise that the problem of Arab-Muslim conspiracy theories became a subject of concern for foreign policy commentators in a post-9/11 political landscape woven through with competing conspiracy narratives, each struggling for legitimacy and standing, all proffering an authoritative interpretation of the origins and significance of 9/11.

The Arab-Muslim paranoia narrative after 9/11: *Foreign Affairs*

I turn now to the discourse analysis of *Foreign Affairs*, focusing in on excerpts from key articles, which are representative of the Arab-Muslim paranoia narrative. These excerpts are drawn from two prominent texts: Fouad Ajami's 'The Sentry's Solitude' and Michael Scott Doran's 'Somebody Else's Civil War'.[28] 'The Sentry's Solitude' was the lead article in the first *Foreign Affairs* issue published after the 9/11 attacks. This pride of place reflected Ajami's status as a sought-after academic and a well-connected Washington insider, who would go on to advise the Bush administration on War on Terror strategy.[29] His ideas have had an important influence on other public intellectuals, including Judith Miller and Thomas Friedman at the *New York Times*, both vocal supporters of the Bush administration's approach to the War on Terror.[30] All of this has led Adam Shatz to claim that Ajami is 'the most influential Arab intellectual of his generation'.[31] 'Somebody Else's Civil War' is often singled out as the best article written after 9/11 on the motivations of Al-Qaeda, and is still widely cited in the terrorism literature.[32] It was this reputation that saw Doran hired by the Bush administration in 2005, as head of Near Eastern and African Affairs at the National Security Council (NSC), and later as Under-Secretary for Public Diplomacy at the US Department of State.[33] According to Steven J. Hadley, National Security Advisor at the time, Doran was sought out in part because of his 'extremely interesting article'.[34]

'The Sentry's Solitude' maps out the origins of 9/11 and points to the complex and difficult dynamics facing US foreign policy makers.[35] Ajami does this by recounting the history of Islamist terrorist attacks against America, from the 1993 World Trade Center bombings, through Khobar Towers and the bombing of the USS *Cole*, to the latest incidents in New York and Washington, situating these events in an explanation of the historical, political and cultural circumstances that animated them.[36] He argues that the anti-Americanism on which Al-Qaeda thrives is the result not so much of America's foreign policy – though this has played a role – but of widespread dissatisfaction among Arab-Muslims with their own political and economic circumstances.[37] America was targeted because Arab-Muslims lacked the political space to criticise their own leaders.[38] At the same time, Arab leaders deliberately used anti-Americanism to deflect criticism from their own policies, although they still kept close ties with America in private.[39] In Ajami's view the coming War on Terror would force these Arab-Muslim elites to choose between their public and their American allies.[40] But, whatever *their* choices, the Bush administration must be cautious about whom to trust in this unfamiliar and anti-American world.[41] Exotic lands and larger than life characters populate this narrative: the dissident terrorist, the Arab crowd, the cunning dictator, Pax Americana. I focus here on several extracts that demonstrate the paranoia narrative and the context from which it emerges.

Who are the conspiracy theorists in 'The Sentry's Solitude'? In this first excerpt, which explains the sources of anti-Americanism in Saudi Arabia through the 1990s, we can identify key actors, their relationship to each other and the role of conspiracy theory:

> The new unrest, avowedly religious, stemmed from the austerity that came to Saudi Arabia after Desert Storm. If the rulers could not subsidize as generously as they had in the past, the foreigner and his schemes and overcharges must be to blame. The

dissidents were not cultists but men of their society, half-learned in Western sources and trends, picking foreign sources to illustrate the subjugation that America held in store for Arabia. Pamphleteering had come into the realm, and rebellion proved contagious. A dissident steps out of the shadows, then respectable critics, then others come forth. Xenophobic men were now agitating against the 'crusaders' who had come to stay.[42]

The term 'conspiracy theory' does not appear in this passage, but connotations of paranoia and misinformation are clear in phrases like 'the foreigner and his schemes' and words like 'blame', 'half-learned' and 'crusaders'. These connotations are activated in concluding sentences of the same paragraph:

'This is a bigger calamity than I had expected, bigger than any threat the Arabian Peninsula has faced since God Almighty created it,' wrote the religious scholar Safar al-Hawali, a master practitioner in the paranoid style of politics. The Americans, he warned, had come to dominate Arabia and unleash on it the West's dreaded morals. Saudi Arabia had been free of the anticolonial complex seen in states such as Algeria, Egypt, Syria, and Iraq. But the simplicity of the Arabian-American encounter now belonged to the past.[43]

The use of the phrase 'paranoid style' is an important marker for concerns about conspiracy theory. As demonstrated at length in Part I of this book, the 'paranoid style' is the way Richard Hofstadter characterised conspiracy theory in his seminal examination of the radical right in American politics, and this paradigm has been an important influence on the Arab-Muslim paranoia narrative.[44]

The 'paranoid style' marker is used here by Ajami to describe the Saudi Arabian religious scholar Safar al-Hawali's warnings about America's intentions in Arabia. But al-Hawali is provided as an example of a broader category. He is representative of the 'dissident' figure introduced early on in the excerpt, whose anti-Americanism proves attractive to the wider Saudi public. The predicates associated with these dissidents and their views are revealing. Their anti-Americanism is 'contagious', they are 'xenophobic' and 'paranoid', and they exhibit an 'anticolonial complex'.[45]

Together, these terms position dissident views as the manifestation of a cognitive illness in the dissident's mind – a spreading disease, a paranoid and irrational fear of foreigners, which is part of a deeper psychological condition. Along with this in-text association with psychological abnormality, the 'paranoid style' provides a potent marker of a broader socio-medical narrative implying pathologisation, irrationality and deviancy, exceptionally familiar to an American audience.[46] Paranoia also acts as the fulcrum for a series of references that support this framework. A subtle rhetoric of disrepute surrounds the more explicit language of pathology: the 'schemes' of foreigners '*must* be to blame'; the 'half-learned' dissidents 'picking sources' selectively, 'agitating' and 'pamphleteering' about 'crusaders'. These predicates all imply the improbability of anti-Americanism. When this background language is put together with the more explicit markers of irrationality and cognitive illness the effect is a powerful negative valence. The implication of wrongheadedness seems to extend out beyond the dissident to the broader Saudi population since Ajami includes 'respectable critics, then others' in the 'contagious' rebellion. For now, the important thing is that, although the term never *actually* appears, there is little doubt that the 'dissident' is motivated by a conspiratorial view of America that is irrational. Even the most obvious terms – 'crusaders', 'anticolonial complex' and 'paranoid style', all common connotations of conspiracy theory – are enough to evoke this understanding.[47]

The relationship between the dissident and America is of obvious importance. Ajami's clearest presentation of this relationship is through the eyes of the dissident, and it is this perspective that he is emphasising for the reader. Here America is 'subjugating' Arabia – an invading Christian army occupying the Holy Land, set to 'dominate Arabia and unleash on it the West's dreaded values'.[48] At the same time, this dissident's Arabia is the passive victim, vulnerable to the subjugation of a threatening America. This is the dissident's view as Ajami relates it. More to the point, it is precisely this view that Ajami attaches to his delegitimising schema, rendering it at best naive and at worst paranoid.

But if this is the dissident's perspective, where is the real America – Ajami's America, which he defends with his subtle framework of paranoia and improbability? And how does this America *really* relate to Saudi Arabia if it is not subjugating it? It becomes clear that Ajami's America is being unfairly accused by unhinged Saudi dissidents; their anti-colonial sentiment is misinformed and unwarranted. The next excerpt gives a fuller sense of Ajami's *actual* understanding of the relationship between American foreign policy and the Arab-Muslim world, as well as extending out his pathologising conspiracy narrative beyond dissidents and Saudis:

John Burns of the New York Times sent a dispatch of unusual clarity from Aden about the Cole and the responses on the ground to the terrible deed. In Yemen, the reporter saw 'a halting, half-expressed sense of astonishment, sometimes satisfaction and even pleasure, that a mighty power, the United States, should have its Navy humbled by two Arab men in a motorized skiff.' Such was the imperial presence, the Pax Americana in Arab and Muslim lands.

There were men in the shadows pulling off spectacular deeds. But they fed off a free-floating anti-Americanism that blows at will and knows no bounds, among Islamists and secularists alike. For the crowds in Karachi, Cairo, and Amman, the great power could never get it right. A world lacking the tools and the political space for free inquiry fell back on anti-Americanism. 'I talk to my daughter-in-law so my neighbor can hear me,' goes the Arabic maxim. In the fury with which the intellectual and political class railed against the United States and Israel, the agitated were speaking to and of their own rulers. Sly and cunning men, the rulers knew and understood the game. There would be no open embrace of America, and no public defense of it. They would stay a step ahead of the crowd and give the public the safety valve it needed. The more pro-American the regime, the more anti-American the political class and the political tumult. The United States could grant generous aid to the Egyptian state, but there would be no dampening down of the anti-American fury of the Egyptian political class. Its leading state-backed dailies crackled with the wildest theories of US-Israeli conspiracies against their country.

On September 11, 2001, there was an unmistakable sense of glee and little sorrow among upper-class Egyptians for the distant power – only satisfaction that American had gotten its comeuppance. After nearly three decades of American solicitude of Egypt, after the steady traffic between the two lands, there were no genuine friends for America in this curiously hostile, disgruntled land.[49]

A good place to begin is with Ajami's characterisation of America as 'Pax Americana' the 'imperial presence', a 'great power' in a foreign land – which seems to contrast with his earlier suggestion that America is not unduly colonial by evoking the imperial Roman Empire, Pax Romana.[50] But 'the great power could never get it right'.[51] Ajami implies here that imperial America was hated *despite* its best intentions – that the United States was damned whatever it did. Thus, the angry crowd 'fell back on anti-Americanism' when their anger *really* belonged elsewhere.[52] America was not the cause of their problems. It had been 'generous' and received in return only 'satisfaction that America had gotten its comeuppance'.[53] It had provided Egypt with 'solicitude' and 'steady traffic' yet garnered 'few genuine friends' in a 'curiously hostile, disgruntled land'.[54] America emerges in this account not as a domineering neo-colonial force subjugating Arab Muslims and spreading its Western values, but as a wrongheaded proxy for local grievances, a well-intentioned power whose best efforts had been rebuffed. A few paragraphs after this excerpt, Ajami confirms this characterisation:

> Policy can never speak to wrath. Step into the thicket (as Bill Clinton did in the Israeli–Palestinian conflict) and the foreign power is damned for its reach. Step back, as George W. Bush did in the first months of his Presidency, and Pax Americana is charged with abdication and indifference.[55]

It is *this* image – of a well-intentioned America – which is under attack from paranoid anti-American dissidents, and, as the second excerpt shows, a broader Arab-Muslim public.

Indeed, it is this curiously amorphous 'crowd' – expanding in Ajami's account to include Islamists and secularists across the entire region, including political, intellectual and upper classes – which are connected with 'the wildest theories of U.S.-Israeli conspiracies'.[56] Once again the delegitimising narrative of paranoia is at work here, linking anti-Americanism to a socio-medical discourse of illness and pathology. But a different predicate web situates this 'crowd' in terms of its conspiratorial anti-Americanism. It is a 'hostile' mass, full of 'rage' and 'wrath' and 'fury'. It 'railed' and 'agitated' against America, and 'crackled' with the 'wildest' views.[57] This 'tumult' was 'frustrated' and 'disgruntled'. Its anger, 'which knows no bounds', was 'free-floating'. These predicates situate the 'crowd' as a roiling, passion-fired mob: unpredictable, unconstrained by reason or government. Indeed, Arab leaders could not engage in 'dampening down' their wildfire publics because anti-Americanism provided a 'safety valve' for their pent-up fury. The point here, then, is that once again anti-Americanism is positioned as the product of irrationality – passion and prejudice and temperament rather than considered judgement. And once again conspiracy theory appears as the most explicit delegitimising marker against a more subtle rhetorical background that works towards the same end.

This background of populist anger connects with the deeper social psychological circumstances that Ajami identifies as the 'roots of Muslim rage', to make the obvious connection with Bernard Lewis's influential work in this area.[58] According to Ajami, anti-Americanism in Egypt is driven by the tension between the Egyptian people's high opinion of themselves and Egypt's current malaise, along with the fact that there is no political space available for criticism of the ruling regime:

> Egyptians have long been dissatisfied with their country's economic and military performance, a pain born of the gap between Egypt's exalted idea of itself and the poverty and foreign dependence that have marked its modern history. The rage against Israel and the United States stems from that history of lament and frustration. So much of Egypt's life lies beyond the scrutiny and the reach of its newspapers and pundits – the ruler's ways, the authoritarian state, the matter of succession to Mubarak, the joint military exercises with U.S. and Egyptian forces, and so on. The animus toward America and Israel gives away the frustration of a polity raging against the hard, disillusioning limits of its political life.[59]

Though this underlying tension, this status anxiety, is identified in the Egyptian case, it is clear from Ajami's sweeping generalisations and his references elsewhere in the article that he means this as a general explanation for a generalised anti-Americanism. Conspiracy theory sits comfortably within this narrative as the extreme version of anti-Americanism. Indeed, as explained in Part I, this narrative had been widely mobilised in media and scholarly accounts well before 9/11 to explain conspiracy theories in the Arab-Muslim world as the emotive delusions of a traumatised civilisation.[60] But its origins also lie with the 'paranoid style' characterisation of American extremism as populist status anxiety and political alienation – a conceptualisation pervasive in American political discourse since the 1970s.[61] This, in turn, rests on a particular brand of Cold War pluralism that sought to marginalise ideologically driven mass politics and reinforce a stable centre focused on the mediation of competing interests through bargain and compromise.[62] Here America stands in for the liberal centre while the roiling 'Arab street' plays the part of emotive populists.[63] Connecting back to the 'paranoid style' in the first extract, and the use of the status anxiety narrative in the second, it is no great leap to suggest that a similar liberalism/populism discourse is once again in action.

Ajami wields this potent delegitimising narrative skilfully in defence of his image of the well-intentioned 'Pax Americana', misunderstood at every turn by ungrateful Arab-Muslims. In both excerpts the conspiracy label focuses the reader on the incompetence of those people making criticisms of American foreign policy. The dissidents and their followers are paranoids advancing improbable claims they lack the wherewithal to make. The generalised crowd is paranoid too, but this emanates from an irrational fury, produced by an underlying social-psychological frustration.

Both of these trajectories point the reader away from the *substance* of Arab-Muslim claims about American power and towards the deeper cognitive or social-psychological conditions of the people making them. In doing so, Ajami neatly condemns and dismisses all criticism of American foreign policy as anti-Americanism, and inoculates his image of benevolent American power.

A similar strategy is at work across *Foreign Affairs*, not least in Michael Scott Doran's article 'Somebody Else's Civil War'.[64] Doran has a more theologically focused approach to the motivations of anti-American terrorism, arguing that Al-Qaeda attacked the United States in order to unite a disparate Muslim world against its own apostate regimes.[65] Here Doran comprehensively delegitimises Salafist anti-Americanism in the same way Ajami undermines dissidents and their views:

> In Salafi writings, the United States emerges as the senior member of a 'Zionist-Crusader alliance' dedicated to subjugating Muslims, killing them, and, most important, destroying Islam. A careful reading reveals that this alliance represents more than just close relations between the United States and Israel today. The international co-operation between Washington and Jerusalem is but one nefarious manifestation of a greater evil of almost cosmic proportions. Thus in his 'Declaration of War' bin Laden lists 10 or 12 world hot spots where Muslims have recently died (including Bosnia, Chechnya, and Lebanon) and attributes all of these deaths to a conspiracy led by the United States, even though America actually played no role in pulling the trigger. And thus, in another document, 'Jihad against Jews and Crusaders', bin Laden describes U.S. policies towards the Middle East as 'a clear declaration of war on God, His messenger, and Muslims.'[66]

Osama bin Laden is connected here with conspiracy theory on account of his view that there is an American conspiracy against Muslims. But bin Laden is only a manifestation of a broader Salafi mindset in Doran's account. Salafist anti-Americanism perceives a 'Crusader-Zionist alliance' that runs beneath all historical events. Its 'manifestations' are 'nefarious', its proportions 'cosmic':

according to Doran, 'Sayyid Qutb, Osama bin Laden, and the entire extremist Salafiyya see Western civilization, in all periods and all guises, as innately hostile to Muslims and to Islam itself'.[67] Though there is less predicate subtlety here, the overt conspiracy markers do the same delegitimising work. Far from being a subjugator of foreign peoples, America is positioned as a benevolent power, subject to the unreliable criticism of religious extremists. Even when Doran later identifies some hypocrisies and blunderings in its approach, these are only significant because they point Muslims away from the fact that America's 'cause is often their cause as well'.[68] At the same time, according to Doran, the anti-American critiques of Salafists seem 'strange' to American audiences.[69] They are doctrinaire, grandiose and paranoid. It is the cognitive competency of Salafists that is under examination here, not the substance of their claims. A few paragraphs later, Doran describes Salafi interpretation as 'a paranoid view', connecting once again to the 'paranoid style' and evoking the full gamut of preconceptions that accompany it in an American readership.[70]

The other face of this paranoia narrative appears not much further on as Doran explains the traction of anti-Americanism for secular Arab-Muslims:

> Indeed, secular political discourse in the Islamic world in general and the Arab world in particular bears a striking resemblance to the Salafi interpretation of international affairs, especially insofar as they speak in terms of Western conspiracies. The secular press does not make references to Crusaders and Mongols but rather to a string of 'broken promises' dating back to World War I, when European powers divided up the Ottoman Empire to suit their own interests. They planted Israel in the midst of the Middle East, so the analysis goes, in order to drive a wedge between Arab states, and the United States continues to support Israel for the same purposes ...
>
> For 80 years – that is, since the destruction of the Ottoman Empire – the Arabs and the Muslims have been humiliated. Although they do not share bin Laden's millenarian agenda, when secular commentators point to Palestine and Iraq today they do not see just two difficult political problems; they see what they consider the true intentions of the West unmasked.[71]

Like Ajami's Arab-Muslim 'crowd', a generalised 'secular Islamic World' is linked here with a paranoid outlook. For Doran the secular Arab discourse shares this conspiratorial mindset with Salafi fundamentalists. Instead of 'Crusaders' and 'Mongols', Doran points to a conspiracy narrative of 'broken promises'. America's 'true intentions' are hidden – they 'planted' and 'divided' in their own interest – though in recent events their intentions have been 'unmasked'.[72] Here the political interpretations of the Islamic world are framed as delusional and linked to a wider Arab-Muslim paranoia theme running through the article. This points readers away from the content of specific criticism and towards the deeper social or psychological motives of the people making them.

And what are these deeper motives in Doran's account? In consonance with Ajami's explanation of the 'crowd', we find a history of Arab-Muslim humiliation at the heart of anti-Americanism. It is because of this humiliation that they see Western conspiracies behind contemporary events in Palestinian territories and Iraq. This connects again with the status anxiety analysis evident in Ajami's assessment. It connects too with that wider understanding of conspiracy theory as the product of a populist fringe operating on the margins of legitimate politics. Here America is situated as a sensible and pragmatic power guided by rational action, while Arab-Muslims – Salafi or secular – are emotive, ideological and irrational.

Drawing the analysis of these *Foreign Affairs* articles together, the Arab-Muslim paranoia narrative enacted a potent delegitimising effect that worked to undermine criticism of American foreign policy and defend an image of a well-intentioned America in the Middle East. It did this by framing all criticism of American foreign policy as anti-Americanism, then connecting this *disposition* to paranoia or social psychological trauma. Under these circumstances, the reader was drawn away from the substance of specific criticisms and refocused on the irrational motives of the people making them. This delegitimising narrative appeared time and again throughout *Foreign Affairs* in articles linking terrorism to anti-Americanism in the year after 9/11.

The Arab-Muslim paranoia narrative after 9/11: the *New York Times*

The same dynamic was carried on in *New York Times* editorials concerned with the connection between terrorism and Arab-Muslim anti-Americanism. I focus on three articles by Thomas Friedman that are representative of the broader Arab-Muslim paranoia narrative in the paper: 'Run, Osama, Run!' and 'Wall of Ideas', published in late January 2002, and the widely cited 'War of Ideas', published three months later, which crystallised his earlier thinking on anti-Americanism into concrete policy proposals.[73] Friedman's articles were the centre of gravity for the Arab-Muslim paranoia narrative in the *New York Times*. He was also by far the most prolific commentator on the link between Arab-Muslim anti-Americanism and terrorism, producing twenty-six editorials on this issue over the year after 9/11. Add to this the fact that he is widely considered *the* most influential foreign policy commentator in America, and Friedman's writing is unavoidable. The section begins with 'Run, Osama, Run', published in late January 2002.[74]

This editorial attempts to explain an apparently widespread belief throughout the Muslim world that Osama bin Laden did not carry out the 9/11 attacks.[75] Friedman contends that although the United States has won the war in Afghanistan it has not won the 'hearts and minds' of Arab-Muslims.[76] There are several reasons for anti-Americanism. One is that America has failed to challenge misperceptions with hard facts.[77] But the most important causes relate to the culture and psychology of Arab-Muslims.[78] This first excerpt gives an indication of how conspiracy theory operates within the text. After telling the reader about a series of interviews he has conducted with notable Muslims he opines:

> All of them were educated, intelligent and thoughtful – and virtually none of them believed Osama bin Laden was guilty.
>
> Let's see, there was the serious Arab journalist in Bahrain who said that Arabs could never have pulled off something as complex as Sept. 11; there was the Euro-Muslim woman in Brussels who looked at me as if I was a fool when I said that the bin Laden tape in which he boasted of the World Trade Center attacks was surely authentic and had not been doctored by the Pentagon; there was the American-educated Arab student who insisted that somehow the C.I.A or Mossad must have known about Sept. 11 in advance, so why didn't they stop it? There was the Saudi businessman who declared there was a plot in the U.S. media to smear Saudi Arabia, for absolutely no reason. And there was the Pakistani who confided that his kid's entire elementary school class believed the canard that 4,000 Jews who worked in the World Trade Center were warned not to go to the office on Sept. 11.[79]

Friedman references conspiracy theory explicitly later on in the editorial, but it is clear that he is using these examples as an indication of a widespread problem in the region. Friedman lists a series of claims around 9/11 that he finds bizarre and fanciful. He leads into this list with a contrast between apparent conspiracy claims and the ostensible competence of the people making them, a rhetorical strategy that positions doubt about 9/11 as the kind of thing the reader would not expect from a competent person. This device is carried on into Friedman's description in the next paragraph, where a 'serious Arab journalist', an 'American-educated student', and an 'entire elementary school' all believe a 9/11 conspiracy. By doing this Friedman produces a relief between sources of authority and beliefs he considers dubious. In the next paragraph Friedman makes the meaning of this contrast between rational people and irrational views explicit:

> And they [these views] add up to a simple point: that while America has won the war in Afghanistan, it has not won the hearts and minds of the Arab-Muslim world. The cultural-political-psychological chasm between us is wider than ever. And if you don't believe that, ask any U.S. ambassador from Morocco to Islamabad – any one of them. They will share with you cocktail party chatter about the 'American conspiracy' against the Muslim world that will curl your ears.[80]

Here Friedman ties scepticism about 9/11 to a broader Arab-Muslim tendency for conspiracy theory, which is a manifestation of a deep 'cultural-political-psychological chasm' between this vast and generalised body of people and the country their conspiracies revolve around.[81] All of this displays the same delegitimising machinery at work in *Foreign Affairs*. Scepticism about 9/11 is connected with a wider Arab-Muslim propensity for conspiracy theories, produced by social-psychological forces, which divide them off from normal interpretations of international affairs. Once again the reader is pointed away from the substance of the claims in question and towards the deeper motivations of the people making them. And this move is not just focused on scepticism about 9/11. It works too on a whole undistinguished range of criticism captured by the category 'American conspiracies against the Muslim world'.[82] The socio-medical predicates evident in more embellished texts, like those from Ajami and Doran, are not evident here, but a clear disdain and dismissal is built into the rhetorical structure of the text, culminating in the explicit use of the term 'conspiracy theory'.

However, a more intense psychologising narrative does emerge towards the end of the piece where Friedman attempts to situate conspiracy theories as a symptom of 'self-loathing', low 'self-esteem' and 'free-floating anger'.[83] It is the 'lagging state' of their economies and politics that is the underlying source of anti-Americanism – implying a disparity between their circumstances and a Western world they 'lag' behind.[84] Here we can see the same social-psychological connotations working to delegitimise the views in question and broader criticism of America from the Arab-Muslim world. It is clear too that Friedman's analysis takes him well beyond a category claim about 9/11 scepticism. He is talking about a broader phenomenon, a general Arab-Muslim's susceptibility to conspiracy thinking:

> Finally, we have to admit that bin Laden touches something deep in the Arab-Muslim soul, even among those who condemn his murders. They still root for him as the one man who was not intimidated by America's overweening power, as the one man who dared to tell certain Arab rulers that they had no clothes on, and as the one man who did something about it.
>
> Quietly today, many in the Muslim world are rooting for bin Laden to get away. They are whispering in their heart of hearts, 'Run, Osama, Run!'[85]

Friedman is speaking about feelings 'deep in the Arab-Muslim soul', 'whispering in their heart[s]'.[86] This diagnosis positions a generalised Arab-Muslim subject as the product of underlying dynamics that determine their thoughts and actions. Whatever else the reader takes away from the editorial, it is clear that questions about 9/11, or Arab-Muslim scepticism of America power, should not be taken at face value or considered on its own terms.

'Wall of Ideas', published a week later, makes this broadening move more explicit by tying conspiracy theory to a wide range of criticisms of American foreign policy – once again emanating from the social-psychology of a generalised Arab-Muslim world.[87] Friedman argues that there is a wall dividing Americans and Muslims, but that this wall is not physical, 'it's in people's heads':

> Just go anywhere – Egypt, Saudi Arabia, Pakistan – and you'll hit your head against this wall. You say the problem is Islamist terrorism; they will say it is Israeli brutality to Palestinians. You say America liberated Afghans from the Taliban; they say we

bombed innocent Afghan civilians. You say Saddam Hussein is evil; they will say Ariel Sharon is worse. You say America is a democracy; they say it is a country whose media and politics are controlled by Jews. You say President Bill Clinton devoted the end of his presidency to creating a Palestinian state; they will tell you that America never showed them the plans. You say the problem is a lack of democracy; they will say that must be what America prefers – given the sorts of Arab-Muslim regimes it backs.

From my own experience, the only thing surprising about last week's Gallup poll from nine Muslim countries – which showed that 61 percent of Muslims believe that Arabs were not involved in the 9/11 attacks and 53 percent view the U.S. unfavourably – is that the numbers are not worse.[88]

The explicit reference to conspiracy theory comes later on it the editorial, but it is already implied here – most notably in the reference to the poll results about Arab involvement in 9/11, but also in the phrases 'controlled by Jews'.[89] The pairing of the poll about 9/11 scepticism with a second one that points to the general unfavourableness of America among Muslims, conflates these categories into a single anti-Americanism. It also makes the oppositional list of criticisms that come immediately before it seem the same as scepticism of 9/11, a position that Friedman had already positioned as a conspiracy theory the week before. It makes broader criticism of American foreign policy the same as doubting the truth of 9/11.

Again, the consequence is to turn the reader's attention away from criticism of American foreign policy and towards the deviancy of the people making the criticism. Friedman's dualisms are actually dichotomies, where his own statements are the obvious truth of the matter and what any sensible reader should think, while any of the retorts he relates – retorts apparently common from Egypt to Saudi Arabia to Pakistan – are patently ridiculous. And, once again, Friedman points the reader to the *real* origin of these sentiments:

But our Arab-Muslim allies have helped erect this wall as well. Their leaders have encouraged their press to print the worst lies about America, as well as blatant anti-Jewish and Holocaust-denial articles, as a way of deflecting the peoples anger away from them. That's why these regimes can now cooperate with us only in secret. And they have let their conspiracy theories about America and Israel become easy excuses for why they never have to look at themselves – why they never have to ask, How is it that we had this incredible windfall of oil wealth and have done so poorly at building societies that can tap the vast potential of our people.[90]

Here conspiracy theory is tied to the anger of the 'people'. It is a way to avoid looking at real problems, a form of denial or self-delusion. On the one hand, the explicit use of the term 'conspiracy theory' buttresses the insinuation of paranoia in the first part of the article, framing criticism of America as both irrational and the product of cognitive deviance. On the other hand, conspiracy theory is presented as a crutch used to prop up and distract Arab-Muslims from their own serious problems. This connects with Friedman's diagnosis in the previous article of resentment and self-loathing, leading to anger against America. This anger, the product of low self-esteem, is actually a protection mechanism (to extend the metaphor) that denies the real issues. Criticism of American foreign policy, framed here as conspiracy theory, now amounts to a form of scapegoating. The same strategy identified in the other texts is at play here too: the Arab-Muslim paranoia narrative delegitimises criticism of American foreign policy by characterising it as anti-Americanism, tying in to conspiracy theory, and situating this as the symptom of a deeper social-psychological ailment. This amounts to a potent disqualifying move that paints a diverse range of views in the colours of irrationality.

The final editorial examined here is Friedman's widely cited article 'War of Ideas' published three months after the previous two editorials, which crystallises his thoughts on the link between terrorism and anti-Americanism.[91] Friedman expands his thinking into a firm policy position that emphasises the need to build partnerships with moderate voices in the Muslim world in order to foster more modern political, economic and cultural values.[92] And, perhaps unsurprisingly, conspiracy theory is central to the framework proposed:

> I'm glad that the F.B.I agents are banging away at all the missed signals that might have tipped us off to 9/11, but we need to remember something: not all signals for 9/11 were hidden. Many were out there in public, in the form of hate speech and conspiracy theories directed at America and preached in mosques and religious schools throughout the Muslim world. If we are intent on preventing the next 9/11, we need to do more than just spy on our enemies better in secret. We need to take on their ideals in public.[93]

Friedman argues that America will never just beat terrorism in a physical battle – it is a 'war of ideas' against 'hate speech and conspiracy theories' that is crucial.[94] From what we know about the Arab-Muslim paranoia narrative around anti-Americanism, it is clear enough that Friedman is carrying out this war of ideas at the same time as he argues for its necessity in the future: delegitimising criticism of American foreign policy by framing it as the product of deeper deviancy. In Friedman's rendering, all anti-Americanism is alike in its quality and pathology.

Conspiracy and modernity

This section focuses on the recurring opposition between Western modernity and Arab-Muslim 'backwardness', which gives the Arab-Muslim paranoia narrative its underlying structure. Friedman's editorials provide an excellent entry point – the manifestation is far more explicit here than in the longer articles from

Foreign Affairs. Rather than adopting the source-by-source treatment, I take a more thematic approach here, which reflects the shared binary structure of the Arab-Muslim paranoia narrative across the texts examined.

A good starting point is Friedman's repeated opposition between the future and the past, development and underdevelopment, conspiracy and irrationality, suicidal violence and progressive politics.[95] Here Western modernity, and specifically America, is the consistent counterpoint to the problems of Arab-Muslims. It is an American author, and an American readership, and an American modernity that looks back and judges apparently benighted Arab-Muslims. This is the base undercurrent to which Friedman's concern about Arab-Muslim paranoia connects. It positions and sustains a vision of America as the model of progress and civilised values, and disciplines criticisms that call this vision into question. Take, for instance, Friedman's support for Dutch anti-Muslim immigration campaigner Pim Fortuyn:

> [he] questioned Muslim immigration to the Netherlands ... not because he was against Muslims but because he felt that Islam had not gone through the Enlightenment and reformation, which separated church from state in the West and prepared it to embrace modernity, democracy, and tolerance.[96]

Friedman implies here that anti-Americanism springs from a lack of Enlightenment, without which Arab-Muslim countries remain mired in intolerance and violence. If only they were more like 'us' there would be no problems. This same logic is evident in 'Wall of Ideas' and 'Run, Osama, Run'. In the first, Friedman opens the article with an analogy to the fall of the Berlin Wall at the end of the Cold War, where, according to him, newly liberated Eastern bloc peoples readily accepted American ideals and perceptions.[97] For Friedman, there is a metaphorical Berlin Wall of misperception and misunderstanding dividing America from the Arab-Muslim world, preventing them, presumably, from accepting America's world-view.[98] In the final paragraph he implores George W. Bush and Hosni Mubarak, who were meeting in Washington that week, to 'tear down this wall':

> We need Mr Mubarak to articulate publicly a progressive modern-looking, Arab-Muslim vision to counter bin Ladenism. We need him to get Egypt's act together, to stop riding on its past and start leading the Arab world into the future. And we need Mr Bush to talk to the Egyptian people, and to Arab societies – not just their leaders – about how that future can also be theirs.[99]

Once again, the future and the past, America and Arab-Muslims, modernity and pre-modernity, progressive liberal democracy and the status quo, are set in opposition. Friedman openly and overtly prioritises the values he ascribes to the modern West over the values he ascribes to contemporary and past Arab-Muslims.

In 'Run, Osama, Run', published the week before, the antecedents of the Berlin Wall metaphor appear in Friedman's use of the 'iron curtain', which does the same rhetorical work.[100] Accordingly, the 'cultural-political-psychological chasm between us is wider than ever' – caused, at least in part, by Arab-Muslim's 'lagging political systems and economies'.[101] This last issue connects narratives about the social-psychological roots of anti-Americanism with the Western/ Arab-Muslim, modernity/pre-modernity, dichotomy set. If there is anger and envy at the West because of a traumatic self-image that cannot deal with the disparity between a glorious past and a disappointing present, then clearly this relies on a contrast between the West and Arab-Muslims. Friedman, at first principles, needs to have drawn up this dichotomy in order to make the argument work. Without these underlying assumptions it would make no sense at all for Arab-Muslims to resent America in itself. The whole position relies on a trajectory from pre-modern to modern that ascribes the former highly negative values and the later unconditional authority as the destination for which the Arab-Muslim world should aim.

What is the point of highlighting this binary set? It is that this too is a deep delegitimising discourse that prioritises the West, and particularly America, over all other things, while marginalising and excluding the experiences of non-Western, non-American people.[102] And it is not just that these oppositional categories are loaded with value; it is also that the categories themselves are a product of a particular Western, liberal self-understanding, projected out on to the world as a latent organising framework for making sense of things.[103] It bears no *necessary* relationship to the experiences of the many millions of human lives it ostensibly situates.[104] Nevertheless, the narrative under examination furnishes these commentators, and their readers alike, with an exceptionally powerful and pervasive suite of dichotomies that flow from the central opposition. The Arab-Muslim paranoia narrative also intersects with and is animated by multiple other dichotomies, among which we must include rational/irrational, reason/emotion, subject/object, masculine/feminine, self/other, progress/tradition and normal/deviant. Articulating these dichotomies is Friedman – the sovereign, authorial voice, not mediating evenly between America and Arab-Muslims as it sometimes appears, but standing with both feet firmly planted within the American liberal tradition, which is both his guiding light and the standard by which he judges the world.

This idea of sovereign presence, of authorial judgement, is particularly important for understanding the delegitimisation underway here. After all, deciding who is deviant and who is normal, which arguments are rational and which are wrongheaded, is a matter of judgement and a matter of interpretation. The modernist discourse Friedman wields provides a framework for making these determinations and the language to make good on them in text. Although the Arab-Muslim paranoia narrative in *Foreign Affairs* is not as explicitly derisive of Arab-Muslims, the same sovereign presence is the unspoken source of authority in the texts – the locus of reason and rationality, where normal cognitive processes and political interpretation emanate from.

But this authorial power is always deployed in consonance with a particular view of the West, and of America especially, at once defended against irrational invectives and affirmed as the ultimate source of modernity. America is positioned as the exemplar – as the healthy, right-minded subject, not susceptible to the same kind of vitriolic and alienated politics. At the same time, it is clear, particularly in Friedman's editorials, that the cure for anti-Americanism is actually America. If the Arab-Muslims world could only adopt American values it would not be so angry about American foreign policy, and it would not be so conspiracy-minded in its interpretations. The important point here, then, is that under these circumstances criticism of American foreign policy is rendered untenable, even deviant, while a particular image of America as benevolent and misunderstood is secured.

But this delegitimising narrative contains significant contradictions, silences and exclusions, all of which point towards its wider significance. First, and most obviously, these binaries rest on generalisations that sweep together all kinds of peoples and experiences. Ajami points to 'rancid anti-Americanism now evident in the Arab world';[105] it is Doran's view that 'the Arabs and Muslims have been humiliated';[106] while for Friedman a 'wall of ideas' now separates 'America' from the 'Arab-Muslim world'.[107] Difference and diversity is occluded in these generic statements. This is matched by the way the many varied viewpoints of the people captured by these categories are subsumed under the equally generalising term 'anti-Americanism', as if being critical of American foreign policy were enough to provide conceptual unity. And, of course, the same thing applies for the categories 'conspiracy theory' and 'paranoia', which also lack conceptual coherence and lump together a variety of different views. Conspiracy theory, like anti-Americanism, becomes a problem to be solved. Of course, when anti-Americanism and conspiracy theory are linked, the many varied critiques and quarrels of a whole spectrum of people blend together as sentiment or pathology.

Moreover, when these categories are located within the modernist binary set that structures the Arab-Muslim paranoia narrative, yet more generalisations, exclusions and obfuscations are added. As multiple scholars have shown, not only are these dichotomies a product of a particular enlightenment discourse, they are not even sustainable in their own cultural context.[108] Over and over they have been implicated in one another. Reason and emotion, rationality and irrationality, normality and pathology are not neat polar opposites as the binaries imply.[109] They are together and inseparable, despite our modernist search for certainty and control. On close examination, each of the oppositional pairings collapse. But, then, this is really the point of the dichotomous structure in the first place: to discipline uncertainty and irrationality, and to produce and reproduce a modern sovereign identity, always in danger of succumbing to the forces of chaos, irrationality, and passion.[110] The important point here is that these dichotomies are about legitimacy and illegitimacy – they are about securing a particular self-image.

At a more practical level it is clear that even the apparent division between Western states, with their modern economies and liberal democratic institutions, and an Arab-Muslim world lacking in these things, is more porous than these foreign policy commentators portray. As Edward Said has argued in response to Huntington's 'Clash of Civilizations', the history of Western civilisation – and specifically the Enlightenment project – has been deeply indebted to cross-cultural influences between these regions and many other places. Here is Said in his own words:

> Huntington is an ideologist, someone who wants to make 'civilizations' and 'identities' into what they are not, shut down, sealed of entities that have been purged of the myriad currents and counter-currents that animate human history and that over the centuries have made it possible for that history to contain not only wars of religion and imperial conquest but also exchange, cross-fertilization, and sharing.[111]

In Said's account the 'West' and 'Islam' are together from the beginning. They are thoroughly indebted to one another – and this continues to be the case despite a recent history of colonialism. However, when the modernist discourse is brought to bear, this interwoven history fades into the background and rigid identity markers are laid out. The difference and diversity and complication and multiple histories are shut off.

This is exactly the significance of the Arab-Muslim paranoia narrative around anti-Americanism. A particular image of America as a benevolent and basically well-intentioned power is at stake.[112] Indeed, Richard Jackson has made a similar point with regards to the broader discourse on terrorism established by Terrorism Studies researchers and counter-terrorism policy makers after 9/11. For Jackson, this discourse acted to 'reinforce and reify existing structures of power in society, particularly that of the state, and to promote particular elite projects', and to produce an image of Western exceptionalism, which positioned Western foreign policy as essentially benign rather than aimed at the reproduction of 'existing structures of power and domination in the international system'.[113] Likewise, beyond the abstract dichotomies and rhetorical strategies, and in the most basic terms, the narrative under examination is about an opposition between authoritative interpretations of foreign policy and illegitimate, unauthorised interpretations – understood here as anti-Americanism, conspiracy theory, and paranoia. Here is Friedman's list of anti-American retorts from the generic 'Arab-Muslim world' again:

> You say the problem is Islamist terrorism; they will say it is Israeli brutality to Palestinians. You say America liberated Afghans from the Taliban; they say we bombed

innocent Afghan civilians. You say Saddam Hussein is evil; they will say Ariel Sharon is worse. You say America is a democracy; they say it is a country whose media and politics are controlled by Jews. You say President Bill Clinton devoted the end of his presidency to creating a Palestinian state; they will tell you that America never showed them the plans. You say the problem is a lack of democracy; they will say that must be what America prefers – given the sorts of Arab-Muslim regimes it backs.[114]

Many of the claims Friedman puts in the mouths of apparently paranoid Arab-Muslims are common on the American left and are advanced by established Western scholars.[115] This is not to argue for the truth of any particular claim. It is just to say that, though Friedman frames these views as anti-American conspiracy theories, produced by the cognitive or social-psychological deviancy of Arab-Muslim people, many of these views are regularly expressed within his *own* political discourse, if not on CNN. Here is Doran with a similar though more subtle passage, which is worth quoting at some length since it demonstrates precisely the issue under examination:

> For 80 years – that is, since the destruction of the Ottoman Empire – the Arabs and the Muslims have been humiliated. Although they do not share bin Laden's millenarian agenda, when secular commentators point to Palestine and Iraq today they do not see just two difficult political problems; they see what they consider the true intentions of the West unmasked.
>
> Arab commentators often explain, for instance, that Saddam Hussein and Washington are actually allies. They ridicule the notion that the United States tried to depose the dictator. After all, it is said, the first Bush administration had the forces in place to remove the Baath Party and had called on the Iraqi populace to rise up against the tyrant. When the people actually rose, however, the Americans watched from the sidelines as the regime brutally suppressed them. Clearly, therefore, what the United States really wanted was to divide and rule the Arabs in order to secure easy access to Persian Gulf oil – a task that also involves propping up corrupt monarchies in Kuwait and Saudi Arabia. Keeping Saddam on a leash was the easiest way to ensure that Iran could not block the project.
>
> Needless to say, this world view is problematic. Since World War I, Arab societies have been deeply divided among themselves along ethnic, social, religious, and political lines. Regardless of what the dominant Arab discourse on broken promises has to say, most of these divisions were not created by the West. The European powers and the United States have sometimes worked to divide the Arabs, sometimes to unify them. Mostly they have pursued their own interests, as have all the actors involved.[116]

Doran frames the views of 'Arab commentators' as problematic and paranoid, in contrast to the author's more sensible appraisal. But it contains several important disjunctions. Doran notes at the outset the long history of colonial intervention and domination in the Middle East, and he references the fact that Western powers broke promises after World War I, when the European states divided up the region in their own interests. But despite this history of self-interested action in the region's affairs, the suggestion by 'Arab commentators' that America's foreign policy intentions might not be transparent is ruled out of court. Moreover, whatever the veracity of the views Doran reports about a continuing US alliance with Saddam Hussein, the broad strategic themes that he ridicules are far from fanciful.

It is a widely held view among international relations scholars that a concern for regional stability and an eye to a potentially revisionist Shiite Iran were both important geopolitical considerations in the decision not to topple Hussein in 1991.[117] Indeed, these are also prominent reasons why America was allied to Iraq in the decade leading up to the Gulf War.[118] Similarly, it is widely accepted – even by Doran later in the article – that America did abandon the Iraqi uprising it had called for because of its reticence to invade.*[119] Moreover, America and other European powers have regularly allied themselves with Arab dictators, precisely because of the strategic importance of the region's energy resources.[120] Thus, whatever other causes there may be for Arab-Muslim problems – and Doran points here to divided societies and civil wars – it is unclear why this undermines the interpretation he finds so improbable. Though it is doubtful that the United States and Iraq remained allies after the Gulf War, the reasoning in this passage is far from outrageous, *even if we disagree.*[121]

Once again, many of the assumptions and arguments are non-controversial positions in American political discourse. But in both these excerpts the Arab-Muslim paranoia narrative delegitimises them and de-emphasises the long, violent and deceptive past. At the same time, it positions these criticisms of American foreign policy as the product of cognitive failure or social-psychological trauma and humiliation rather than evidence and reasoning. But, of course, these criticisms were always already on the inside of the Western political identity.

---

*In 1991, Friedman, who by 2002 can ridicule Arab-Muslim cynicism about America's intentions towards Iraq, openly acknowledged the strategic orthodoxy at the end of the first Gulf War: 'The war was, instead, fought to restore the status quo. And, as every American policymaker knows, before Mr. Hussein invaded Kuwait he was a pillar of the gulf balance of power and status quo preferred by Washington. His iron fist simultaneously held Iraq together, much to the satisfaction of the American allies Turkey and Saudi Arabia, and it prevented Iranian Islamic fundamentalists from sweeping over the eastern Arab world. It was only when the Iraqi dictator decided to use his iron fist to dominate Kuwait and Saudi Arabia that he became a threat. But as soon as Mr. Hussein was forced back into his shell, Washington felt he had become useful again for maintaining the regional balance and preventing Iraq from disintegrating.

That was why Mr. Bush never supported the Kurdish and Shiite rebellions against Mr. Hussein, or for that matter any democracy movement in Iraq. ... Sooner or later, Mr. Bush argued, sanctions would force Mr. Hussein's generals to bring him down, and then Washington would have the best of all worlds: an iron-fisted Iraqi junta without Saddam Hussein.'

However, the most telling collapse in this opposition between legitimate and illegitimate interpretations of international politics occurs around the idea of conspiracy itself. Throughout many of the texts linking terrorism to anti-Americanism the use of conspiracy theory to characterise criticism of American foreign policy is paralleled by the identification of *actual* terrorist conspiracies against America. Look again at the introduction to 'War of Ideas':

> I'm glad that the F.B.I agents are banging away at all the missed signals that might have tipped us off to 9/11, but we need to remember something: not all signals for 9/11 were hidden. Many were out there in public, in the form of hate speech and conspiracy theories directed at America and preached in mosques and religious schools throughout the Muslim world. If we are intent on preventing the next 9/11, we need to do more than just spy on our enemies better in secret. We need to take on their ideals in public.[122]

The article ends by tying this theme back in:

> Zacarias Moussaoui, accused of being the 20th hijacker, told a U.S. court that he 'prayed to Allah for the destruction of the United States.' That is an ugly idea – one many Muslims would not endorse. But until we and they team up to fight a war of ideas against those who do, there will be plenty more Moussaouis where he came from – and there will never be enough F.B.I agents to stop them.[123]

The opening line here identifies a secret terrorist conspiracy that was hidden from American authorities. The next line alleges that the terrorists were motivated by the perception that America is involved in a secret conspiracy against the Arab-Muslim world. The parallel is repeated in the final paragraph. But, plainly, only one of these conspiracy narratives is held to be an acceptable interpretation of international politics. This dynamic is repeated throughout all the sources analysed in this chapter – and is particularly obvious where the literal/legal meaning of conspiracy appears alongside conspiracy theory. Ajami repeatedly refers to dissidents working in 'the shadows' – to 'the plotters life' and 'men in the shadows pulling of spectacular deeds'.[124] Doran points to the men that 'masterminded the attacks on September 11th'.[125] In this formulation the conspiracy signifier is paradoxical. From the point of view of these authors, to conduct conspiracies against America and to suspect America of conspiracies are *both* deviant. The terrorists are pathological for their thoughts and actions. But the conspiracy acts and allegations of Americans are unimpeachably sound and sensible.

To make this formulation work requires a few basic moves. First, an official conspiracy narrative has to be established and secured. Second, a deep forgetting needs to occur – one that blocks out the many examples of covert US power in the Middle East, and the world generally; one that denies the well-established geostrategic imperatives of America's regional foreign policy.[126] If we recognise the authority required to establish an official conspiracy narrative, and remain open to this broader historical context, then the paradox unravels. It becomes clear that 'conspiracy' operates from the commanding heights. It is imbricated with power; the power to point to the unseen enemy, to sketch out the dark forces at work in the world, to act covertly on the basis of these perceptions; and the power to dismiss the attempts of others to do the same. Indeed, the texts examined in this case study were full of references to covert actions, secret dealings, suspicious activities, looming threats, nightmare scenarios, plots and sleeper agents and spies. Sensible foreign policy experts regularly interpreted ambiguous circumstances and divined the motives and meanings behind events, not least of which was 9/11. But this was not conspiracy theory. It never even seemed to be, despite regularly sharing the rhetoric and structure of a conspiracy narrative. And it would have been quite ridiculous to suggest that it was. These interpretations were given by foreign policy aficionados, plying their trade in some of the most reputable forums in America. The authority and legitimacy that enabled their interpretation of opaque international affairs is also what allowed them to delegitimise the interpretations of others, however apt or incorrect, insightful or obtuse these may have been.

Conspiracy discourse in the War on Terror

This issue of power and legitimacy points to the necessity of reconnecting the Arab-Muslim paranoia narrative to a wider conspiracy discourse composed of competing conspiracy narratives, each intimately connected to debates about the meaning and consequences of 9/11. One way to do this is to trace the foregoing narratives about Arab-Muslim cultural dysfunction into the highly contentious field of political controversy present in the months before the outbreak of the Iraq War, a time when suspicion of double-dealings and ulterior motives was rife. The place to start is with the influence of a small group of Arabist experts on the Bush administration in the aftermath of 9/11. According to Bob Woodward, Deputy Secretary of Defence Paul Wolfowitz asked the American Enterprise Institute to convene a group of intellectuals to provide historical context and policy advice to the Bush administration: 'among those invited to help in generating the appropriate public response were Bernard Lewis, journalist and former *Newsweek* editor Fareed Zakaria, and Johns Hopkins professor Fouad Ajami, as well as several other neocons'.[127] Here we see key purveyors of the orientalist narrative, flagged for their concern with Arab-Muslim paranoia across this chapter, speaking into the ear of power in a time of crisis and ambiguity. The message taken away by the Bush administration's inner circle was that the Muslim world was undergoing an internal struggle between the forces of modernisation and tradition, and that the United States should prepare for a generation long war against radical Islam.[128] For Edward Said this perspective was integral to the administration's subsequent thinking:

95

The major influences on George W. Bush's Pentagon and National Security Council were men such as Bernard Lewis and Fouad Ajami, experts on the Arab and Islamic world who helped the American hawks to think about such preposterous phenomena as the Arab mind and centuries-old Islamic decline that only American power could reverse.[129]

Indeed, Both Lewis and Ajami conducted private meetings with leading administration figures, including Vice-President Richard Cheney, National Security Advisor Condoleezza Rice and Wolfowitz.[130] But Lewis stands out as the most powerful intellectual force shaping the Bush administration's response to 9/11, which has sometimes been dubbed the 'Lewis Doctrine'.[131] As Wolfowitz explained in the lead-up to the Iraq War, 'Bernard [Lewis] has taught how to understand the complex and important history of the Middle East, and use it to guide where we will go next to build a better world.'[132] The advice Lewis gave was that, much as Atatürk had successfully imposed secular modernity on Turkey through forceful top-down measures, the United States needed to address the underlying anti-modernism of Islam by bringing secular democracy to the Arab-Muslim world – through force, if necessary.[133]

This policy recommendation was unavoidably implicated in the wider controversy about the Bush administration's case for war with Iraq, which ostensibly rested on the imminent threat posed by Iraq's Weapons of Mass Destruction (WMDs). The administration argued that WMDs could easily be handed off to terrorist groups who would be unswayed by the logic of deterrence, and that Iraq was already in collaboration with Al-Qaeda. Yet the account given above, concerning the influence of orientalist narratives about democratic transformation, suggests that other policy ambitions were at play in the drive towards war. Indeed, even before 9/11 or the advice of Lewis and others, regime change in Iraq was a key administration priority, outlined in its inaugural national security meeting eight months before the terrorist attacks.[134] The leaked Downing Street memo, minutes of a high-level British government meeting in July 2002, confirms what many critics had argued in the lead in to the Iraq War: 'that the intelligence and the facts were being fixed around the policy'.[135] More than a decade later, it is a historical fact that the alleged conjunction between Iraqi WMDs and Al-Qaeda terrorism was a confected conspiracy, the political pretext for a decision to go to war with Iraq that had already been made.

Of course, this reality was more contentious in the months leading up to Operation Iraq Freedom. The political discourse at that time was driven by a forceful public diplomacy campaign aimed at selling the war, along with commentators and public intellectuals making the same case. A confluence of pro-war advocacy and authoritative scepticism, not least from within the diplomatic and intelligence bureaucracy, constituted a field of political controversy where the assertions of credible actors were in tension – where the language of intelligence assessments, geostrategic planning, secret alliances, clandestine programmes, informants, defectors and spies, pointed below the surface to the covert machinations of Saddam Hussein, Al-Qaeda and the Bush administration.

Below the surface, for critics of the case for war, lay the administration's ulterior motives for regime change, including, for instance, President Bush's complicated relationship with his father; the geopolitics of energy security and regional stability; the long-running ideological commitments of neoconservative foreign policy hawks; and, complimentary to all these objectives, orientalist policy prescription for democratic transformation in a recalcitrant region. Paradoxically, then, the issue of Arab-Muslim conspiracy theories emerged from a narrative about the anti-modern dysfunctions of Arab-Muslim culture, which was itself implicated, via the influential advice of Lewis, Zakaria, Ajami and others, in the secret history of America's intervention in Iraq.

The point of tracing these connections is to demonstrate that concerns about Arab-Muslim paranoia must be understood as part of a broader conspiracy discourse: the competing and interrelated conspiracy narratives woven through the post-9/11 political landscape. It should be clear that concerns about Arab-Muslim paranoia involved the delegitimisation of one set of conspiracy narratives, those proffered by Arab-Muslims sceptical of American power in the Middle East, out of a foreign policy discourse comprised of suspicions about secret dealings and deep politics. The suspicion and cynicism expressed by Arab-Muslim people about US power had little standing in America's foreign policy discourse, where it regularly came up as conspiracy theory and paranoia and the rage of 'the Arab street'. The Arab-Muslim paranoia narrative produced a potent delegitimising effect that disqualified criticism of American foreign policy. Readers were directed away from the substance of specific claims and towards the cognitive or social-psychological deviancy of the people making them. This swept together a whole range of different grievances and tied them to more fundamental pathologies. While the categories and oppositions at the heart of the Arab-Muslim paranoia narrative collapse on close examination, this merely demonstrates that its power is precisely that it provides certainty and stability, rational politics and a stable sovereign; a liberal, progressive, democratic and, above all, benign America.

NOTES

1   The title of this chapter is drawn directly from Keith Goshorn's incisive review of key contributions to the conspiracy culture literature. See K. Goshorn, 'Strategies of Deterrence and Frames of Containment: On Critical Paranoia and Anti-Conspiracy Discourse', *Theory & Event*, 4:3 (2000).
2   A. Roy, 'The Algebra of Infinite Justice', *Guardian*. Available at www.theguardian.com/world/2001/sep/29/september11.afghanistan (accessed 6 January 2015).

3　J. George, *Discourse of Global Politics: A Critical (Re)Introduction to International Relations* (Boulder, CO: Lynne Rienner, 1994), p. 191; M. Shapiro, 'Textualizing Global Politics', in J. Der Derian and M. Shapiro (eds), *International/Intertextual Relations: Postmodern Readings of World Politics* (Lexington, MA: Lexington Books, 1989), pp. 12, 19; R. Jackson, 'Constructing Enemies: "Islamic Terrorism" in Political and Academic Discourse', *Government and Opposition*, 42:3 (2007), pp. 394–426, 395–397; and B. Paltridge, *Discourse Analysis: An Introduction* (London: Continuum, 2006), pp. 179–197. See also, V. Dijik, 'Principles of Critical Discourse Analysis', *Discourse and Society*, 4:2 (1993), pp. 249–283.

4　Richard Jackson has taken a similar approach in his examination of key texts produced by terrorism studies scholars after 9/11, along with a parallel analysis of media commentary and government policy discourse. See R. Jackson, 'Knowledge, Power and Politics in the Study of Political Terrorism' in R. Jackson, M. B. Smyth and J. Gunning, *Critical Terrorism Studies: A New Agenda* (Hoboken: Taylor & Francis, 2009); and R. Jackson, 'Culture, Identity and Hegemony: Continuity and (the Lack of) Change in US Counterterrorism Policy from Bush to Obama', *International Politics*, 48:2/3 (2011), pp. 390–411.

5　For the impact of these two publications particularly see, Dolan, 'The Shape of Elite Opinion on US Foreign Policy, 1992 to 2004'; M. Baum and P. Potter, 'The Relationship between Mass Media, Public Opinion and Foreign Policy: Towards a Theoretical Synthesis', *Annual Review of Political Science*, 11 (2008), pp. 39–65; 'The Role of Think Tanks in US Foreign Policy', *US Foreign Policy Agenda: An Electronic Journal of the Department of State*. Available at http://usinfo.state.gov/journals/itps/1102/ijpe/ijpe1102 .pdf (accessed 6 January 2015); C. H. Weis, 'What America's Leaders Read', *The Public Opinion Quarterly*, 38:1 (1974), pp. 1–22; and Abbas Malak, 'New York Times Editorial Positions and United States Foreign Policy: The Case of Iran Revisited', in Malak (ed.), *News Media and Foreign Relations: A Multifaceted Perspective* (Norwood, NJ: Abex, 1996).

6　*9/11 Commission Report* (Washington DC: US Government Printing Office), p. 1.

7　M. Shapiro, 'Wanted, Dead or Alive', *Theory & Event*, 5:4 (2001).

8　P. L. Bergen, *The Osama Bin Laden I Know: An Oral History of Al Qaeda's Leader* (New York: Free Press, 2005), p. 205.

9　A. Roy, 'The Algebra of Infinite Justice'.

10　S. P. Huntington, 'The Clash of Civilizations', *Foreign Affairs*, 72:3 (1993), pp. 22–59.

11　Sandra Silberstein, *War of World: Language and Politics After 9/11* (London: Routledge, 2002)

12　'The Carlyle Group: C is for Capitalism', *Economist* (26 June 2006).

13　R. Jackson, *Writing the War on Terror*. Jackson suggests that it was the insidious treachery of the terrorist plot, as much as its violence, which was often associated with morally deviancy. See also D. Campbell, *Writing Security*; R. Goldberg, *Enemies Within: The Culture of Conspiracy in Modern America* (New Haven: Yale University Press, 2001).; J. Rogin, *Ronald Reagan the Movie*.

14　J. Butler, 'Explanation and Exoneration, Or What We Can Hear', *Social Text*, 20:3 (2002), p. 178.

15　P. J. Buchanan, 'Whose War?', *The American Conservative*. Available at www.the americanconservative.com/articles/whose-war/ (accessed 6 January 2015).

16　C. Krauthammer, 'The Neoconservative Convergence', *Commentary* (July–August 2005), p. 26. Another good example of this labelling procedure is the way critiques of neo-liberal globalization have been described as conspiracy theory in mainstream international relations journals. See, for instance, M. Strauss, 'Globalization's Jewish Problem', *Foreign Policy*, 130 (2003), pp. 58–67.

17 Indeed, there was a great deal of suspicion about the official narrative of 9/11. For instance, a Zogby International Poll conducted in 2004 found that 49 per cent of New Yorkers believed that the US government knew about the 9/11 attacks in advance and failed to act, while a nationwide poll from Scripps Howard in 2006 showed that 36 per cent of Americans thought that it was 'somewhat likely or very likely' US government officials had assisted in the attacks or took no action to prevent them. Zogby polls carried out around the same period show similar results. A 2006 poll showed 42 per cent of Americans thought that the 9/11 Commission was a cover-up and 45 per cent think the attacks should be reinvestigated; and a 2007 poll shows that 51 per cent of Americans wanted Congress to investigate President Bush and Vice-President Cheney regarding 9/11, while 30 per cent wanted them immediately impeached. See respectively, 'Half of New Yorkers Believe US Leaders had Foreknowledge of Impending 9/11 Attacks and Consciously Failed to Act; 66% Call for New Probe of Unanswered Questions by Congress or the New York's Attorney General Poll Reveals', *Zogby International*. Available at www.911truth.org/zogbypoll-50–percent-nyc-says-u-s-govt-knew/ (accessed 6 Janaury 2015); T. Hargrove and G. Stempel, 'Third of Americans Suspect 9–11 government Conspiracy', *ScrippsNews*. Available at www.911truth.org/new-poll-a-third-of-u-s-public-believes-911–conspiracy-theory/ (accessed 6 January 2015); 'A Word about our Poll of American Thinking Toward the 9/11 Terrorist Attacks', *Zogby International* (24 May 2006); A. Shatz, 'The Native Informant', *Nation* (10 April 2003) and 'Zogby Poll: 51% of Americans Want Congress to Probe Bush/Cheney Regarding 9/11 Attacks; Over 30% Seek Immediate Impeachment', *Zogby International*. Available at www.911truth.org/zogby-poll-51–of-americans-want-congress-to-probe-bushcheney-regarding-911–attacks-over-30–seek-immediate-impeachment/ (accessed 6 January 2015).

18 T. Friedman, 'Wall of Ideas', *New York Times* (3 March 2002), p. 15. See also C. Torcher, '9/11 Conspiracy Theories Rife in Muslim World', *Washington Post*. Available at www.washingtonpost.com/wp-dyn/content/article/2010/10/02/AR2010100200663.html (accessed 6 January 2015). The countries surveyed were Turkey, Kuwait, Saudi Arabia, Jordan, Lebanon, Morocco, Pakistan and Indonesia. More specifically, 86 per cent of Pakistanis and 89 per cent of Kuwaitis thought that Arabs had not been involved in the 9/11 attacks.

19 Indeed, an analysis of *Foreign Policy*, another important forum for elite foreign policy opinion, revealed relatively few articles deploying the Arab-Muslim paranoia narrative. For a full content analysis of terrorism-related articles dealing with anti-Americanism in *Foreign Affairs*, *New York Times* and *Foreign Policy*, see Tim Aistrope, *Conspiracy Theory and American Foreign Policy* (PhD diss., University of Queensland, 2013), pp. 108–149.

20 Fifty-five per cent of terrorism/anti-Americanism articles mentioned conspiracy theory. Nine of these articles deployed the Arab-Muslim paranoia narrative extensively. These were: F. Ajami, 'The Sentry's Solitude', *Foreign Affairs*, 80:6 (2001), pp. 2–16; M. S. Doran, 'Somebody Else's Civil War', *Foreign Affairs*, 81:1 (2002), pp. 22–42; P. L. Bergen, 'Review: Picking up the Pieces: What We can Learn From – and About – 9/11', *Foreign Affairs*, 81:2 (2002), pp. 169–175; G. E. Fuller, 'The Future of Political Islam', *Foreign Affairs*, 81:2 (2002), pp. 48–60; D. Hoffman, 'Beyond Public Diplomacy', *Foreign Affairs*, 81:2 (2002), pp. 83–95; E. Rouleau, 'Trouble in the Kingdom', *Foreign Affairs*, 81:4 (2002), pp. 75–89; M. Hirsh, Bush and the World', 81:5 (2002), pp. 18–43; P. G.

Peterson, 'Public Diplomacy and the War on Terrorism', *Foreign Affairs*, 81:5 (2002), pp. 74–94; B. Rubin, 'The Real Roots of Arab Anti-Americanism', 81:6 (2002), pp. 73–85.

21   Bergen, 'Review: Picking up the Pieces', p. 174. This review of post-9/11 books engages with two edited collections drawing together contributions from authors across the political spectrum, including conservatives like Fouad Ajami, Michael Scott Doran, George Shultz and Fareed Zakaria, and liberals like Strobe Talbot, Anthony Blinken and Nayan Chandar. Bergen highlights concerns about Arab-Muslim conspiracy theory from Hill and Blinken in constructing his own post-9/11 narrative, but it is interesting to note that many of the contributors to the edited collections he reviews have exhibited similar concerns, including Ajami, Doran and Zakaria.

22   Twenty-three of these exhibited extensive conspiracy discourse, seventeen with the Arab-Muslim paranoia discourse. These were S. Rushdie, 'Yes, This is About Islam', *New York Times* (2 November 2001), p. 25; F. Rich, 'Wait Until Dark', *New York Times* (24 November 2001), p. 27; 'Editorial Desk: Censorship in Pashto and Arabic', *New York Times* (10 October 2001), p. 18; F. A. Gerges, 'A Time of Reckoning', *New York Times* (8 October 2001), p. 17; N. Kristof, 'All-American Osamas', *New York Times* (June 7 2002), p. 27; D. I. Kurtzer, 'The Modern Uses of Ancient Lies', *New York Times* (9 May 2002), p. 39; N. Kristof, 'The War on Terror Flounders', *New York Times* (10 May 2002), p. 35; K. Abou El Fadl, 'Moderate Muslims Under Siege', *New York Times* (1 July 2002), p. 15; M. Dowd, 'I'm With Dick! Let's Make War!', *New York Times* (28 August 2002), p. 19; B. Keller, 'The 40–Year War', *New York Times* (6 October 2001), p. 23; T. Friedman, 'Rights in the Real World', *New York Times* (2 December 2002), p. 15; T. Friedman, 'Dear Saudi Arabia', *New York Times* (12 December 2001), p. 31; T. Friedman, 'Someone Tell the Kids', *New York Times* (6 January 2002), p. 15; T. Friedman, 'Run, Osama, Run', *New York Times* (23 January 2002), p. 19; T. Friedman, 'Blunt Questions, Blunt Answers', *New York Times* (10 February 2002), p. 15; T. Friedman, 'A Traveller to Saudi Arabia', *New York Times* (24 February 2002), p. 13; T. Friedman, 'The Core of Muslim Rage', *New York Times* (6 March 2002), p. 21; T. Friedman, 'Wall of Ideas', *New York Times* (3 March 2002), p. 15; T. Friedman, 'No Mere Terrorist', *New York Times* (24 March 2002), p. 15; T. Friedman, 'The Free Speech Bind', *New York Times* (27 March 2002), p. 23; T. Friedman, 'Listening to the Future?', *New York Times* (5 May 2002), p. 15; T. Friedman, 'Global Village Idiocy', *New York Times* (12 May 2002), p. 15; T. Friedman, 'Nine Wars Too Many', *New York Times* (15 May 2002), p. 23; and T. Friedman, 'War of Ideas', *New York Times* (2 June 2002), p. 19.

23   Of the fifty-five articles Friedman wrote on terrorism over the twelve months after 9/11, twenty-six focused on anti-Americanism, making him easily the most prolific editorial commentator on this topic at the *New York Times*. Add to this the fact the thirteen editorials referencing the problem of Arab-Muslim conspiracy theories were published between 2 December 2001 and 2 June 2002, a six-month period immediately after 9/11 where Friedman established and repeated these connections. His articles account for 54 per cent of *New York Times* texts with extensive references to the problem of conspiracy theory. On Friedman's public profile and influence see, for instance, M. Welch, 'Capturing Tom Friedman', *Reason*. Available at http://reason.com/archives/2005/08/01/capturing-tom-friedman (accessed 7 January 2015); G. M. Graff, 'Thomas Friedman is On Top of the World', *Washingtonian* (1 July 2006). Available at www.washingtonian.com/articles/people/thomas-friedman-is-on-top-of-the-world (accessed 24 July 2015); D. M. Pink, 'Why the World is Flat', *Wired* (May 2005). Available at www.wired.com/wired/archive/13.05/friedman.html (accessed 24 July 2015). Friedman recently appeared on *Foreign Policy*'s Top 100 global thinkers list at number 33. See, 'The FP

Top 100 Global Thinkers', *Foreign Policy*. Available at www.foreignpolicy.com/articles/2010/11/29/the_fp_top_100_global_thinkers (accessed 7 January 2015).
24 Zakaria, 'The Politics of Rage'.
25 B. Lewis, 'The Roots of Muslim Rage', *Atlantic* (September 1990).
26 *Ibid.*
27 D. Pipes and Jonathan Schanzer, 'Denial is a River', *New York Post* (14 January 2002).
28 F. Ajami, 'The Sentry's Solitude', pp. 2–16; and M. S. Doran, 'Somebody Else's Civil War', *Foreign Affairs*, 81:1 (2002), pp. 22–42.
29 *Ibid.*
30 Shatz, 'The Native Informant'.
31 *Ibid.*
32 See Wright, 'An Eye for Terrorist Sites'. The article also appears in *Foreign Affairs*' ten-year anniversary collection on the War on Terror. See Gideon Rose and Jonathan Tepperman (eds), *The US Vs. Al Qaeda: A History of the War on Terror* (New York: Council on Foreign Relations, 2011).
33 See Doran's White House Biography, 'Michael Doran: Senior Director for Near East and African Affairs, National Security Council', *The White House*. Available at http://web.archive.org/web/20080307004410/http://www.WhiteHouse.gov/government/doran-bio.html (accessed 8 January 2015).
34 Cited in Wright, 'An Eye for Terrorist Sites'.
35 Ajami, 'The Sentry's Solitude', pp. 22–42.
36 *Ibid.*
37 *Ibid.*
38 *Ibid.*, p. 9.
39 *Ibid.*, pp. 9–10.
40 *Ibid.*, pp. 14–16.
41 *Ibid.*, pp. 15–16.
42 *Ibid.*, pp. 6–7.
43 *Ibid.*, pp. 6–7.
44 See M. Fenster, *Conspiracy Theories: Secrecy and Power in American Culture* (Minneapolis: University of Minnesota Press, 2008), pp. 1–22.
45 Ajami, 'The Sentry's Solitude', pp. 6–7.
46 J. Dean, 'Theorizing Conspiracy Theory', *Theory & Event*, 4:3 (2000), pp. 1–15; G. Hustings and M. Orr, 'Dangerous Machinery: 'Conspiracy Theorist' as a Transpersonal Strategy of Exclusion', *Symbolic Interaction*, 30:2 (2007), pp. 127–150; K. Goshorn, 'Strategies of Deterrence and Frames of Containment: On Critical Paranoia and Anti-conspiracy Discourse', *Theory & Event*, 4:3 (2000); and J. Bratich, *Conspiracy Panics: Political Rationality and Popular Culture* (New York: State University of New York, 2008).
47 *Ibid.*
48 *Ibid.*
49 Ajami, 'The Sentry's Solitude', pp. 8–9.
50 *Ibid.*
51 *Ibid.*, p. 8.
52 *Ibid.*
53 *Ibid.*, p. 9.
54 *Ibid.*
55 *Ibid.*, p. 10.
56 *Ibid.*, p. 8.
57 *Ibid.*, pp. 8–9.

58   For a short version of this thesis see Lewis, 'The Roots of Muslim Rage'. For Lewis's response to 9/11, which shares many of the themes at play in Ajami's account, see B. Lewis, 'What Went Wrong', *Atlantic* (January 2002).

59   Ajami, 'The Sentry's Solitude', pp. 9–10.

60   See, for instance, D. Pipes, *The Hidden Hand: Middle East Fears of Conspiracy* (London: Macmillan Press, 1998).

61   See Fenster, *Conspiracy Theories*, pp. 1–22; and Bratich, *Conspiracy Panics*, pp. 1–50.

62   I deal with these issues extensively in Chapters 1 and 2.

63   Ajami, 'The Sentry's Solitude', pp. 8–9.

64   Doran, 'Somebody Else's Civil War'.

65   *Ibid.*

66   *Ibid.*, pp. 29–30.

67   *Ibid.*, p. 30.

68   *Ibid.*, p. 31.

69   *Ibid.*, p. 30.

70   *Ibid.*, p. 34.

71   *Ibid.*, p. 39.

72   *Ibid.*

73   T. Friedman, 'Run, Osama, Run', *New York Times* (23 January 2002); T. Friedman, 'Wall of Ideas', *New York Times* (March 3 2002); and T. Friedman, 'War of Ideas', *New York Times* (June 2 2002).

74   Friedman, 'Run, Osama, Run'.

75   *Ibid.*

76   *Ibid.*

77   *Ibid.*

78   *Ibid.*

79   *Ibid.*, p. 19.

80   *Ibid.*

81   *Ibid.*

82   *Ibid.*

83   *Ibid.*

84   *Ibid.*

85   *Ibid.*

86   *Ibid.*

87   Friedman, 'Wall of Ideas'.

88   *Ibid.*, p. 15.

89   *Ibid.*

90   *Ibid.*

91   Friedman, 'War of Ideas'.

92   *Ibid.*

93   *Ibid.*, p. 19.

94   *Ibid.*

95   Friedman, 'War of Ideas', p. 19.

96   *Ibid.*

97   Friedman, 'Wall of Ideas'.

98   *Ibid.*

99   *Ibid.*, p. 15.

100 Friedman, 'Run, Osama, Run'.

101 *Ibid.*, p. 19.

102 E. Said, 'Orientalism', in A. Easthope and K. McGowen (eds), *A Critical Cultural Studies Reader* (Toronto: University of Toronto Press, 1997), pp. 59–66.

103 *Ibid.* See also J. George, *Discourses of Global Politics* (Boulder, CO: Lynne Rienner, 1994), pp. 139–169.

104 *Ibid.*

105 Ajami, 'The Sentry's Solitude', p. 2.

106 Doran, 'Somebody Else's Civil War', p. 39.

107 Friedman, 'Wall of Ideas', p. 15.

108 Friedrich Nietzsche provides the most provocative critique of this tradition. A good starting place here is F. Nietzsche, *The Gay Science* (Cambridge: Cambridge University Press, 2007). For a summary of the most important critiques of this modernist discourse see, George, *Discourses of Global Politics*, pp. 139–169; and also, R. Tarnas, *The Passion of the Western Mind* (London: Pimlico, 1991), pp. 325–441.

109 Nietzsche, *The Gay Science*, pp. 109–131.

110 See R. Ashley, 'Untying the Sovereign State: A Double Reading of the Anarchy Problematique', *Millennium: Journal of International Studies*, 17:2 (1988), pp. 227–262; and also, Campbell, *Writing Security*, pp. 9–12, 61–72, 75–90.

111 E. Said, 'Adrift in Similarity', *Al-Ahram* (11 October 2001).

112 See Jackson, 'Knowledge, Power and Politics in the Study of Political Terrorism', pp. 67 and 78–79.

113 *Ibid.*

114 Friedman, 'Wall of Ideas', p. 15.

115 See, for instance, the work of Noam Chomsky (apparently, the most cited scholar in the world and, for some, the most important intellectual alive), which regularly calls in to question the kinds of orthodoxies advanced by Friedman here. A good starting point here is N. Chomsky, 'Middle East Terrorism and the American Ideological System', *Race and Class*, 28:1 (1986), pp. 1–28; and, more recently, N. Chomsky, 'Who are the Terrorists?', in Ken Booth and Tim Dunne (eds), *Worlds In Collision* (London: Palgrave Macmillan, 2002), pp. 128–137.

116 Doran, 'Somebody Else's Civil War', p. 39.

117 See, for instance, J. Mearsheimer and S. Walt, 'An Unnecessary War', *Foreign Policy*, 134:1 (2003), pp. 50–59.

118 See, for instance, B. Jentleson, *With Friends Like These: Reagan, Bush and Saddam, 1982–1990* (New York: Norton, 1994).

119 See, for instance, T. Friedman, 'A Growing Sense that Saddam must go', *New York Times* (7 July 1991).

120 Anthony Burke gives an excellent account of the strategic logic and the devastating costs associated with US policy on Iraq since before the first Gulf War in 1991. See A. Burke, 'Iraq: Strategy's Burnt Offerings', *Global Change, Peace and Security*, 17:2 (2005), pp. 202–209.

121 For a review of the varied Islamic responses to the Gulf War see J. Piscatori, 'Religion and Realpolitik: Islamic Responses to the Gulf War', *Bulletin of the American Academy of the Arts*, 45:1 (1991), pp. 17–39.

122 Friedman, 'War of Ideas', p. 19.

123 *Ibid.*

124 Ajami, 'The Sentry's Solitude', pp. 4, 7, 9, 14, 15.

125 Doran, 'Somebody Else's Civil War', p. 26.

126 See, for a starting point on US covert action, William Blum, *Killing Hope: US Military and CIA Interventions Since World War II* (Monroe, ME: Common Courage Press, 1995).

127 B. Woodward, *State of Denial: Bush at War, Part III* (New York: Simon & Schuster, 2006), p. 84.

128 *Ibid.*

129 E. Said, *Orientalism*, preface to the revised edn (London: Penguin Books, 2003), pp. xiv–xv.

130 J. Marshal, 'Remaking the World: Bush and the Neoconservatives', *Foreign Affairs*, 82:2 (2002), pp. 142–146; E. Said, 'The Academy of Lagado', *London Review of Books*, April 2003. Available at www.lrb.co.uk/v25/n08/edward-said/the-academy-of-lagado (accessed 7 January 2015; and Shatz, 'The Native Informant'.

131 See P. Waldman, 'A Historian's Take on Islam Steers U.S in fight on Terrorism', *Wall Street Journal* (3 February 2004); M. Hirsh, 'Bernard Lewis Revisited', *Washington Monthly* (November 2004); F. Kempe, 'Lewis's 'Liberation' Doctrine Faces New Tests', *Wall Street Journal* (13 December 2005); and E. Said, *Orientalism*, pp. xiv–xv.

132 Waldman, 'A Historian's Take on Islam Steers US Fight on Terrorism'.

133 Hirsh, 'Bernard Lewis Revisited'.

134 See R. Leung, 'Bush Sought 'Way' to Invade Iraq', *CBS* News (9 January 2004); and R. Suskind, *The Price of Loyalty* (New York: Simon & Schuster, 2004). See the open letter sent by the Project for the New American Century to President Clinton in February 1998, which advocated regime change in Iraq. Eighteen signatories later joined the Bush administration including, notably, Donald Rumsfeld, Paul Wolfowitz, Douglas Feith, Richard Armitage, Eliot Abrams and Richard Perle. See 'Open Letter to the President', *Project for the New American Century* (19 February 1998).

135 'The Downing Street Memo' (July 2002), reproduced in M. Danner, 'The Secret Way to War', *New York Review of Books*, 52:10 (2005).

4

The War of Ideas

T HIS CHAPTER SHIFTS THE focus from foreign policy commentary to War on
Terror doctrine. It does so by engaging with the Bush administration's
War of Ideas strategy, which aimed to undermine the cultural drivers of
terrorism by winning the 'hearts and minds' of Arab-Muslims thought vulnerable to radicalisation. The strategic significance of this approach was first spelled
out by then National Security Advisor Condoleezza Rice in 2004, as Arab-Muslim
resentment towards America soared – provoked, for instance, by concerns about
the justification and conduct of the Iraq War; extraordinary rendition to 'black
sites'; extra-judicial detention at Guantanamo Bay; 'enhanced interrogation' of
detainees, including waterboarding, stress positions and sleep deprivation; and
the obscene physical and psychological degradation inflicted at Abu Ghraib
prison. According to Rice, polls taken across Muslim countries indicated that
'large majorities of Muslims fear American power or misunderstand American
values'.[1] But for Rice, these sentiments were often based in distortions:

> many in the Muslim world see the worst of American popular culture and assume
> that American-style democracy – or any democracy for that matter – inevitably leads
> to crassness and immorality. Others believe democracy is inherently hostile to faith,
> and corrosive to cherished traditions. And many more are fed a steady diet of hateful
> propaganda and conspiracy theories that twist American policy into grotesque
> caricatures.
>   These views pose a serious challenge for our country. At their worst and most
> intense, they create a climate of bitterness and grievance, in which extremists find
> a sympathetic ear. And such views can hold entire societies captive to failed ideolo-
> gics and prevent millions of people from joining in the progress and prosperity of
> our time. The consequences for much of the Muslim world are stagnation, persistent
> poverty and a lack of freedom.[2]

In this narrative, a perception of American cultural decadence, a fear of
liberalism's secularising influence, and paranoia about US power played into a
broader culture of disillusionment and blame. While terrorists would always
hate America, bitterness and grievances had rendered otherwise ambivalent
communities vulnerable to terrorist indoctrination. Rice laid out a two-pronged

strategy for addressing this situation: 'First, we must work to dispel destructive myths about American society and about American policy. Second, we must expand dramatically our efforts to support and encourage voices of moderation and tolerance and pluralism within the Muslim world.'[3]

This policy articulation takes as its starting point the Arab-Muslim paranoia narrative so familiar from post-9/11 foreign policy commentary – conspiracy theory, bitterness, blame, politico-economic failure and social stagnation are all key markers here. This is perhaps unsurprising given the intellectual influence of foreign policy thinkers like Bernard Lewis, Fouad Ajami and Fareed Zakaria (whom Rice references directly in the above speech) on the administration's understanding of terrorism and its origins.[4] Indeed, Michael Scott Doran took up a position as Head of Near Eastern and African Affairs for the National Security Council in early 2005.[5] The particular understanding of the 'roots of Muslim rage' promulgated by these thinkers achieved policy significance in the context of a growing consensus about the link between anti-Americanism and terrorist recruitment. The 'long war' would be won, it was thought, not on the battlefield, but through soft power engagement and democracy promotion.

The presence of the Arab-Muslim paranoia narrative in US counter-terrorism doctrine is particularly interesting, given the powerful identity politics associated with this perspective in the preceding chapters. The fact that this narrative, as it appeared in post-9/11 foreign policy commentary, helped delegitimise criticism of American power and limit interpretation of 9/11, while simultaneously sanctifying an image of America as benign and misunderstood, is highly pertinent for thinking about the effects of a policy approach explicitly propounding the virtues of ideational engagement with disaffected Arab-Muslims. At the very least, the conceptual grounds on which this framework operated were already loaded against the reasonable consideration of Arab-Muslim perspectives on US foreign policy in the region. Indeed, the broader modernist discourse in which the issue of Arab-Muslim paranoia was embedded centres on an opposition between a rational, morally superior West and irrational others of one stripe or another, usually mired in backward traditions or superstitions. Chapter 3 demonstrated that the power of the modernist discourse, and the paranoia theme specifically, was to secure these positions as stable and unproblematic – to perform boundary maintenance against the destabilising forces of contrary interpretation and ideological dissent.

These potent identity politics dynamics stand in direct contrast with the sober precision often associated with national security doctrine. I examine the highly charged Arab-Muslim paranoia narrative as it appeared in speeches from the US President and his National Security Advisor, and in the most important high-level articulations of US counter-terrorism strategy: the National Security Strategy (NSS) 2006 and the National Strategy for Combatting Terrorism (NSCT) 2006.[6] It is important to recognise that these texts were highly significant and visible not just to government officials, but also to wider audiences at home and abroad.[7] The disjuncture between this high-powered policy setting and the discursive economy circulating around the Arab-Muslim paranoia narrative present an intriguing way into the Bush administration's War of Ideas. It suggests that latent cultural drivers animated US national security policy as much as sober calculation and rational action.

This chapter uses the tensions brought out by the Arab-Muslim paranoia narrative to show how the War of Ideas strategy tended to produce the conditions it sought to address. Its delegitimising dynamics embedded a strong countervailing force against successful engagement with Arab-Muslim people, who were framed here as inherently problematic. At the same time, the War of Ideas accentuated the contrast between America's purported ideals and the often ruthless pursuit of American interests. Under these circumstances, the War of Ideas had the potential to provoke suspicion of conspiracies, double-dealing and ulterior motives, as well as cynicism about American values. The first section begins by introducing the War of Ideas as counter-terrorism strategy, before exploring these underlying tensions.

'Hearts and minds' in the long war

In the wake of 9/11, anti-Americanism was highlighted as a key problem for American foreign policy. Al-Qaeda's terrorism was horrific and extreme, but it was often situated as an outgrowth of an underlying antipathy towards America common throughout the Arab and Muslim world.[8] This view was captured in strategic terms in the NSS 2002, which included a paragraph pointing to the importance of complementing the military components of US counter-terrorism strategy by 'wag[ing] a war of ideas'.[9] Some core assumptions underlying the strategy discourse on the origins of terrorism are set out here: the importance of promoting moderate governments in the Arab-Muslim world; the need to address the underlying conditions that produce terrorism; and the role of public diplomacy in encouraging the free flow of information and ideas.[10] These concerns were by no means new to elite debates about the origins of 9/11, which often centred on the appropriate method for 'draining the swamp' that terrorists recruit from.[11] Indeed, this is precisely the context in which the connection between conspiracy theory and Arab-Muslim anti-Americanism was made by foreign policy commentators immediately after 9/11.

While the Arab-Muslim paranoia narrative did not appear in strategy documents or infuse key Bush administration speeches in the early War on Terror years, it was always present in the administration rhetoric on terrorism. For instance, as early as November 2001 Rice explained that anti-Americanism was stoked by 'a tendency to allow the spewing of propaganda – propaganda and conspiracy theories – that are not helpful or true'.[12] President Bush, in his address to the United Nations General Assembly two days later, made a similar connection:

> We must speak the truth about terror. Let us never tolerate outrageous conspiracy theories concerning the attacks of September 11; malicious lies that attempt to shift blame away from the terrorists themselves, away from the guilty. To inflame ethnic hatred is to advance the cause of terror.[13]

This passage acts as both a reference to anti-Americanism and as a rebuke to claims that Mossad, the Israeli intelligence service, had carried out the attacks – a view at that time prevalent throughout the Middle East.[14] Bush repeated this language in his radio address to the American public the same day, though this time he recalibrated to focus on governments that 'encourage malicious lies and conspiracy theories' about 9/11.[15] While these conspiracy references do not form part of an intense strategic discourse until at least 2004, it is significant that both the National Security Advisor and the President used this language in the same context, the President in a major speech before the United Nations and an address to the nation. More broadly, Congressional hearings on public diplomacy after 9/11 repeatedly noted the prevalence of conspiracy theories and propaganda about America and Israel as an important aspect of the radicalisation process. Of particular concern to committee members was the allegation widespread among Arab-Muslims that Jewish workers in the World Trade Center had been warned not to go to work on 9/11, as well as a general allegation that Israel was behind the attacks.[16]

The Arab-Muslim paranoia narrative was drawn to the heart of Bush administration thinking with the increasing importance of public diplomacy in the War on Terror strategy. The context for this rise was resurgent resentment towards America in the Muslim world and an emerging policy consensus that military force could not on its own defeat terrorism. This strategic recalibration was captured in the *9/11 Commission Report* release in July 2004:

> The first phase of our post 9/11 effort rightly included military action to topple the Taliban and pursue Al Qaeda. This work continues. But long term success demands the use of all elements of national power: diplomacy, intelligence, covert action, law enforcement, economic policy, foreign aid, public diplomacy, and homeland defence. If we favour one tool while neglecting others, we leave ourselves vulnerable and weaken our national effort.[17]

This report was the last in a long line pointing to the need for an approach aimed at the broader context from which terrorists emerge. Among these were the Djerejian Report, calling for a bureaucratic restructuring and renewed funding for public diplomacy,[18] and 'Finding America's Voice' a Council on Foreign Relations report that advocated a renewed focus on strategic communication, effective bureaucratic structures, public diplomacy, and relationship building.[19] Though not necessarily prominent in either report, both the 9/11 Commission

Report and 'Finding America's Voice' made the link between anti-Americanism and Arab-Muslim paranoia. The 9/11 Commission accounted for the appeal of bin Laden's world-view like this:

> For those yearning for a lost sense of order in an older, more tranquil world, he offers his caliphate as an imagined alternative to today's uncertainty. For others, he offers simplistic conspiracies to explain their world.[20]

This reference to conspiracy theories was embedded in a broader account of cultural dysfunction, bitterness and blame. 'Finding America's Voice' was more focused on expanding the range of messengers explaining America's policy and values:

> In thus fostering the free flow of ideas, the Administration should be fully aware that these messengers will sometimes be critical of the United States. By the same token, however, these dialogues should in no way shrink from countering vigorously the various conspiracy theories and lies that are disseminated about the United States and, of course, themselves.[21]

The point here is that the Arab-Muslim paranoia narrative was always present in official foreign policy discourse after 9/11, complementing its widespread promulgation in foreign policy commentary. It was in this context that the Bush administration devised its War of Ideas strategy.

Although Condoleezza Rice initially articulated this policy shift, its formulation into strategic doctrine was left to Steven Hadley who replaced Rice after she was promoted to Secretary of State.[22] Speaking to the Council on Foreign Relations in late 2005, Hadley establishes the causal link between Arab-Muslim cultural dysfunction, anti-Americanism and terrorism:

> The appeal [from terrorists] is not to the world's destitute, based on their poverty. Muhammed Atta and the other 9/11 hijackers were predominately middle class and well-educated. They and many Islamic terrorists like them are clearly alienated from their societies. Unable to visualise a meaningful future within their own political system, they are susceptible to radical alternatives to it. When people have been denied their fundamental rights, they have little stake in the existing order. The terrorists capitalize on this discontent and stake it with a narrative of Arab and Muslim grievances and victimization at the hands of the infidel West and the Zionists. The terrorists offer a radical vision of a totalitarian system brought about through violence and the killing of innocents.[23]

We can locate this excerpt in the familiar story of Arab-Muslim cultural failure and anti-modernist sentiment identified across the preceding chapters. In the full account political alienation goes along with economic stagnation, which together produces a stifling and frustrating social malaise.[24] Instead of dealing with these issues head on, Arab-Muslim people are said to blame their problems on others – notably the colonial forces that dominated them in the recent past and, more recently, America. At the same time, in this narrative the historical decline of Muslim civilisation has fuelled a sense of humiliation, and yet more resentment towards foreign powers for their perceived part in this. Such grievances are allegedly articulated in conspiracy theories and misinformation that seek to explain these unsatisfactory circumstances by pointing to the hidden hand of power that keeps the decks stacked against Arab-Muslims. The capstone of this narrative is that the culture of blame is an unhelpful and self-denying distraction from the real source of Arab-Muslim problems: themselves. From this perspective, Arab-Muslims should acknowledge their own failure and seek to modernise their political and economic institutions – liberal democracy and the free markets being the obvious models. But whereas foreign policy commentators writing after 9/11 deployed these ideas to provide a historical and cultural context for Arab-Muslim resentment towards America, Hadley goes a step further by integrating it into an assessment of Al-Qaeda's organisational structure and operational capacity:

> From the beginning the War on Terror has been both a Battle of Arms and a Battle of Ideas. As the president has said, 'We're fighting terrorists and we're fighting their murderous ideology.' In the short run, we must use our military forces and other instruments of national power to fight terrorists, deny them safe haven, and cut off their resources and support. But in the long run, to win the War in Terror we must win the Battle of Ideas. We must counter the grim totalitarian visions of the terrorists with positive visions of freedom and democracy. As we make progress in the Battle of Arms and the terrorist network becomes more decentralized, the need to present an alternative vision becomes even more critical. For what increasingly links these groups is not some central chain of command, but a common ideology.[25]

Hadley provides some clear signposts here indicating how this account might be mobilised in US counter-terrorism strategy. The Battle of Ideas is linked to the changing security environment – to decentralised, self-sustaining, self-radicalising terrorists.[26] For Hadley counter-terrorism strategy needed an ideational dimension that could challenge terrorist ideology and present an alternative to it:

> The antidote to this radical vision is democracy, justice and the freedom agenda. This agenda offers empowerment as an alternative to enslavement. It offers participation in place of exclusion. It offers the marketplace of ideas to counter the dark world of conspiracy theory. It offers individual rights and human dignity instead of violence and murder. Fundamentally, it means people participating in governing themselves, rather than being governed by others they never choose, never change, and never influence.[27]

President Bush presented this Freedom Agenda in a series of four speeches through October and November of 2005, where he repeatedly produced the same narrative of Arab-Muslim cultural dysfunction in his stock explanation of the evolving terrorist threat:

> Defeating the militant network is difficult because it thrives, like a parasite, on the frustrations of others. The radicals exploit local conflicts to build a culture of victimization, in which someone else is always to blame and violence is always the solution. They exploit resentful and disillusioned young men and women, recruiting them through radical mosques as the pawns of terror. And they exploit modern technology to multiply their destructive power. Instead of attending far-away training camps, recruits can now access online training libraries to learn how to build a roadside bomb or fire a rocket propelled grenade – and this further spreads the threat of violence even within democratic societies.[28]

The strategic link between an Arab-Muslim culture of victimisation, blame and frustration and terrorist recruitment is again tied to the role of ideology and technology in the evolving terrorist threat. And once again it is in this context that the distorting effect of conspiracy theories, misinformation and propaganda emerge as an issue of concern:

> The influence of Islamic radicalism is also magnified by helpers and enablers. They have been sheltered by authoritarian regimes, allies of convenience like Syria and Iran, that share the goal of hurting America and moderate Muslim governments, and use terrorist propaganda to blame their own failures on the West and America, and on the Jews ... The militants are aided, as well, by elements of the Arab news media that incite hatred and anti-Semitism that feed conspiracy theories and speak of a so-called 'war on Islam' – with seldom a word about American action to protect Muslims in Afghanistan, and Bosnia, Somalia, Kosovo, Kuwait and Iraq.[29]

Later in the speech Bush explains the policy implications of this situation: America is engaged in 'a global ideological struggle' against terrorism which it will prosecute by 'standing for hope and freedom'; encouraging US allies with repressive governments to reform; supporting dissidents in their struggle against dictatorial regimes; and making America's case through public diplomacy.[30] The Freedom Agenda aimed to represent liberal democratic America as an alternative for alienated Arab-Muslims, who might otherwise be seduced by terrorist ideology. What we see here is the transformation of the Arab-Muslim paranoia narrative from a general account of 'the roots of Muslim rage' into a counter-terrorism doctrine. The Arab-Muslim paranoia narrative provided a description of the policy problem and implied a course of action that was subsequently elaborated into a broader strategic logic.

Identity politics and the War of Ideas

This section explores tensions embedded in the Bush Administration's ideational strategy via an analysis of the NSS 2006. The NSS is the central US policy document on national security.[31] It is hard to over-emphasise its importance as an articulation of high-level strategic thinking.[32] Developed over months of consultation, review and refinement, it is the settled doctrine of the US government. In what follows I explore the countervailing forces that undermined the 'hearts and minds' objective of the War of Ideas, all of which flow from the underlying identity politics dynamics implicit in the Arab-Muslim paranoia narrative.

The following excerpt is the most extensive, coherent and high-profile articulation of the War of Ideas. It is the framework that guided America's counter-terrorism strategy for the remaining years of the Bush administration. The passage is drawn from section three of NSS 2006, titled 'Strengthen Alliances to Defeat Global Terrorism and Work to Prevent Attacks against Us or our Friends'. This same text also appeared in NSCT 2006, providing a broad framework for the more specific approach set out there.[33] It is worth reproducing it at some length because of the strategic significance of NSS 2006, and because the texts hangs together conceptually in such a way that its full force can be better understood when it is considered as a whole:

> The terrorism we confront today springs from:
>
> - Political Alienation. Transnational terrorists are recruited from people who have no voice in their own governments and see no legitimate way to promote change in their own country. Without a stake in the existing order, they are vulnerable to manipulation by those who advocate a perverse vision based on violence and destruction.
> - Grievances that can be blamed on others. The failures the terrorists feel and see are blamed on others, and on perceived injustices from the recent or sometimes distant past. The terrorists' rhetoric keeps wounds associated with the past fresh and raw, a potent motivator for revenge and terror.
> - Sub-cultures of conspiracy and misinformation. Terrorists recruit most effectively from populations whose information about the world is contaminated by falsehoods and corrupted by conspiracy theories. The distortions keep alive grievances and filter out facts that would challenge popular prejudices and self-serving propaganda.
> - An ideology that justifies murder. Terrorism ultimately depends upon the appeal of an ideology that excuses or even glorifies the deliberate killing of innocents. A proud religion – the religion of Islam – has been twisted and made to serve an evil end, as in other times and places other religions have been similarly abused.
>
> Defeating terrorism in the long run requires that each of these factors be addressed. The genius of democracy is that it provides a counter to each:
>
> - In place of alienation, democracy offers an ownership stake in society, and a chance to shape one's future.

- In place of festering grievances, democracy offers the rule of law, the peaceful resolution of disputes, and the habit of advancing interests through compromise.
- In place of a culture of conspiracy and misinformation, democracy offers freedom of speech, independent media, and the marketplace of ideas, which can expose and discredit falsehoods, prejudice and dishonest propaganda.
- In place of an ideology that justifies murder, democracy offers a respect for human dignity that abhors the deliberate targeting on innocents.[34]

This excerpt is remarkable for the extent to which it reproduces in crystallised form the Arab-Muslim paranoia narrative identified in accounts of anti-Americanism after 9/11.

While the aim of the War of Ideas was to allay the circumstances that rendered Arab-Muslims vulnerable to radicalisation, I have shown repeatedly that the Arab-Muslim paranoia narrative involved a highly delegitimising view of Arab-Muslims and their political grievances. Thus underlying the clear lines of strategic logic aimed at persuasive engagement, a current of connotations and counter-narratives pulled in the other direction. Criticism and disaffection towards America was positioned as conspiracy theory, misinformation, distortion, falsehood, propaganda and perceived injustice. In the War of Ideas, the ideas of Arab-Muslims were not only wrong, but were manifestations of a particular culture characterised by decline and failure, frustration and blame. Arab-Muslim understandings critical of America were illegitimate, but so too was the political, economic and cultural context that produced them. Moreover, we can see here a casual interchange between delegitimising terms, highlighting a much wider discourse that went well beyond the issue of Arab-Muslim paranoia – a discourse that operated in manifold configurations and assemblages to imply irrationality and improbability. But the conspiracy theory issue is a useful marker for the underlying mechanism at play here: attention is directed beyond the specifics of particular claims and towards the competency of the people making them. The point here is that this framing worked against the persuasive soft power engagement called for in the War of Ideas, to the extent that it denied Arab-Muslim people standing as reasonable interlocutors in a dialogue about American foreign policy.

Indeed, the relative position of the actors identified in NSS 2006 indicates a definite power relationship that reinforced this delegitimising process. While Arab-Muslim people were associated with irrational beliefs and cultural dysfunction, America's liberal democratic values were associated, by contrast, with human dignity, respect, freedom, independence, peacefulness and ownership. This dichotomy animated and limited the actions of each identity. A pertinent example for our purposes is the curious passivity imputed on to what is once again presented as an amorphous and undifferentiated Arab-Muslim world. Agency resides with terrorists who 'exploit' and 'recruit' and 'kill', and democracy – read American democracy, and specifically America – which is 'empowering' and transformative, which 'confronts', 'challenges', 'exposes', 'discredits' and 'counters'.[35] On the other hand, Arab-Muslim populations were 'vulnerable to manipulation', recruited and propagandised by terrorists, and rescued from their misapprehensions and dysfunction by the power of democratic values:

> Democracy is the opposite of terrorist tyranny, which is why the terrorists denounce it and are willing to kill innocents to stop it. Democracy is based on empowerment, while the terrorists' ideology is based on enslavement. Democracies expand the freedom of their citizens, while the terrorists seek to impose a single set of narrow beliefs. Democracy sees individuals as equal in worth and dignity, having the inherent potential to create and govern themselves. The terrorists see individuals as objects to be exploited, and to be ruled and oppressed.[36]

In this account, Arab-Muslims are acted upon, but never act. This is a battle between terrorists and America for the 'hearts and minds' of a seemingly helpless, passive population, mired in a history of decline and a culture of failure and blame.[37] Terrorists have agency, and offer it, because they are motivated by the desire to change the political order, albeit through illegitimate means. American democracy has agency, and offers it, because this is entailed in its very definition, and because American democracy exists outside an Arab-Muslim world bound by time and history.

The dynamic of action and passivity was also carried out in the language of NSS 2006, where Arab-Muslims were introduced in terms of their alienation – a term with deep social-psychological roots in accounts not just of political disaffection and populism, but also in explanations of prejudice and criminality.[38] Its connotations are status anxiety, frustration, disconnection, isolation and resentment. It is a psychological state produced by social conditions. It is a psychological state that just *happens* to Arab-Muslims. This socio-psychological parlance continues with terrorists exploiting these damaged psyches, keeping the 'wounds' of past grievances 'fresh and raw' and 'festering' in the minds of Arab-Muslims.[39] Blame, denial and distortion are all layered onto this profile. It is a profile of Arab-Muslims produced by circumstances beyond them – political, cultural, historical and psychological. These circumstances fold together with an apparent Arab-Muslim understanding of the world 'contaminated' and 'corrupted' by conspiracy theory and misinformation – maladies of the mind that infect Arab-Muslim understanding and render them susceptible to untoward influences.[40] At the same time, while democracies are not 'immune' to terrorists and the conditions that produce them, the 'antidote', as Condoleezza Rice framed it, is always more liberal democracy.[41] Indeed, liberal democracy, and America by implication, is presented as the unspoken counter to this image of a damaged Arab-Muslim population – healthy, clear-eyed, empowered, authentic and rational. This socio-psychological framing points to the active diagnosis of the Arab-Muslim condition underway here. Rather than engagement or dialogue, the very premise of the War of Ideas is that there is something inherently wrong with Arab-Muslim people; that this is why they express resentment towards America; and that, far from being the cause of their problems, American style liberal democracy will be the solution.

However, this formulation must be read in the wider context of a US foreign policy tradition often directed by an understanding of regional cultures as, in one way or another, on the steady march to liberal democratic modernity.[42] Indeed, there is a rich literature in postcolonial studies that has identified the same kind of narrative at play in the development context – and, indeed, in accounts of Middle Eastern political culture, particularly through the Cold War.[43] In the super-power imaginary, two systems, capitalism and communism, vied for the hearts and minds of similarly passive Middle Eastern states in need of the right kind of progress.[44] More broadly, this mindset pervades even culturally sensitive left-liberal aspects of America's international normative engagement – for instance, the Peace Core and Human Rights advocacy.[45] The point here is that the deep discourses of America's liberal political culture resonate with and informs all these instances.

This becomes clear in relation to the NSS 2006 if we remember the importance of the post-war liberal discourse around populism for understanding the paranoid style paradigm. I showed how this framework, which divided a rational, pluralist centre from an irrational, populist fringe, had been extrapolated from American politics out on to the world at large. Here conspiracy theory could move to the heart of Middle Eastern political communities in the Arab Muslim paranoia narrative, because these polities remained on the fringe of international power and legitimacy in a Western geopolitical world-view. In the NSS 2006, we can see the same schema at play:

> Democracies are not immune from terrorism. In some democracies, some ethnic or religious groups are unable or unwilling to grasp the benefits of freedom otherwise available in society. Such groups can evidence the same alienation and despair that the transnational terrorists exploit in undemocratic states. This accounts for the emergence in democratic societies of home grown terrorists such as were responsible for the bombing of London in July 2005 and the violence in some nations. Even in these cases the long term solution remains deepening the reach of democracy so that all citizens can enjoy its benefits.[46]

From this viewpoint, in democracies (read the West, and particularly America) the conditions of alienation, perceived grievances, blame, misinformation and conspiracy theory exist on society's fringes, where the leavening influence of democracy has not taken hold. By contrast, in the absence of democracy, Arab-Muslims experience these conditions as the basic historical, political and cultural reality of their existence. Put simply, the War of Ideas doctrine rests on the same pluralist framework sketched out by Hofstadter and his Cold War liberal contemporaries, though now combined with a specific narrative about Arab-Muslim dysfunction and decline advanced by Bernard Lewis and contemporary advocates of the Arab-Muslim paranoia narrative.

The point here is that the War of Ideas objective of remedying the conditions that enable radicalisation was undermined by this deep culture and structure embedded in America's liberal political imaginary. Potent and historically rich scripts around populism, ideology and dissent, along with a reservoir of related associations like irrationality, emotion, ideology and alienation worked against a persuasive encounter with Arab-Muslims critical of American foreign policy, when these people were framed as the problematic product of a dysfunctional culture. Indeed, it is critical to acknowledge that although the identities and relations highlighted here existed as discursive positions within this specific policy discourse and wider liberal cosmology, they bore no necessary relationship to the lived experience of differentiated Arab-Muslims, or even specific Americans, who no doubt refused classification in these terms. In the end it is the disjuncture between the self/other understandings of interpretive communities – a particular segment of the US foreign policy establishment and specific Arab-Muslim publics or groups – that is most problematic for the War of Ideas.

From a broader standpoint, the identity politics underlying the NSS 2006 can be understood in terms of maintaining stable identity.[47] Self and other, identity and difference, are mutually constituted in this policy discourse, such that a coherent, stable, authoritative American identity can only exist if an Arab-Muslim identity possesses antithetical qualities. In short, opposition produces self-definition. In this context, the contradiction between the objectives of the War of Ideas and the delegitimising effects woven into the doctrine's framing can be understood in terms of sovereign anxiety. As James Der Derian noted incisively, anxiety about boundary failure also provides the impetus for hypervigilance, extreme suspicion, heightened security, a reductive representation of nefarious others and violent counter-measures. The language of paranoia and alienation can be positioned as discursive counter-measures against a loss of control, authority, credibility, and indeed the potential loss of a disreputable, irrational other to counterpoise these things against. The next section shows how the impulse to uncover and secure opens up the potential for renewed insecurity.

Ideational weaponry

The problem of sovereign authority was particularly relevant in the War of Ideas since the authenticity of American values and US government information were at stake. Yet this authenticity was undercut by the instrumental logic of this soft power strategy. Indeed, we have seen already how the promotion of democratic values worked alongside other instruments of state power: 'these inseparable priorities – fighting and winning the War on Terror and promoting freedom as the alternative to tyranny and despair – have guided American policy for more than four years'.[48] While the military and ideational dimensions seem distinct in this formulation, there remains a tension here between the notion of sincerely held ideas and the notion of strategic intent.

This tension is more explicit in the NSCT 2006, which added detail to the broad vision set out in the NSS.[49] Here ideational elements were integrated into counter-terrorism doctrine. According to the NSCT, limiting Al-Qaeda's capacity to operate involved six key areas: leadership, foot soldiers, weapons, funds, communications and propaganda operations.[50] For our purposes leadership, communications and propaganda are particular important in terms of the interplay between ideas and military strategy. For instance, terrorist leaders were targeted because of their organisational and planning abilities, but also because of their ideological capacity.[51] They 'provide vision that followers strive to realise'.[52] In this sense, the ideas motivating terrorism took on a material existence in the bodies of terrorist leaders, who could be targeted for capture or killed outright. Similarly, the ideological battle was waged militarily in the material context of communications technology:

> This is especially true of the Internet, which they exploit to create and disseminate propaganda, recruit new members, raise funds and other material resources, provide instructions on weapons and tactics, and plan operations. Without a communications ability, terrorist organizations cannot effectively organize operations, execute attacks, or spread their ideology. We and our partners will continue to target the communications nodes of our enemy.[53]

Like the approach to terrorist leaders, the ideational dimension of the War on Terror is embedded in the military. Leaders are killed and communications disabled as much for the ideas they transmit as their traditional logistical value. This comes across clearly when the NSCT describes propaganda operations

> which are used by terrorists to justify violent actions as well as inspire individuals to support or join the movement. The ability of the terrorists to exploit the internet and 24/7 worldwide media coverage allows them to bolster their prominence as well as feed a steady diet of radical ideology, twisted images, and conspiracy theories to potential recruits in all corners of the globe. Besides a global reach, these technologies allow terrorists to propagate their message quickly, often before an effective counter to the terrorist message can be co-ordinated and distributed. These are force multipliers for our enemy.[54]

A force multiplier is defined by the US Department of Defence as 'a capacity that, when added to and employed by a combat force, significantly increases the combat potential of that force and thus enhances the probability of successful mission accomplishment'.[55] Classic examples include armour, cannons and machine guns. Propaganda operations utilising the Internet and the global media quite literally multiply the force size and legitimacy of terrorist organisations by radicalising more Muslims. These technologies are deployed in the service of specified strategic ends of recruitment and radicalisation. Yet framing of ideas as 'propaganda' tends to push them into the same strategic frame, where ideas are instrumental rather than authentic, weapons of terrorists in the service of their military objectives rather than genuinely held belief systems.

The instrumental use of ideas was also evident in the strategic framework proposed in NSS 2006, where the transformative effects of democratic values were understood to be central for long-term victory over the terrorist enemy. More specifically, NSCT 2006 positions ideals as tools of strategy when it proposes ideational counter-measures: 'through outreach programs and public diplomacy we will reveal the terrorist's violent extremist ideology for what it is – a form of totalitarianism following in the path of fascism'.[56] According to the NSCT,

> To counter the use of the Internet as a virtual sanctuary, we [the US government] will discredit terrorist propaganda by promoting truthful and peaceful messages. We will seek ultimately to deny the Internet to terrorists as an effective safe haven for their propaganda, proselytising, recruitment, fundraising, training and operational planning.[57]

The key question is 'what happens when a truthful and peaceful message conflicts with broader strategic imperatives?' For instance, will such accounts be given even where they portray the United States negatively or inflame antagonisms? Ambiguity is introduced by the way these categorical values are positioned alongside strategic elements like the disruption of enemy financing, training and operational planning. This ambiguity is increased when we consider that the NSCT is by definition a strategic doctrine. Taking strategy on its own terms, we might consider Clausewitz's influential account of war as 'a mere continuation of policy by other means'.[58] Here the weapons of war and the strategies that coordinate them are secondary to the political objectives of the conflict, among which we may certainly include winning.[59]

The gap opened up here between militarised ideas and political objectives is not just abstract. It manifested practically in the many incidents where military or intelligence operations and the language of freedom and equality were in tension. For instance, it may have been deemed necessary, in the context of defeating Al-Qaeda, to detain suspected terrorists indefinitely, without recourse to judicial review, and in some cases torture them, but this hardly conformed to the high ideals deployed in the War of Ideas.[60] These ideals were deployed nevertheless. At the same time, it seems relevant to suggest that if the Bush

administration was willing to be pragmatic in its military and intelligence operations, the same might be true of its ideational engagements.

This line of thinking resonates with the delegitimising function of the Arab-
Muslim paranoia narrative embedded in the NSS 2006. The War of Ideas was
carried out through the labelling of Arab-Muslim grievances, with disciplinary
effects both abroad and in American political culture. But on the foregoing
account the bedrock ideas that this disciplinary narrative operated in defence of
– a benign America, liberal democracy and free market capitalism – operated as
the secondary means of more primary political ends, for which they were
deployed and manoeuvred and maintained. From this perspective, the whole
ideational 'field of battle' set out in the NSS and NSCT 2006 were not only political and politicised but also fundamentally instrumental.

Of course the perception that there is a contradiction between values and
interests, high ideals and cold calculation, truthfulness and strategic deceptions
is one of the most common and recurring critiques of American foreign policy
– and is no doubt a source of resentment for people whose lives these policies
affect.[61] Ironically, then, the War of Ideas, a policy aimed at quelling anti-
Americanism thought to be motivating terrorists and their sympathisers, had
the potential to produce the conditions under which critics could call the motives
of American foreign policy into question, by accentuating America's purported
ideals, which were everywhere flouted in the conduct of the War on Terror.
Likewise, it should have come as no surprise if, in these circumstances of empty
rhetoric and ulterior motives, Arab-Muslim people, and people generally, were
reinforced in their suspicions of America's foreign policy, to the extent that they
continued to speculate about its *actual* aims. From this standpoint, the suspicion
of America's secret plots and plans was not the product of Arab-Muslim cultural
dysfunction or social-psychological pathology, but just the ordinary consequences of structural hypocrisy.

This circularity brings us back to where we started: to the Arab-Muslim
paranoia narrative as an explanation for widespread suspicion and speculation
about American foreign policy. Indeed, the War of Ideas can also be understood
as the formalisation of a conspiracy discourse, which I have described as the
multiple narratives that spring up around foreign policy controversy and vie for
legitimacy and standing. The Bush administration occupied the commanding
heights in this policy setting, such that it could say authoritatively which interpretations of America's opaque and controversial engagement in the Middle East
were legitimate and which were the product of paranoia and misinformation.
But I have also highlighted latent ruptures and disjunctions in this War of Ideas
framework that point to a more complicated and contested political landscape
beyond the rarefied confines of US national security doctrine.

It is crucial to remember that Arab-Muslim people situated in their own
political cultures, with their own institutions and resources for interpreting US

foreign policy, and their own sources of legitimacy and standing, were ultimately the audience of this soft power strategy. A fuller assessment of the political landscape in question would have to centre not on Arab-Muslim misperception, but on the object of controversy around which these competing interpretations congregated. It would have to take seriously the complicated origins of 9/11 and the wider imperatives for US involvement in the Middle East. In the absence of this broader view, attempted engagement with Arab-Muslim people cynical about America's foreign policy and values will be open to scepticism and the charge of propaganda.

This chapter has followed the Arab-Muslim paranoia narrative to the heart of Bush administration counter-terrorism doctrine, where it was integrated into the strategic logic of the War on Terror. I have shown that the paranoia narrative worked against the stated objective of the War of Ideas, which was to allay the conditions of bitterness, resentment and blame thought to render Arab-Muslims vulnerable to radicalisation. On the one hand, Arab-Muslim criticism of American policies and values were framed in a highly delegitimising way, as the product of cultural dysfunction, political alienation, misinformation and paranoia. These delegitimising dynamics shut down room for meaningful communication with differentiated Arab-Muslims by denying them standing as reasonable interlocutors, while holding the US government out as a paragon of rational authority. On the other hand, this framework situated ideas as instruments of counter-terrorism strategy – as a strategic capacity in the service of more fundamental priorities. As a consequence, the rhetoric of liberty and democracy espoused for Arab-Muslim consumption was brought into tension with less savoury practices of the War on Terror. This tension connected with a widespread perception in the Arab-Muslim world of a contradiction in US foreign policy between purported values and the national interest, between idealistic grandiloquence and ruthless pragmatism. Thus, the War of Ideas had embedded in its conceptual foundations the potential to inspire the very circumstances it sought to address, not least of which was suspicion about the secret operation of American power in the region.

NOTES

1   The White House, Office of the Press Secretary, 'Remarks by the National Security Advisor Condoleezza Rice Followed by Question and Answer to the US Institute of Peace', Washington DC, 29 August 2004. Available at www.mtholyoke.edu/acad/intrel/bush/usip.htm (accessed 25 January 2015).
2   *Ibid.*
3   *Ibid.*
4   Indeed, the War of Ideas framing was surely drawn from Thomas Friedman's Pulitzer Prize winning series of Op-Ed columns written in the year after 9/11 which dealt with

precisely these issues, including a widely cited article titled 'The War of Ideas'. See T. Friedman, 'War of Ideas', *New York Times* (2 June 2002), p. 19.

5　See R. Wright, 'An Eye for the Terrorist Sites', *The Washington Post*. Available at www.washingtonpost.com/wp-dyn/content/article/2005/11/16/AR2005111602120.html (accessed 25 January 2015).

6　The White House, *The National Security Strategy of the United States of America* (Washington, DC: Government Printing Office, 2006); and The White House, *The National Strategy for Combating Terrorism* (Washington, DC: Government Printing Office, 2006).

7　Jackson argues that presidential rhetoric after 9/11 was a potent force setting out the official view and the parameters of the emerging War on Terror discourse. More recently, Jackson has used presidential speeches to demonstrate US foreign policy on terrorism in the Obama administration. See respectively, R. Jackson, *Writing the War on Terrorism* (Manchester: Manchester University Press, 2005), pp. 1–5, 16–19, 26–28; R. Jackson, 'Culture Identity and Hegemony: Continuity and (the Lack of) Change in US Counterterrorism Policy from Bush to Obama', *International Politics*, 48:2/3 (2011); R. Jackson, 'Continuity and (the Lack of) Change in US Counterterrorism Policy from Bush to Obama', *International Politics*, 48:2/3 (2011), pp. 403–404; and, for a complementary account, S. Silberstein, *War of World: Language and Politics After 9/11* (London: Routledge, 2002), pp. 1–3. For a good summary of the National Security Advisor role and its significance see J. P. Burke, *Honest Broker? The National Security Advisor and Presidential Decision Making* (Texas: Texas A&M Press, 2009), pp. 1–7. John Lewis Gaddis argues that the post-9/11 grand strategy set out in NSS 2002 and NSS 2006 were far more a reflection of a decisive policy direction from the Executive branch than previous NSS, which had tended towards bureaucratic compromise and the formalisation of existing positions. On NSS 2002, see Gaddis, 'A Grand Strategy of Transformation', pp. 50–57. On NSS 2006, see Gaddis, 'Grand Strategy in the Second Term', pp. 2–15.

8　I identified this concern with anti-Americanism as a key theme for American foreign policy commentators in their attempt to explain the origins of 9/11. A common starting point in post-9/11 discussions of anti-Americanism was a Gallup poll conducted in nine predominantly Muslim countries that indicated a 53 per cent disapproval of American foreign policy. See F. Newport, 'Gallup Poll of the Islamic World', *Gallup Poll*. Available at www.gallup.com/poll/5380/gallup-poll-islamic-world.aspx (accessed 25 January 2015).

9　The White House, *The National Security Strategy of the United States of America* (Washington, DC: Government Printing Office, 2002), p. 6.

10　*Ibid.*

11　For instance, this language has a heavy resonance with Thomas Friedman's commentary on the links between terrorism and anti-Americanism. It also connected with the early post-9/11 discourse around public diplomacy. See, for example, P. G. Peterson, 'Public Diplomacy and the War on Terrorism', *Foreign Affairs*, 81:5 (2002), pp. 74–94.

12　The White House, Office of the Press Secretary, 'Press Briefing by National Security Advisor Condoleezza Rice'. Available at www.presidency.ucsb.edu/ws/index.php?pid=79214 (accessed 25 January 2015).

13　The White House, Office of the Press Secretary, 'Address by George W. Bush' (10 November 2001), available at www.state.gov/documents/organization/18967.pdf (accessed 25 January 2015).

14　Congressional hearings on public diplomacy after 9/11 repeatedly noted the prevalence of the idea that Jewish workers in the World Trade Center had been warned not to go to work on the day of the attack, as well as a general allegation that Israel was behind the attacks. See, for instance, 'Words Have Consequences: The Impact of Incitement and

Anti-American and Anti-Semitic Propaganda on American Interests in the Middle East', Hearing Before the House Subcommittee on the Middle East and South Asia (April 2002).

15 The White House, Office of the Press Secretary, 'The President's Radio Address' (November 10 2001). Available at www.presidency.ucsb.edu/ws/index.php?pid=24993 (accessed 25 January 2015.

16 See, for instance, 'Words Have Consequences'.

17 National Committee on Terrorist Attacks Upon the United States, *The 9/11 Commission Report* (New York: W. W. Norton & Co., 2004), pp. 263–264.

18 Advisory Group on Public Diplomacy in the Arab and Muslim World, *Changing Minds, Winning Peace: A New Strategic Direction for U.S Public Diplomacy in the Arab-Muslim World* (Washington: Advisory Group on Public Diplomacy in the Arab and Muslim World, 2003).

19 Independent Task Force on Public Diplomacy, *Finding America's Voice: A Strategy For Reinvigorating US Public Diplomacy* (New York: Council on Foreign Relations, 2003).

20 *The 9/11 Commission Report*, p. 51. The report also refers to the anti-Semitic belief in a Jewish world conspiracy. See *ibid.*, pp. 20 and 562.

21 Independent Task Force, *Finding America's Voice*, p. 41. Peterson produced the same language in a *Foreign Affairs* article in 2001. See Peterson, 'Public Diplomacy and the War on Terrorism', pp. 74–94.

22 Rice became a driving force for the War of Ideas strategy within the State Department, where public diplomacy was a key soft power vector.

23 Council on Foreign Relations, 'Prepared Remarks by Stephen Hadley, Assistant to the President for National Security Affairs' (18 October 2005). Hadley gave the same speech to the American Israel Public Affairs Committee later in October 2005. See The White House, Office of the Press Secretary, 'Remarks by Stephen Hadley to the American Israeli Public Affairs Committee National Summit, 2005' (31 October 2005).

24 I have explored this narrative at length in Chapters 1 and 3 but it is worth reiterating it again here as a central context for this strategic doctrine. See, again, Bernard Lewis, 'The Roots of Muslim Rage', *The Atlantic* (September 1990), pp. 1–8; and, for the updated post-9/11 version, see Lewis, 'What Went Wrong', *The Atlantic* (January 2002), pp. 43–45.

25 *Ibid.*

26 *Ibid.*

27 *Ibid.*

28 The White House, Office of the Press Secretary, 'President Bush's Address to the Joint Services 'Wives' Luncheon' (25 October 2005). The same stock paragraphs appeared in three more presidential speeches in the lead up to NSS 2006. See The White House, Office of the Press Secretary, 'President Discusses War on Terror at National Endowment for Democracy' (8 October 2005); The White House, Office of the Press Secretary, 'President Commemorates Veteran's Day, Discusses War on Terror' (11 November 2005); and The White House, Office of the Press Secretary, 'Remarks on the War on Terror' (28 October 2005).

29 White House, 'President Bush's Address to the Joint Services 'Wives' Luncheon'.

30 *Ibid.*

31 The NSS is mandated by the Goldwater-Nichols Act of 1986, which requires the Executive branch to produce a statement of grand strategy for the information of Congress. The chief concern animating this legislation was that, although a clear continuity ran through the containment policies of the Cold War, the various resources and capabilities of the US government where not brought to bear in a coordinated way. See J. L. Gaddis,

'A Grand Strategy of Transformation', *Foreign Policy*, 133 (2002), pp. 50–57; and D. M. Snyder, *The National Security Strategy: Documenting Strategic Vision* (Carlisle Barracks, PA: Strategic Studies Institute, 1995). Snyder was responsible for drafting the Regan administration's NSS in 1988.

32 According to Snyder the NSS has five principle aims: 1) to provide Congress with a strategic overview and set out a logic for resource allocations; 2) to communicate US policy to foreign audiences; 3) to appeal to selected domestic constituencies; 4) to produce, through the development process, policy consensus within the executive; and 5) to reinforce the policy agenda of the president. See Snyder, *The National Security Strategy*, pp. 5–6.

33 See National Security Council, *The National Strategy for Combating Terrorism* (Washington DC, 2006), pp. 9–14.

34 The White House, *The National Security Strategy of the United States of America*, pp. 10–11.

35 *Ibid.*, p. 9.

36 *Ibid.*

37 *Ibid.*

38 For a broader account of the links between alienation and psychology in society see Michel Foucault, *Madness and Civilization: A History of Insanity in the Age of Reform* (Oxford: Routledge, 2001).

39 The White House, *The National Security Strategy of the United States of America*, p. 9.

40 *Ibid.*

41 *Ibid.* See also The White House, Office of the Press Secretary, 'Remarks by the National Security Advisor Condoleezza Rice Followed by Question and Answer to the US Institute of Peace'. Available at www.mtholyoke.edu/acad/intrel/bush/usip.htm (accessed 29 January 2015.

42 The understanding of American as a 'city on the hill' and 'humanity's last, best hope' is a powerful theme in America's foreign policy tradition. And this theme explicitly positions American liberal democracy as the exemplar model for humanity. For an incisive account of the way liberal democracy has operated normatively in US foreign policy, see J. Moten, 'The Roots of the Bush Doctrine: Power, Nationalism, and Democracy Promotion in US Strategy', *International Security*, 29:4 (2005), pp. 112–156. For the broader contexts, see C. Coker, *Reflections on American Foreign Policy Since 1945* (New York: St Martin's Press, 1989); and W. R. Mead, 'The American Foreign Policy Tradition', *Foreign Affairs*, 81 (2002), pp. 163–176.

43 The classic Cold War liberal development account is W. Rostow, *The Stages of Economic Growth: A Non-Communist Manifesto* (Cambridge: Cambridge University Press, 1971). For a good summary of the liberal development model see R. Higgott, *Political Development Theory: The Contemporary Debate* (London: Taylor & Francis, 2005); B. Hindess, 'The Past is Another Culture', *International Political Sociology*, 1:4 (2007), pp. 325–338; and T. A. McCarthy, 'From Modernism to Messianism: Liberal Developmentalism and American Exceptionalism', *Constellations*, 14:1 (2007), pp. 3–30.

44 Higgott, *Political Development Theory*; and Hindess, 'The Past is Another Culture', pp. 325–338.

45 *Ibid.*

46 The White House, *The National Security Strategy of the United States of America*, pp. 9–10.

47 D. Campbell, *Writing Security: United States Foreign Policy and the Politics of Identity* (Manchester: University of Manchester Press, 1998); and J. Der Derian, 'The CIA, Hollywood, and the Sovereign Conspiracy', in James Der Derian (ed.), *Critical Practices in International Theory: Selected Essays* (New York: Routledge, 2009).

48 The White House, *The National Security Strategy of the United States of America*, p. 1.

49 National Security Council, *The National Strategy for Combating Terrorism* (Washington DC, 2006), pp. 9–14.
50 *Ibid.*, pp. 11–12.
51 *Ibid.*, p. 11.
52 *Ibid.*
53 *Ibid.*, p. 12.
54 *Ibid.*, p. 12–13.
55 Joint Education and Doctrine Division, *Department of Defence Dictionary of Military and Associated Terms* (Washington, DC: United States Department of Defence, 2010), p. 119.
56 National Security Council, *The National Strategy for Combating Terrorism*, p. 11. The NSCT also points to the promotion of liberal democratic values and moderate Arab-Muslim voices as a key element of this approach.
57 *Ibid.*, p. 17.
58 C. Von Clausewitz, *On War*, trans. J. J. Graham (Radford, VA: Wilder Publications, 2008), p. 42.
59 Anthony Burke has identified the strategic logic entailed in the Clausewitzian tradition with a pernicious means–ends approach that never resolves in any ultimate end. Here the world is turned into a 'standing reserve' for the technologies of security. See A. Burke, 'Iraq: Strategy's Burnt Offerings', *Global Change, Peace and Security*, 17:2 (2005), pp. 203–205.
60 For a comprehensive account of detentions at Guantanamo Bay see 'Guantanamo Bay: Get the Facts', *Amnesty International*. Available at www.amnesty.org.au/hrs/comments/2218 (accessed 29 January 2015). See also, 'Unlock the Truth: Europe, Renditions, and Secret Detention', *Amnesty International*. Available at www.unlock thetruth.org (accessed 29 January 2015). For a lucid account of the gap between rhetoric and policy see F. Rich, ' "We Do Not Torture" and other Funny Stories', *New York Times*. Available at www.informationclearinghouse.info/article10985.htm (accessed 29 January 2015).
61 See for instance the survey based conclusions about the motivations of anti-American sentiment in J. L. Esposito and D. Mogahed, 'Battle for Muslims' Hearts and Minds: The Road Not (Yet) Taken', *Middle East Policy*, 14:1 (2007), p. 36, pp. 38–42.

5

Conspiracy, misinformation
and public diplomacy

T HIS CHAPTER EXAMINES the practical manifestation of the War of Ideas strategy in United States (US) State Department public diplomacy, as well as more recent counter-radicalisation efforts under the Obama administration. It does so by focusing on several programmes involved in direct engagements with anti-Americanism and extremist ideology: the Counter-Misinformation Team, tasked with debunking instances of misinformation and propaganda, and the Digital Outreach Team (DOT), which engaged online with Muslim people thought vulnerable to radicalisation, as well as attempting to discredit jihadi recruiters.

Public diplomacy is usually understood as the 'systematic effort to communicate not with foreign governments but with the people themselves'.[1] It has a long history in US foreign policy, particularly during the Cold War, when the United States Information Agency (USIA) was a key advocate of liberal democracy in America's ideological confrontation with communism.[2] Public diplomacy became increasingly important to US War on Terror strategy as the Bush administration began to formulate its War of Ideas by late 2004. Indeed, it was former National Security Advisor Condoleezza Rice (who had initially articulated the new approach to counter-terrorism) who now oversaw its implementation at the State Department as Secretary of State from 2005 to 2009. This public diplomacy campaign centred on three core principles: producing a positive vision of hope; advancing universal human rights, while isolating violent extremists; and fostering common interests and values.[3] According to the State Department, these principles would be pursued by vigorously engaging foreign publics to explain and advocate US policies.[4]

I show that the Arab-Muslim paranoia narrative flowed through into this public diplomacy effort and infused it with the same delegitimising dynamics identified in the War of Ideas doctrine, undermining the purported aim of engagement with Arab-Muslim people. This influence is clear in the framing evident in the State Department's Country Report on Terrorism, which catalogues terrorist activity each year and reports on counter-terrorism programmes:

Responding to a quickly debunking misinformation, conspiracy theories, and urban legends is crucial to success in the war of ideas. The State Department maintains a public 'Identifying Misinformation' website in English and Arabic, devoted to countering false stories that appear in extremist websites and other web sources. The site focuses on disinformation likely to end up in the mainstream media. Embassies have used information from this site to counter disinformation in extremist print publications in Pakistan and other countries. One article, 'A Trio of Disinformers', was the subject of a 1,100 word front page story in an issue of the influential pan-Arab newspaper *al-Sharq al-Awsat*. 'Identifying misinformation' is featured on the usinfo. state.gov website, and listed first of 17.6 million sites in a search for the term misinformation. At least 49 websites have direct links to it.[5]

The State Department's public diplomacy output cannot be reduced to this counter-misinformation programme; it also involved educational exchanges, extensive print publications, multimedia promotions and substantial foreign aid. Yet focusing on the paranoia narrative provides an incisive way into the underlying power relations animating the broader enterprise, particularly since it was intimately involved in the diagnosis of Muslim animosity towards America. Most obviously, in the above extract resentment towards America is associated with delusion and incompetence, while the US government is positioned as the source of authoritative knowledge about international affairs. This dichotomy pervaded the State Department's understanding of Muslim resentment. For instance, the term 'conspiracy' appeared twenty-five times in the Country Report 2005: on twenty-four occasions it was used to describe terrorist acts, including the criminal charge of conspiracy; on one occasion it was used as a characterisation of ill-founded and potentially delusional claims made by Arab-Muslim. These contrasting uses of 'conspiracy' reflect deeper assumptions about the legitimacy, authority and rationality of American foreign policy.

Of course, the War of Ideas was explicitly involved in strategic communication, which entailed carving out room to deliver a message, mustering the trappings of credibility, staking the high ground in ideological encounters, building audience fidelity and undermining the ability of competing narratives to do these self-same things. Richard Holbrooke, one of the America's most senior diplomats during this period, alludes to the instrumental nature of this enterprise in his description of the counter-radicalisation context:

> Call it public diplomacy, or public affairs, or psychological warfare, or – if you really want to be blunt – propaganda. But whatever it is called, defining what this war is really about in the minds of the 1 billion Muslims in the world will be of decisive and historic importance. Bin Laden could well spawn a new generation of dedicated, fanatical terrorists if his message takes root. The battle of ideas therefore is as important as any other aspect of the struggle we are now engaged in. It must be won.[6]

Scholars and practitioners of public diplomacy have often sought to distinguish it from the less savoury practices of psychological warfare and propaganda by pointing to Edward Murrow's famous quip that 'the truth is the best propaganda and lies are the worst'.[7] While public diplomacy can clearly partake in propaganda, it is most effective, they argue, when it relies on accurate information. However, it remains the case that there is an underlying set of power relations in action that imply superiority/inferiority, legitimacy/illegitimacy, rationality/ delusion, and so on. These problematic dynamics are obvious in the practice of the Counter-Misinformation Team and the DOT, two programmes ostensibly dedicated to engagement and dialogue. I show that the recurring language of paranoia and misinformation is likely to offend and rebuff rather than connect, and highlight the extent to which the credibility of the US government was a matter of serious contention for the Arab-Muslim audiences who were highly sensitive to hypocrisy and propaganda.

The counter-misinformation team

The 'Identifying Misinformation' website flagged in the Country Report extract above was produced by the State Department's Counter-Misinformation Team. Established along with the USIA during the Cold War, its early focus was identifying and dispelling Soviet disinformation aimed at tarnishing America's international reputation.[8] One of the few records of its Cold War output is a 1988 report titled 'Soviet Active Measures in the Era of Glasnost', prepared for the US House of Representatives, which outlines various false stories produced by the USSR about America.[9] After the Cold War, the Counter-Misinformation Team's focus shifted to countering Iraqi propaganda during the First Gulf War, and to rebutting misinformation about the US, like the 'body parts' rumour alleging that Americans kidnap children to harvest their organs.[10] Wound down in 1996 when the USIA was disbanded, it was reconstituted at the State Department after 9/11 in order to rebut misinformation thought to be fuelling Arab-Muslim resentment towards America.[11] I take two snapshots of Counter-Misinformation Team output as a representative sample: the first is the initial fourteen-month roll-out phase of the programme from December 2004, during which twenty-seven texts were posted to the State Department's 'Identifying Misinformation' website (see Table 1); the second is the web feature 'Conspiracy Theories and Misinformation', posted in October 2009, which draws together texts from across the life of the program with new interviews and diagrammatic illustrations (see Figure 1).

It is easy enough to see how the Counter-Misinformation Team operated as a delegitimising enterprise, actualising the Arab-Muslim paranoia narrative embedded in the War of Ideas. In this narrative terrorists achieve their goals by deploying disinformation and propaganda to recruit new members and sympathisers, while Arab-Muslim people are rendered vulnerable by a culture of embitterment, blame and misinformation. Here Counter-Misinformation amounts to

Table 1 'Identifying misinformation' web series texts, December 2004–January 2006

Date	Title	Claim debunked
December 2004	'US forces Not Using Outlawed Weapons in Iraq'[12]	Chemical weapons were used in Iraq.
	'Life of Mohammed Book *not* Authored by Grandfather or Ancestor of President Bush'[13]	President Bush's grandfather authored a disparaging book about the life of Muhammad.
January 2005	'False Allegations Regarding the South Asian Tsunami'[14]	The United States had forewarning of the South Asian tsunami and failed to alert anyone but the US base at Diego Garcia.
	'Exaggerated Concerns about Anti-AIDS Drug Nevarapine'[15]	The AIDS drug Nevarapine is unsafe and this has been covered up.
	'Saddam's Disinformation'[16]	Provides a link to a report on Iraqi disinformation around the 1991 Gulf War and a report on Iraqi disinformation between 1990 and 2003.
	'AIDS as a Biological Weapon'[17]	AIDS was developed by the US military as a biological weapon.
	'About US'[18]	The 'body parts' myth that Americans are kidnapping children to harvest their organs.
	'Al Qaeda Confirms it Carried out 9/11'[19]	Al-Qaeda did not carry out 9/11.
	'Depleted Uranium'[20]	Uranium tipped munitions used by the US military cause health side effect.
	'Definitions'[21]	This article covers a range of claims: AIDS as a biological weapon; Hamid Karzai was a consultant to the oil Company UNACOL when it was exploring the viability of a pipeline across Afghanistan; the 'body parts' myth; a man survived the 9/11 attacks of the WTC by surfing a concrete slab down from the 80th floor; and a missile, not a plane, hit the Pentagon.

Table 1 continued

Date	Title	Claim debunked
	'Soviet Disinformation'[22]	A link to a report titled 'Soviet Active Measures in the Era of Glasnost'.
	'About Us'[23]	The 'body parts' myth.
	'Countering Misinformation'[24]	This article covers a range of claims: the United States had forewarning of the South Asian tsunami; the United States created Osama bin Laden; the United States is using chemical weapons in Iraq; President Bush's grandfather; depleted uranium; 4,000 Jews failed to show up to work at the WTC on 9/11; AIDS as a biological weapon; the cover-up about the AIDS drug Nevaripine; and the 'body parts' myth.
February 2005	'Countering Misinformation'[25]	This article covers a range of claims: depleted uranium; AIDS as a biological weapon; the 'baby parts' myth; and the 4,000 Jews on 9/11 allegation.
March 2005	'About Us'[26]	Addresses the 'body parts' myth and links to the Soviet Active Measures report.
April 2005	'United States Involved in Lebanese Assassination'[27]	Hariri was assassinated by the United States because he opposed US bases in Lebanon.
	'A Trio of Disinformers'[28]	Jihadist websites are spreading disinformation: exaggerated body counts; mustard gas was used in Fallujah; and a letter from a girl named Fatima claiming she and other women have been raped and tortured in Abu Ghraib prison.
June 2005	'Burned Quran not a Hate Crime'[29]	A burned Koran left outside a mosque was an anti-Muslim act.
July 2005	'The US Take-Over of the Amazon Myth'[30]	The United States and UN have taken control of the Amazon to preserve it for all humanity.

Table 1 continued

Date	Title	Claim debunked
	'How to Identify Misinformation'[31]	This article covers a range of claims: AIDS as a biological weapon; the 9/11 missile theory; a man surfed down the WTC; a bible was found undamaged in the wreckage at the Pentagon on 9/11; the 'baby parts' myth; organ harvesting in Iraq; depleted uranium; chemical weapons in Iraq; and the claim that Iraqi children playing soccer were killed by US soldiers.
September 2005	'9/11 Revealed'[32]	A drone or a small 757 under remote control hit the Pentagon on 9/11; the WTC was brought down by controlled demolition.
November 2005	'North Korea Persists in 54 Year Old Disinformation'[33]	The US used chemical and biological weapons in the Korean War.
	'US is *not* Harvesting Organs in Iraq'[34]	The 'body parts' myth in Iraq.
	'United States has no Plans for a Military Base in Paraguay'[35]	America plans to build a military base in Paraguay.
January 2006	'Plan 'Balboa' not a US Plan to Invade Venezuela'[36]	The US plans to invade Venezuela.
	'Misinformation about the "Gladio/Stay Behind" Networks Resurfaces'[37]	Stay behind networks, established during the Cold War as clandestine resistance movements to be activated in the event of a Soviet invasion of Europe, have been used to conduct domestic terrorist operations in Greece.
	'September 11 Conspiracy Theories'[38]	A missile hit the Pentagon; the WTC was blown up in a controlled demolition. Also links to a Popular Mechanics article debunking *Loose Change*.

a calculated effort to delegitimise the dangerous views of extremists and correct the misperceptions of vulnerable Arab-Muslims. The terms conspiracy theory, misinformation, urban legend, myth, false story, misperception, distortion, propaganda and lies, used repeatedly across the Identifying Misinformation series, all have highly negative connotations that draw attention away from the substance of claims and towards the problematic motivations of the people making them. Indeed, the presentation of specific claims was so prejudiced from the outset that no genuine engagement was possible. Take the following extract from 'AIDS as a Biological Weapon', a document that points to the origins of this claim in a Soviet disinformation programme, and its latter day propagation by some doubtful individuals:

> In addition to the Soviet disinformation specialists, a tiny handful of fringe group conspiracy theorists also espoused the false charge that the AIDS virus had been created as a biological weapon. One of them was Mr. Theodore Strecker, an attorney in the United States ... . Theodore wrote a manifesto, 'This is a Bio-Attack Alert', on March 28, 1986. He imagined that traitorous American doctors, United Nations bureaucrats, and Soviet officials were involved in a gigantic conspiracy to destroy the United States with biological warfare. He wrote 'we have allowed the United Nations World Health Organisation to combine with traitors in the United States National Institute of Health to start a Soviet attack ...'
>
> Mr. Strecker saw the Soviet Union at the heart of this alleged conspiracy: This is an attempt to exhaust America with hatred, struggle, want, confusion, and inoculation of disease. The enemy intends to control our population with disease, make us dependent on their remedies, engineer each birth, and reduce America to a servant of the Supreme Soviet.
>
> Mr. Strecker sent his manifesto to the President and Vice President of the United States, governors of several states, and various US Government Departments, urging them to 'retake the various labs using force if necessary' and other dramatic emergency measures. It did not have the galvanising effect he had hoped.
>
> Other conspiracy theorists have espoused confused theories similar to those of the Streckers.[39]

Whatever the veracity of the claims dealt with by the Counter-Misinformation Team, they were situated and understood within an all too familiar framework of irrationality, deviance and marginality. Indeed, there is a clear resonance here with the recurring 'paranoid style' understanding of conspiracy theory, where a rational political centre is contrasted with an irrational, emotive and paranoid periphery. Mr Strecker is a lone character, selectively quoted and otherwise dismissed. His ideas are not explored and his views are contrasted with the sensible political elites on whom his conspiracy allegations 'did not have the galvanising effect he had hoped'.[40] Moreover, the brief account of his claim is surrounded by negative terms – 'fringe', 'imagined', 'gigantic conspiracy', 'manifesto', 'confused' – which have strong connotations with psychological deviance, delusion and radicalism.[41] This delegitimising web is even more strik-ing when it is deployed against more orthodox claims. This was clear from the way suspicion about the operation of elite financial power was treated on the 'Conspiracy Theory and Misinformation' web feature published in 2009 (Figure 1). In the middle of a Global Financial Crisis that directly implicated powerful financial elites in massive and systematic duplicity, the Counter-Misinformation Team had this to say:

> Economic conspiracy theories are often based on the false, but popular, idea that powerful individuals are motivated overwhelmingly by wealth, rather than the wide variety of human motivations we all experience. This one dimensional, cartoonish view of human nature is at the heart of Marxist ideology, which once held millions under its sway.[42]

At exactly the time when scepticism of financial elites was both warranted and necessary, the very thought of this was framed as conspiracy theory.[43] This and other issues of pressing concern were also delegitimised through the conspiracy theory association, flagged in twenty-point bold at the top of the page (See Figure 1). Beneath this, a web of negative connotations did more delegitimising work, associating 'false claims' with a 'realm of myth, where imaginations run wild, fears trump facts, and evidence is ignored'.[44] Across the 'Conspiracy Theory and Misinformation' web feature claims were framed as 'nonsense', 'fearful', 'deep-seated', 'one dimensional', 'fantasy', 'simplistic', 'unimaginative', 'exaggerated', and 'irrational'.[45] At the same time, these claims were contrasted with fact, reason, evidence, and rationality, which were always on the side of the govern-ment line. The Counter-Misinformation Team is presented as the source of authoritative knowledge, in possession of the proper facts and methodologies for making judgements about international politics.

The selection of claims for analysis presented another barrier to engage-ment with Arab-Muslim publics, since the Counter-Misinformation Team did not analyse the most significant issues of controversy informing resentment towards US foreign policy. Claims regarding a disparaging account of Muham-mad penned by George W. Bush's grandfather; allegations about a burned Koran left outside a Christian church in America; assertions that the US military had forewarning of the South-Asian tsunami and did not pass it on to affected countries (see Table 1) – these were not core concerns of Arab-Muslim people angry about American foreign policy.[46] A list of substantive issues would need to have included: the relationship between America and repressive dictatorships in the Middle East; America's role in regime change, particularly in Iran; Amer-ica's relationship with Israel, with particular reference to military and diplo-matic support; the influence of the America's Israel lobby on American foreign policy; America's historical relationship with Iraq, including the issue of Iraqi civilian deaths caused by US sponsored sanctions; and, most recently, the

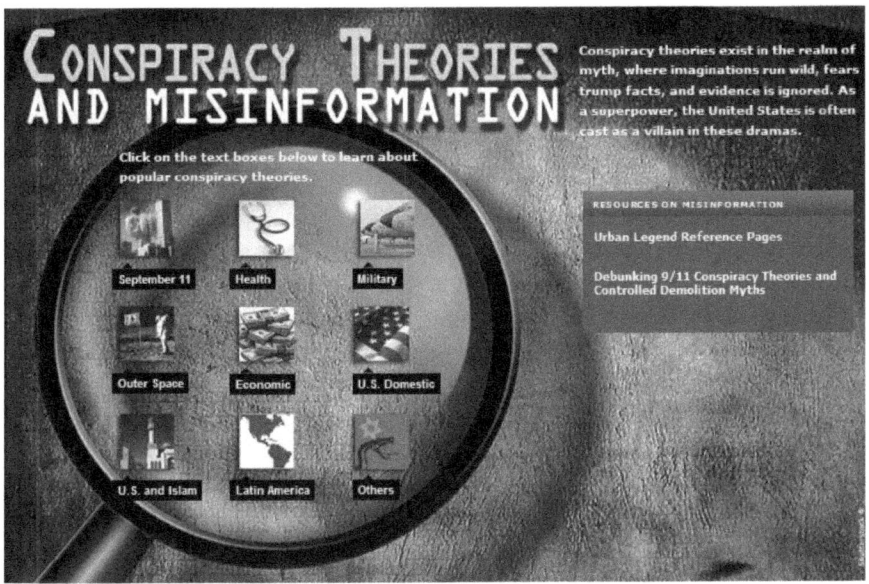

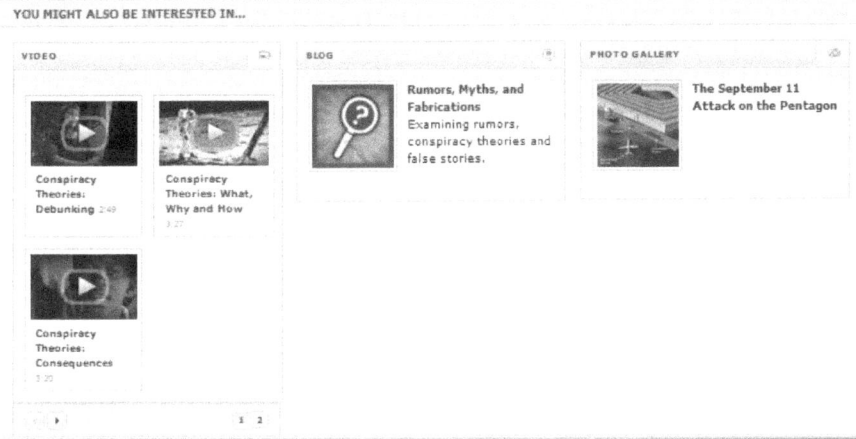

Figure 1 'Conspiracy Theories and Misinformation' web feature on the site America.gov

justification and conduct of the Iraq War.[47] Whatever truth or misperception there was around these issues areas, there is a strong scholarly consensus that they were among the most serious concerns motivating animus toward America in the Arab-Muslim world at that time. Yet they were never dealt with by the Counter-Misinformation Team, which focused instead on more peripheral issues.[48]

Moreover, while some issues that did bear directly on Arab-Muslim perception of America were dealt with, they were surrounded with, and diluted by, outlandish and unconnected topics. For instance, the 'Conspiracy Theories and Misinformation' web feature published in 2009 included two topic headings – 'September 11' and 'US and Islam' – that were directly related to the War on Terror (see Figure 1). But they appeared alongside the topic headings 'Health', 'Military', 'Outer Space', 'Economics', 'US Domestic', 'Latin America', and 'Other'. Some of the claims dealt with under these headings did relate to the War on Terror and the core concerns of some Arab-Muslim people – for instance, the debunking of the infamous 'Protocols of the Elders of Zion', the prolific anti-Semitic screed, or the treatment of fears about depleted uranium, which was particularly relevant to US military operations in Iraq.[49]

But overwhelmingly the issues raised were unconnected to Arab-Muslim radicalisation.[50] Under 'Health', fears about AIDS, SARS, H1N1 flu, and the 'body parts' myth were listed.[51] Under 'Military', the allegation that the US army used biological weapons in the Korean War was highlighted. Under 'Outer Space' fears of alien abduction were canvassed, along with moon landing scepticism.[52] Under 'Economic', fears of wealthy power elites, Marxism and John Perkins's book *Confessions of an Economic Hit Man* were examined.[53] Under 'US Domestic', the JFK assassination, claims that Barack Obama was not born in America and the anti-Semitic Franklin Prophecy were explored.[54] Under 'Latin America', claims about US bases in Paraguay, a looming US and UN annexation of the Amazon and an alleged Cuban spy ring arrested in America were addressed.[55] Under 'Other', the South Asian tsunami claims from 2005 were reproduced.[56] The implication here is that issues like the alleged use of chemical weapons or alleged atrocities by US military are of the same character and quality as these more fanciful claims. Under these circumstances it is difficult to see how an engagement with the genuine concerns of Arab-Muslim people could have been effective.

The broader point here is that the War of Ideas doctrine and the Counter-Misinformation Team programme therein tended to divide Arab-Muslim political culture between 'cultures of conspiracy and misinformation', and acquiescence to American foreign policy in the region. This division obscures genuine grievances of differentiated Arab-Muslims and reduces diverse political cultures to simplistic caricature. It delegitimises resentment by tying it to distortion and misunderstanding. Clearly, this dynamic was in tension with the aim of changing Arab-Muslim perceptions of America's regional engagement. Lacking a forthright discussion about core policy issues, the work of the Counter-Misinformation Team remained superficial in its approach. The lack of standing afforded to Arab-Muslim audiences, the derisive labelling and patronising diagnostics, rendered genuine dialogue unlikely.

At the same time, the Counter-Misinformation Team's own credibility and standing was put into question by the strategic and ideological nature of the enterprise. Consider the methodology for judging the legitimacy of claims outlined by the Counter-Misinformation team in a document titled 'How to Identify Misinformation':

> Does the story fit the pattern of a conspiracy theory? Does the story fit the pattern of an 'urban legend'? Does the story contain shocking revelations about a highly controversial issue? Is the source trustworthy? What does further research tell us?[57]

While these questions might be useful starting points for thinking about the accuracy of information, the instrumental character of the Counter-Misinformation Team is drawn out when these criteria are turned back on ostensibly authoritative US government narratives from the recent past. On the first question, even a cursory examination of the historical record shows that foreign policy discourses have often been shaped by conspiracy narratives. As Murray Edelman points out, the mythology of the conspiratorial enemy is common.[58] From communist world domination to terrorist attacks on Western civilisation, political leaders, security commentators and everyday people have regularly found in world events the outlines of diabolical schemes which threaten to undermine our security and our very way of life. This was certainly the logic driving George W. Bush's description of the terrorist threat in his 2002 State of the Union address as a 'terrorist underworld' comprised of 'thousands of dangerous killers, schooled in the methods of murder ... now spread throughout the world like ticking time bombs, set to go off without warning'.[59] It was nothing less than an alleged conspiracy between Saddam Hussein and this 'terrorist underworld' that formed the central justification for the Iraq War. Did these catastrophic plots of global proportions 'fit the pattern of a conspiracy theory?'

Conversely, the power dynamic at play here is plain enough when we consider the kinds of claims that have been written off as conspiracy theory in the broader American foreign policy milieu since 9/11. Glenn Greenwald makes this point in relation to a counter-misinformation strategy focused on domestic American subjects proposed by Cass Sunstein:

> who is it that demonized as 'conspiracy mongers' people who warned that the U.S. government was illegally spying on its citizens, systematically torturing people, attempting to establish permanent bases in the Middle East, or engineering massive bail out plans to transfer extreme wealth to the industries that own the government? The most chronic and dangerous purveyors of 'conspiracy theory games' are the very people Sunstein thinks should be empowered to control our political debates ... namely, the government itself and Enlightened people like him.[60]

From this perspective, the Counter-Misinformation Team's suggestion that readers should be sceptical about 'issues of controversy' seems particularly problematic, since uncovering elite malfeasance would very likely be controversial.[61] Indeed, as Keith Goshorn notes incisively, 'strategies of deterrence and frames of containment', like the allegation of paranoia, tend to congregate around issues of political controversy for precisely this reason.[62] The impetus to dampen down controversy highlights the strategic function of the Counter-Misinformation Team, which inevitably defended official policy positions and forswore critical engagement. The important point here is to highlight the blatant self-interest that informed the Counter-Misinformation Team's activities.

This dynamic flowed on into the issue of source reliability. Were discerning Arab-Muslim people really in a position to take statements from the US government at face value? In making this determination they would have to consider a laundry list of sanctioned illegality and official deception, for instance, around the US government's direct or indirect involvement in covert regime change and other clandestine activities in, for example, Iran, Guatemala, Cuba, Chile and Nicaragua;[63] or the US government's involvement in the funding and support of covert torture centres in Iraq from 2003 to 2006;[64] or the revelations from Edward Snowden about the activities of the US National Security Agency. At the more improbable end of historical US government transgressions one might consider the Tuskegee syphilis experiments carried out without consent on poor African American sharecroppers over a 40-year period beginning in 1932;[65] the LSD mind control experiments conducted by the Pentagon through the 1960s;[66] the plans drawn up, though never implemented, by the Pentagon for false flag operations inside the United States, designed to justify a war against Cuba;[67] and the Nixon administration's bugging operation against the Democratic National Committee offices at the Watergate Hotel.[68]

Aside from covering up controversial policies, there is evidence that the US government has sought to deliberately propagandise both domestic and foreign audiences.[69] Some relevant examples of covert influence include the Pentagon secretly paying retired generals to appear on TV news and current affairs programmes as 'independent' commentators on US national security, having provided them with synchronised talking points;[70] and the Pentagon contract with the communications firm Lincoln Park to plant pro-American articles in Iraqi newspapers, while pretending they were written by ordinary Iraqis.[71] Taken together, all these examples, themselves only samples of a much wider pool, suggest that the US government is not a reliable source of impartial information, particularly around issues of foreign policy controversy. This position is supported by a growing scholarly literature that examines propaganda in the context of the Pentagon's 'full spectrum dominance' strategy.[72] The space opened up here between the official accounts of foreign policy controversy proffered by the Counter-Misinformation Team and the historical practices of American power parallels the broader disjuncture in the War of Ideas doctrine between the rhetoric of liberal democratic idealism and the ruthless pursuit of national interest. In both settings this tension undermined the credibility of US government policies, programmes and public statements, and in doing so made successful engagement with Arab-Muslim publics less likely.

Nevertheless, the Counter-Misinformation Team held itself out as a source of sober analysis, such that it could debunk the misinformation of others and then set the record straight. Indeed, the 'How to Identify Misinformation' document suggested this as a last measure: 'Finally, if the Counter-Misinformation Team can be of help, ask us. We can't respond to all requests for information, but if the request is reasonable and we have time, we will do our best to provide accurate, authoritative, information.'[73] One such request, asking if the absence of WMDs in Iraq suggests a conspiracy to mislead the country into war, received this response: 'I have not found any evidence of conspiracy. Instead, I believe Iraq's consistent pattern of concealment, evasion and lying about WMD led Western governments to believe that Iraq was concealing WMD. Iraq did not, in fact, have WMD stockpiles, but its behaviour fed suspicions that it did.'[74]

This response was in keeping with the general standard of evidence and research on display throughout the 'Identifying Misinformation' series.[75] For instance, in a document addressing the allegation that US soldiers killed unarmed Iraqi children who were playing soccer, the main source of evidence provided was the log records of the soldiers themselves, which did not mention any anomalies and maintained that the fatalities were all insurgents.[76] This may well have been the case, but these records were hardly impartial evidence that could be relied upon – as if the US military in Iraq had not on other occasions mistakenly targeted civilians and then suppressed the incident.[77] Indeed, military controversies of this kind have often required whistleblower testimony that contradicts official records as an impetus to further investigation.[78] Likewise, the document 'A Trio of Disinformers', released in late 2005, argued that claims about the multiple rape of a woman named Fatima in Abu Ghraib prison were false, based on the prison's own records of detainees, with no mention of the covert interrogation and rendition programmes in operation, or the horrific physical and sexual assault of multiple prisoners by US personnel at Abu Ghraib, which were by then public knowledge.[79]

Thus, the credibility and authority of Counter-Misinformation Team information was undermined by the US government's own propensity for covert action, sanctioned illegality, cover-ups and propaganda, which went unacknowledged in the supposedly sober analysis promulgated to Arab-Muslim people already sceptical about American power in the region. This situation invited allegations of hypocrisy and duplicity, not to mention an understandable suspicion about the *actual* facts of the matter. Coupled with a delegitimising narrative centred on alleged cultural dysfunction, including highly charged language that implied disrepute and irrationality, it is reasonable to suggest that the Counter-Misinformation Team's approach entailed serious barriers against genuine engagement with a disaffected Arab-Muslim public.

The digital outreach team

These barriers were readily evident in the operation of the State Department's Digital Outreach Team (DOT), a group of bloggers tasked with countering anti-Americanism via direct engagement with online users in Persian, Urdu, Arabic, Pashto, Punjabi and English. Indeed, the interactive back-and-forth character-istic of DOT work provides an excellent practical example of the problematic dynamics inherent in the War of Ideas framework. The DOT can certainly be positioned as the manifestation of that strategic vision. Established in 2006 by then Under-Secretary for Public Diplomacy Karen Hughes the DOT's stated mission was to 'explain US foreign policy and counter misinformation'.[80] More specifically, according to the State Department, 'the Digital Outreach Team con-trasts objective facts with the often emotive, conspiracy-laden arguments of US critics in the hope that online users will take a fresh at their opinions of the US'.[81] The same Arab-Muslim paranoia narrative is evident here, entailing an opposi-tion between an authoritative, right-minded US government and misguided, emotionally affected Arab-Muslims. The DOT is a particularly useful site for analysis for two reasons: there is some direct evidence about how target audi-ences have responded to DOT interventions; second, whereas the Counter-Misinformation Team was rolled up in late 2009, the DOT continued on and expanded under the Obama administration with the explicit backing of Secre-tary of State Clinton, and is still in operation today.

But to begin with it is important to recognise that the DOT was one element of a broader and more covert US government attempt to counter-misinformation using digital outreach techniques.[82] Immediately after 9/11 the US Department of Defense established the Office of Strategic Influence, which aimed to support the War on Terror by influencing public sentiment and foreign policy makers, including planting false stories in foreign media.[83] According to Douglas Feith, the Under-Secretary for Defense responsible for managing the programme, the aim was to 'preserve our ability to deceive the enemy'.[84] Another programme within the Pentagon called the Office of Global Engagement aimed to confront jihadists online, as well as work to increase Internet connectivity globally.[85]

Neither of these programmes came to fruition – the first was rolled up after a media outcry, the second was shelved in DOD budgetary wrangling – but the intended function of online engagement found a home at the US Special Opera-tions Command (CENTCOM) in Tampa, with a 70-strong unit called the Joint Psyops Support Element (JPSY).[86] By 2011 news of Operation Earnest Voice, a program run by JPSY that engaged directly with critics of US foreign policy in online forums and comment sections, had made its way into mainstream media.[87] Of particular concern was the revelation that JPSY had contracted a Californian corporation to produce 'persona management' software that would allow a single Psyops operative to control up to ten online identities with convincing backgrounds and characterisation.[88] According to CENTCOM spokesman Bill Speaks, 'the technology supports classified blogging activities on foreign language websites to enable CENTCOM to counter violent extremists and enemy propaganda outside the United States'.[89] The contract called for up to 50 platforms, and personas with the look and feel of real people, the ability to withstand sophisticated scrutiny, and full deniability for the US government.[90]

While this programme is similar to the State Department's DOT, there are several key differences. First, DOT bloggers are required to identify themselves as US State Department employees, whereas the appearance of independence was a key feature of the JPSY programme. Second, the DOT argues for the presentation of accurate and truthful information, whereas strategic deception was implicit in the JPSY approach. Finally, the scale of the DOT enterprise was relatively small, whereas JPSY could potentially use 'persona management' software to coordinate up to 500 distinct identities.[91] There is limited information about JPSY or Operation Earnest Voice. But what there is indicates that the DOT is part of a wider US government counter-misinformation effort that was often engaged in strategic deception online, which involved so-called 'sock puppet' avatars and calculated disinformation. Of course, the US Department of Defense is not alone in this approach. The propaganda operations of China's so-called '50 cent army' have been widely reported, and Russia, Israel, France and the UK have all been implicated in similar programmes.[92] Thus, while the US State Department claimed the moral high ground of full disclosure and truthful messaging, this was undermined by the duplicitous approach to online engagement taken elsewhere in the national security bureaucracy.

Relatively little systematic research has been done on the effectiveness of the DOT, and even the State Department admits that its performance is difficult to measure. The best indication comes from a case study analysis of DOT activity in the months after President Obama's Cairo Address in June 2009, which sought to reset US relations with the Middle East by focusing on engagement and partnership building. Khatib, Dutton and Thelwall analysed posts in 30 discussion threads across 19 websites, including 181 posts from the DOT and 459 posts from other users.[93] What they found was bad news for the DOT:

> The findings show that DOT posts generate more negativity and that the DOT itself is not popular on the sites analyzed. On the surface, it seems that the DOT is counterproductive because the result of its participation is so negative (including driving more expressed negativity towards US foreign policy [general negativity] and negativity towards the DOT itself [posts that express negative opinions about the DOT]).[94]

Overall, only 4.8 per cent of posts expressed a positive view of America.[95] The most extensive DOT engagement took place on *Talk to Al Jazeera*, where 86.8 per cent of posts took a negative view of US foreign policy.[96] The overwhelming impression from this, albeit snapshot, study is that the DOT was not well received and actually generated more animus and negativity towards US foreign policy than might otherwise have been the case. Khatib et al. are at their most interesting, though, when they drill down and highlight the key themes and attitudes of the various posts. DOT posts generally challenged negative perceptions of US foreign policy, particularly on Iraq and the Israel/Palestine issue, stressed that the US is not at war with Islam, and emphasised a more compassionate Islamic tradition, as well as the multiculturalism of American society. More tellingly, the DOT also dedicated time to 'ridiculing myths and conspiracy theories and calling users with extreme views radicals, but claiming to enjoy engaging with users who post objective views.'[97] DOT bloggers also found themselves 'defending DOT members as US civil servants when accused of being spies or traitors'.[98]

DOT posts converged on the following themes:[99]

- challenging perceptions of US foreign policy towards the Middle East
- stating that the United States is supportive of establishing a Palestinian state
- stating that the United States wants to withdraw from Iraq
- stressing that the United States is not at war with the Muslim world
- stressing US multiculturalism and religious tolerance
- presenting Islam as a religion of compassion and describing Islamic extremists as foreign to Islam and to what most Muslims think
- presenting Obama's speech as a new beginning for US-Arab relations
- ridiculing myths and conspiracy theories and calling users with extreme views radicals but claiming to enjoy engaging with users who post objective views
- defending DOT members as US civil servants when accused of being spies and traitors.

Responses to the DOT converged around:

- describing them as slaves and traitors, suggesting that they have little or no credibility
- posting photos of dead children and dead and injured American soldiers
- refuting views on American foreign policy by citing Palestine and Iraq as examples
- posting doctored sarcastic photos of Obama
- posting photos of Osama bin Laden and other Al-Qaeda figures
- posting a YouTube video of Obama's speech to AIPAC where he calls Hamas a terrorist organisation
- citing verses from the Koran
- saying that the United States will be destroyed
- posting myths and conspiracy theories (like saying the date of Obama's speech was chosen because it is the day before that of the Nakba of 1967 [the Arab– Israeli War of 1967]).[100]

Meanwhile the vast majority of people who expressed a view about the DOT were negative in their comments, with half openly 'ridiculing and condescending'.[101] When we look at these comments more closely, outside of outright hostility, it is suspicion of US intentions, brought on by a disconnection between words and actions that stands out. Questioning DOT credibility, providing counter-examples to undermine DOT statements about US foreign policy, forwarding conspiracy narratives about the ulterior motives and secret actions of the United States – these were the key issues at stake for the DOT's respondents. The DOT has argued that the negative reactions generated by their posts do not reflect the responses of silent observers, so-called 'lurkers', who may be quietly weighing arguments and forming a view. The DOT contests space formerly dominated by extremists, it is argued, by providing an alternative perspective.[102] Yet of the 27.2 per cent of respondents who expressed no view about American foreign policy, the common sentiment was 'wait and see' and a recurring phrase was 'actions not words', suggesting it is precisely a historically grounded suspicion of US foreign policy actions that needs to be overcome.[103] Of course, we have seen already that online users were well founded in their scepticism of US government information, if not the DOT then certainly from the wider set of programmes aimed at strategic influence through deceptive methods. This is the same scepticism identified in the overarching War of Ideas strategy, where a disjunction between rhetoric and action drove suspicion of US foreign policy in the Middle East.

More recently, the focus of the DOT has shifted to discrediting so-called digital jihadists and their message, rather than promoting a positive account of US foreign policy and American values per se. This change in emphasis began in the last months of the Bush administration under the stewardship of James Glassman, who argued that it was not necessary for Arab-Muslim people to like American policy, they just needed to dislike violent extremists like Al-Qaeda.[104] This approach gained traction under the Obama administration as Secretary of State Clinton consolidated the public diplomacy operations of the US government at the State Department in a new interagency task force.[105] The Centre for Strategic Counterterrorism Communication (CSCC) was established in 2011 by Executive Order 13584 to coordinate messaging on counter-radicalisation from a whole-of-government perspective.[106] Drawing together representatives from across the national security bureaucracy, the CSCC expanded the DOT's online effort to a 50-strong staff with a budget of 6 million dollars by 2014.[107] Operating accounts across Twitter, Facebook, YouTube and other social media platforms, according to Alberto Fernandez the head of the CSCC 'the goal is to make Al-Qaeda look bad'.[108]

Zooming forward to the confrontation with the Islamic State of Iraq and Syria (ISIS), the DOT has mobilised a significant online effort to stem the flow of radicalised Muslims to the battlefields of Syria and Iraq. The power of online recruitment has been a key area of concern for the US government in this context, with the ISIS media unit exhibiting slick production values and savvy popular culture references to influence target audiences, and a growing number of online sympathisers willing to share ISIS content with their network.[109] According to the State Department, the ISIS message has three components:

> tapping into a deep-seated sense of grievance and persecution among Muslims, particularly as the civil war in Syria continues; an assurance that ISIS actually has the ability to right the wrongs others have imposed on the community, recruiting young men and women to join the movement and dirty their hands; and harnessing the religious aspect of their cause, promoting the rise of the caliphate and a sense of inevitability.[110]

The target of DOT blogging has been on the way ISIS presents itself as a vehicle for social and political justice against the oppressors of Muslim people, as well as its claims about religious legitimacy and military success. The DOT campaign is organised around the hashtag #thinkagainturnaway, which is attached to DOT posts questioning the credibility of ISIS messages (see Figure 2).[111] The DOT highlights that ISIS kills mainly Muslim people; is rejected by key Muslim scholars; and has presided over a 'rape culture', where women are forced into marriage or worse.[112]

For instance, addressing a specific ISIS post, the DOT replied 'you can best show you're your sincerity by not murdering women and children with suicide bombs' and 'teaching small, innocent children how to kill and get killed isn't

Figure 2   DOT (Digital Outreach Team) Twitter post

jihad. Where is your moral judgment?'[113] Likewise, the DOT attempted to address disillusioned and alienated youth looking for adventure or a rebel cause by pointing toward the regretful testimony of former ISIS fighters, and by contesting claims about military victory with facts about ISIS defeats and body counts.[114] In this context #thinkagainturnaway aims to sow the seeds of doubt in the minds of potential jihadists, such that ISIS propaganda loses traction.

While less concerned with engagement and persuasion, this more confrontational mode of online counter-radicalisation has nevertheless attracted similar criticism around the issue of credibility and hypocrisy. One recurring critique of the DOT in the era of the CSCC is that it lacks the rhetorical skill set to convincingly participate in the spontaneous to-and-fro of social media, where wit, sarcasm and cultural reference are crucial.[115] Whereas ISIS social media is often in touch with its audience's attitudes and sensibilities, the DOT risks appearing out of touch when its posts are cumbersome and overly contrived. This was certainly case with one DOT video production titled 'Caravan of Jihad', which attempted to parody an ISIS recruitment film. Posted on YouTube, the video flopped, achieving only a small number of shares and generating a much more popular spoof response from ISIS supporters.[116]

A more consequential criticism is forwarded by Rita Katz, an expert in jihadist activities online, who argues that the DOT give a voice to otherwise low-level jihadists by engaging them directly, as well as drawing attention to US mistakes by entering into a combative and defensive argument about them.[117] Katz gives the example of a DOT exchange with @de_blackRose, an ISIS-friendly account on Twitter, that posted images of tortured prisoners from Abu Ghraib prison and the message 'REMEMBER HOW YOU AMERICANS TORTURED AND HUMILIATED OUR BROTHERS IN IRAQ AND HUMILIATED THEM IN THEIR OWN COUNTRY!!'[118] The DOT responded with the following: 'US troops are punished for misconduct, #ISIS fighters are rewarded', accompanied by images of US soldiers talking with children.[119]

Such interventions are lightning rods for ISIS supporters eager to dwell on the admittedly horrendous US record of prisoner abuse. Katz's view is that this is unhelpful, first, because it catapults an innocuous post by a little-known user to the centre of attention; and second, because public diplomacy should avoid such antagonisms and direct attention towards the positives.[120] Yet a more critical view might be that the existence of controversy like torture at Abu Ghraib undermines from the outset the standing of the DOT bloggers when they advance criticisms against jihadists. Indeed, this point is acknowledged obliquely by one senior State Department official who explained that ISIS propaganda is often difficult to combat because it is built around an element of truth – for instance, regarding ISIS opposition to the Assad regime in Syria or its military victories there and in Iraq. A grain of truth also works against the DOT bloggers when the historical record of US foreign policy in the Middle East informs interpretations of US government information.

More broadly, like the Counter-Misinformation Team, the DOT was always an instrument of state power, its purported authenticity mobilised in the service of US interests. This instrumental quality set the scene for extreme scepticism about DOT activities among online users, where the gap between rhetoric and US foreign policy practice was readily appreciated. Stepping back from the issue of effectiveness, we can also position the DOT, digital jihadists and online users vulnerable to radicalisation, as participants in the interpretation of controversial international political circumstances that were opaque and often deceptive. This interpretive dynamic resonates with the post-9/11 conspiracy discourse evident in US foreign policy commentary, where competing conspiracy narratives vied for credibility and standing, and the conspiracy theory *position* marked the outer limit of acceptable opinion. Yet unlike that conspiracy discourse, in the online struggle between competing narratives there is no foreign policy establishment or institutional authority to provide the interpretive high ground, to sanctify some claims and dismiss others. In this setting, credibility and authenticity are currency and everything is up for grabs.

Public diplomacy, identity and difference

I want to finish the chapter by connecting these State Department counter-misinformation programmes to the broader themes of modernity, identity and difference that have run through the book, in order to highlight potentially more productive modes of engagement. Whatever misgivings we might have about US public diplomacy after 9/11, there is a consensus on all sides of the debate that effective communication and mutual understanding are crucial ingredients for successful counter-radicalisation. The Arab-Muslim paranoia narrative, I have contended, is centred on stark oppositional configurations that foreclose this possibility, not least of which are self/other, sovereignty/anarchy, reason/emotion, rationality/irrationality, modernity/tradition and, of course, West/Islam. As we have seen, these dichotomies have had a chilling effect on dialogue. I want to suggest that the nature of the failure of communication between State Department officials and specific Arab-Muslim people also points towards a more fruitful approach to public diplomacy centred on the experience of cross-cultural encounters.

The West vs Islam trope has been a particularly powerful barrier against dialogue since Arab-Muslim publics have often perceived precisely this prejudice behind US foreign policy. Leonard and Smewing noted as early as 2003 that 'most pernicious is the pervasive sense that Western policy is motivated by hatred or fear of Muslims. In Arab eyes, attempts to link Saddam Hussein to Osama bin Laden read like a racist conspiracy theory.'[121] The War of Ideas framework reinforced the impression of a civilisational confrontation through its contrast between liberal democratic modernity and dysfunctional Arab-Muslims.

This view was confirmed in DOT and Counter-misinformation Team engagements with jihadists and their supporters online. As Marc Lynch explains:

> The focus on violent extremism as the primary mission of engagement privileges and reinforces al Qaeda's conception of the nature of the confrontation ... The United States should not be in a tacit dialogue with al Qaeda on its own terms, entertaining its fantasies of a global caliphate or offering any sustenance to its conceptions of an essential clash of civilizations between the West and Islam. Al Qaeda should be marginalized, recognized for the radical fringe movement that it is, and not allowed to dominate our vital dialogue with the mainstream of the Arab and Muslim worlds.[122]

The point here is that counter-radicalisation should be aimed at undermining the recruiting narrative of Al-Qaeda and ISIS, not confirming it. These groups thrive when they can present themselves as the standard bearers for widely held grievances in a confrontation with the US state. The US government should focus its efforts on disaggregating these broad identity categories, showing the tensions and contradictions between different groups, thus weakening their civilisational narrative and showing that there are alternatives to extremist violence on issues of social justice and resistance to the regional status quo.[123] The task is to show that categories like Islam and the West are meaningless, not just by pointing to diversity in the Arab-Muslim world (though that is very important), but also by emphasising the plurality of American society.[124] Policies that promote education about Islam in American schools and combat Islamophobia can undermine perceptions of monolithic civilisations or religions still common in sections of American society, while education exchanges and cultural information programmes provide similar benefits abroad.

Still, there is much to suggest that efforts to better explain American foreign policy and American values do not connect with the main sources of Arab-Muslim animus towards America. Rather than misinformation about 'who we are', it is concrete policy disagreements that drive this resentment. As Lynch explained in the wake of Operation Iraqi Freedom:

> The failure to find dramatic evidence of Iraqi weapons of mass destruction has spurred widespread debate in the Middle East about the real purpose of the recent war, which most Arab commentators now see as a bid by the United States to consolidate its regional and global hegemony. U.S. threats against Iran and Syria play into this fear, increasing a general determination to resist. And the chaos that followed the fall of Baghdad, the escalating Iraqi anger at what is always described as an American occupation, and the seemingly ambivalent U.S. attitude toward Iraqi democracy have reinforced deep pre-existing scepticism about Washington's intentions.[125]

Without an acknowledgement of these serious antagonisms, an engagement in sustained self-reflection about the strengths and limitations of US foreign policy, and a willingness to countenance policy change where appropriate, public diplomacy will be in danger of speaking past Arab-Muslim people. Comor and Bean capture the broader significance of the situation when they write that in the War of Ideas doctrine

> [e]ngagement ... is perhaps better understood as a relatively participatory form of persuasion; a form of persuasion crafted to generate some amount of tolerance for otherwise entrenched US policies. In Washington, to carry this argument forward, the discourse of engagement soothes American policymakers (and publics) who seek the symbolism of dialogue yet find some kind of psychic security in the fact that its outcome will not destabilize the status quo.[126]

It is easy to see how this attitude and approach might reinforce perceptions of the United States as patronising and hypocritical.

The broader point here is that elite foreign policy discourse around the character of Arab-Muslim resentment towards America was plainly unsuccessful in practice. The Arab-Muslim paranoia narrative and its manifestation in the War of Ideas could not survive the encounter with *actual* Arab-Muslim people, fully differentiated and endowed with agency, perspective and ideas about the world based in their own lived experience. This highlights the way encounters with ostensibly incommensurate others can problematise seemingly fixed identities. As Edward Said made plain in his critique of orientalism and its modernist predilections, there have always been such encounters across regions, religions and traditions; encounters which undercut the neat civilisational boundaries between the 'West' and 'Islam'.[127] For Said it was clear that different traditions and identities were implicated in each other – ideas and technologies and cultural forms spread down trade routes, through migration and travel, via the translation of 'great books', and through violent conquests in both directions.[128]

Perhaps surprisingly, though, it is the shared experience of an increasingly globalised modernity that provides the clearest common ground between disparate traditions and locales. As Susan Buck-Morss has pointed out, there is an important postcolonial literature that charts the way secularisation, modernisation and nationalism 'change not their conceptual meaning as they move from West to non-West, but their material referent, and with it, their political value':

> the object does not go into its concept without leaving a remainder: how lived experience escapes the names we attach to it – how, for example, 'progress' as actually lived by the Muslim world has not been progressive; how Afghanistan's so-called 'backward' condition is precisely the effect of global modernity; how the alliance of Arab regimes with the 'democratic' West has worked to repress democracy.[129]

Thus, the Arab-Muslim experience of colonialism is inextricably linked to the spread of ideas about liberty, equality, democracy and market capitalism, while the same ideas can form the bedrock of a triumphalist narrative about the steady march to a better world in the minds of liberal elites and neoconservative foreign policy hawks alike. Roxanne Euben gives a sense of the multiplicity of modernities at play even within a particular religious tradition via an engagement with Islamism, which she describes as intimately involved in negotiating modernity.[130] Euben contrasts the writings of two figures from this diverse tradition to make her point.[131] The first is Muhammad 'Abduh, a nineteenth-century Muslim scholar who sought to forestall the apparent decline of the Muslim umma in the face of European expansion, which he thought was the product of technological innovation and military strength.[132] For 'Abduh rationalism was not to be rejected; but neither was secularism to be embraced. Instead, he advocated the revival of an earlier Islamic 'golden age' that was once at the cutting edge of scientific discovery and philosophic sophistication, and where reason was positioned as part of God-given human nature.[133] Thus 'Abduh looked to a modernity that positioned science and rationality as a feature of Islamic tradition.

By contrast, Euben explores the writings of Sayyid Qutb, widely recognised as the intellectual progenitor of contemporary Sunni jihadists, including Al-Qaeda and ISIS.[134] Qutb's thought is centred on a scathing critique of Western modernity. He argues that Western regimes and their Eastern allies are corrupt and that Muslims have been led astray by false idols, decadent lifestyles and nihilistic secularism.[135] Though these are just brief snapshots of complex thinkers, the contrast here is between a compatibilist attitude to modernity and a violent critique of modernity. The point for Euben is to recognise that:

> these comparisons at the very least challenge explanations of Islamic fundamentalism that portray the current purchase of Islamic ideas as the resistance of a static and essentially premodern 'Islamic essence' to the imperatives of modernity; it makes little sense to characterise as premodern a phenomenon parasitic upon and profoundly engaged with modernity. Moreover, I argue that it is not particularly illuminating to characterize Islamic fundamentalist political thought as antimodern unless we are willing to call all critiques of modernity antimodern. On the contrary, both these comparisons reveal only a glimpse of the diversity of understandings of what it means to be modern within and across cultures, including the sense that to live in the modern world may by definition entail serious criticisms of and ambivalence towards modernity. This means that Islamist fundamentalist thought such as Qutib's is part of an ongoing and multivocal critique of modernity and rationalism in particular, a critique which 'Westerners' not only recognise but participate in.[136]

What Euben points to here is the simultaneous presence of a common modernity *and* very different interpretations of what modernity means – a simultaneity that exceeds the macro tectonics of a conflict between hermetically sealed civilisations. While there are clearly incommensurable aspects between many cultures, there are also similarities that work across cultural horizons. Euben and Buck-Morrs both point to the resonance of the Islamist critique of modernity with the scepticism of critical theorists and poststructuralists about the dark side of modernity. Take, for instance, the way Robert Bellah sums up the broad problematic of modernity to which critical social theory is addressed:

> There is a widespread feeling that the promise of the modern era is slipping away from us. A movement of enlightenment and liberation that was to have freed us from superstition and tyranny has led in the twentieth century to a world in which ideological fanaticism and political oppression have reached extremes unknown in previous history. Science, which was to have unlocked the bounties of nature, has given us the power to destroy all life on earth. Progress, modernity's master idea, seems less compelling today when it appears that it may be progress into the abyss.[137]

In an international relations context Jim George describes a parallel concern about the intrinsic relation between the violence and domination that has often characterised international politics, and modernity, which has been so crucial for the production of international politics and the set of relations it entails. According to George,

> The celebration of the age of rational science and modern technological society cannot simply be disconnected from the weapons of mass slaughter and the techniques of genocide. Nor can the language and logic of liberty and emancipation be easily detached from the terror waged in their names by, for instance, the major Cold War foes, each proclaiming itself the natural systemic heir to the Enlightenment.[138]

None of this is to claim that Islamist political thought and critical social theory are the same, or that Islamists are postmodern in any respect. There are big differences here, not least of which is that the Islamist critique ultimately leads to religious fundamentalism. It is to point out those similar experiences of modernity, similar problems, similar ambivalences, that complicate simplistic oppositions between 'West' and 'Islam'.

Paradoxically, the propensity for crisis and trauma to push interpretations of modernity towards rigid caricatures is also a common dynamic across cultural horizons. So, for instance, while critical engagements with modernity in the Islamist tradition have often been subtle, violent jihadists have built their political outlook around a hard occidentalism that trades in monolithic stereotypes. Likewise, in the wake of 9/11, US neoconservatives, among others, often pointed to a threatening Islam, antithetical to Western values, sketched out in equally reductive orientalist tropes. Although it is important to acknowledge the very real power relations entailed in the colonial experience and its ongoing consequences, there is also a certain mirroring between these occidental and oriental responses. And, of course, in both settings, discourses of enemy others entailed a range of disciplinary dynamics that stifled difference and dissent within the respective political communities and undercut shared experiences between them.

Throughout this chapter I have illustrated the way the association of particular claims with the Arab-Muslim paranoia narrative delegitimised Arab-Muslim resentment towards America, denying differentiated subjects standing as reasonable interlocutors. But it should be clear too that this narrative of paranoia and irrationality disciplined American political culture, when the personal and professional costs of critical engagement with elite power and foreign policy controversy could be potentially catastrophic. All the same connotations and hierarchies entailed in the Arab-Muslim paranoia narrative are at play here, but the unspoken threat is that one may move from the 'inside' to the 'outside'. For instance, the taint of irrationality can be devastating, even by association – undermining credibility, calling motivations into question, positioning the subject in the pejorative against all that is rational and ordered in liberal modernity. Indeed, this is the 'slippery slope' of liberal subjectivity, where the precious resource of agency is always in danger of receding into passion and impulse and incoherency. The forces of anarchy hang like a spectre over the liberal subject, such that suspected outbreaks of irrationality and delusion need to be quarantined off and relegated to abnormality. Moreover, still rational, still coherent subjects are incentivised to guard their thoughts and utterances against these kinds of indiscretions and to monitor the behaviour of others. Of course, this account of liberal subjectivity is embedded in the wider discourse of modernity, which emphasises the production of sovereignty – the sovereign individual, the sovereign state, the sovereign source of knowledge – surrounded on all sides by a world of anarchy and darkness, which must be subdued and controlled and brought into the light. These powerful conforming effects provided the very conditions of possibility for interpretation of 9/11, particularly with regard to the origins and motivations of resentment towards America.

Though the purpose of this book is not to give an account of the delegitimising dynamics at play in Arab-Muslim political culture around the interpretation of American foreign policy, the association of dissent and difference with an abominable other can be clearly discerned in the rhetoric of Islamic fundamentalists. Thus, rather than helping to see the common ground and mutual affinities that run between ostensibly incommensurable political culture, or the diversity within these polities, the mutual tendency towards extreme self/other stereotypes closes down the space for such encounters.

One way to draw the discussion back to the issue of political communication is to think about it in terms of the way these contending narratives comprise a conspiracy discourse. In the conspiracy discourse we have been examining across this book, international political controversy can be understood as a common object shared across cultural horizons. But it is an object encountered and interpreted in particular material circumstances, and in the context of specific lived experiences, which exceed the names and categories available for their description. In the case of American foreign policy controversy in the

Middle East, Arab-Muslim interpretations are informed by particular experiences of modernity, potentially including colonial exploitation, a neo-colonial client state order, and numerous examples of violent, often covert intervention from foreign powers. The point here is that although conspiracy discourse centres on a specific event or circumstance, it is not sealed off from the broader historical encounter with modernity. Under these circumstances, there is a temptation to posit a kind of psychological over-determination in the minds of Arab-Muslim people, where the interpretation of foreign policy controversy resembles a kind of Rorschach test for these more general attitudes. But this misses the way historical experience inevitably and quite reasonably informs future practice for just about everyone. Thus, cynicism, suspicion and caution may be entirely appropriate guiding principles for many Arab-Muslim people, with regard to international political controversy. Moreover, whatever the differences in political vision or the specific claims advanced, these attitudes are shared with many critics of international power and order the world over, not least from within American political culture.

What does this mean for US public diplomacy efforts aimed at disaffected Arab-Muslims? As Lynch notes incisively, as it is 'the United States, whether the Pentagon or the State Department, is almost uniquely poorly positioned to "reform Islam", to "promote moderate readings of the Qur'an", to "combat Salafi interpretations of Islamic tradition", or any of the other ideas often on offer in the "War of Ideas" industry – and trying to do so is likely to discredit the approved carriers of the message and to ignite opposition'.[139] A more limited approach based in the values of self-reflection and mutual respect would instead focus on developing fidelity between foreign policy deeds and public diplomacy rhetoric; openly acknowledging the historical effects of US foreign policy in the region, including its benefits; and speaking honestly about the full range of interests at play in US foreign policy strategising. At the same time, rather than messaging and direct engagement, the US government should continue to ramp up policies that act indirectly by building relationships between civil society actors with genuine independence from government. Examples here include cultural and education exchanges, the promotion of curriculum-based learning around Islamic history and culture in American schools, and engagement with diaspora communities in a civil society context.

However, the most important task (outside of actual foreign policy reform) the US government can perform is to help open up space in Middle Eastern polities where civil society can flourish and a vibrant political debate can take place. But this is about creating space *not* shaping the ensuing debate. US foreign policy must be the subject of authentic debate among credible voices, many of whom will be fierce critics. Yet as foreign policy deeds begin to match foreign policy rhetoric, moderate voices will find it easier to gain traction – though even moderate views may fall well short of celebrating American power. More broadly, the discussion above suggests that public diplomacy may ultimately be best carried out within and between publics, where common interests, tolerance of difference and the plurality of life build genuine connections between people. Implicit here are the virtues of pluralism and solidarity, which disdain intolerance and unitarianism in both the violence of religious zealots and the foreign policies carried out in our names.

Notes

1 This definition comes from Henry Hyde, Chair of the House Committee on International Relations and chief sponsor of the Freedom Promotion Act 2002, which sets out a new public diplomacy approach for the emerging security environments after 9/11. Hyde, cited in 'Public Diplomacy Bill Authorizes Islamic Exchanges', *The Centre for Global Education*. Available at http://globaled.us/now/fullstatementhyde.html#5 (accessed 28 February 2015).

2 See L. Kennedy and S. Lucas, 'Enduring Freedom: Public Diplomacy and US Foreign Policy', *American Quarterly*, 57:2 (2005), pp. 309–333.

3 US Department of State, Office of the Coordinator for Counterterrorism, Washington, DC, 'Country Report on Terrorism 2006', April 2007, pp. 32–33.

4 *Ibid.*

5 Office of the Coordinator for Counterterrorism, 'Country Report on Terrorism 2006', p. 33. The same excerpt appeared in this annual report in the years 2005–8, with the only variation being the addition in 2008 of a new feature website, America.gov, and the aforementioned Digital Outreach Team. See Office of the Coordinator for Counterterrorism, 'Country Report on Terrorism 2006', p. 192; US Department of State, Office of the Coordinator for Counterterrorism, Washington, DC, 'Country Report on Terrorism 2007', April, 2008, p. 223; and, US Department of State, Office of the Coordinator for Counterterrorism, Washington, DC, 'Country Report on Terrorism 2008', April, 2009, p. 233.

6 R. Holbrooke, 'Get the Message Out', *Washington Post* (28 October 2008), p. B7.

7 Edward Murrow was a broadcasting giant famous for his work as a journalist and news presenter. He also served as a director of the USIA from 1961 to 1963 under the Kennedy administration. See 'The Edward R. Murrow Center for Public Diplomacy', The Fletcher School, Tuft University. Available at http://fletcher.tufts.edu/murrow (accessed 28 January 2015).

8 The Counter-Misinformation Team was part of the Bureau of International Information Programs, a section of the State Department's Public Diplomacy secretariat.

9 Bureau of International Information Programs, US Department of State, Washington, DC, 'Soviet Active Measures in the Era of Glasnost' (1988).

10 See Bureau of International Information Programs, US Department of State, Washington, DC, 'Soviet Active Measures in the "Post-Cold War" Era' (1992); Bureau of International Information Programs, US Department of State, Washington, DC, 'Iraqi Disinformation: Allegations and facts' (4 February 1991); and Bureau of International Information Programs, US Department of State, Washington, DC, 'The Child Organ Trafficking Rumour: A Modern 'Urban Legend' (December 1994).

11 See Bureau of International Information Programs, US Department of State, Washington, DC 'About Us: Counter-misinformation Team' (January 2005). According to this document, in the early years of the War on Terror the Counter-misinformation

Team participated in presenting the Bush Administration's case for war with Iraq in 2003.

12 Bureau of International Information Programs, US Department of State, Washington, DC, 'US forces Not Using Outlawed Weapons in Iraq' (December 2004).

13 Bureau of International Information Programs, US Department of State, Washington, DC, 'Life of Mohammed Book *not* Authored by Grandfather or Ancestor of President Bush' (December 2004).

14 Bureau of International Information Programs, US Department of State, Washington, DC, 'False Allegations Regarding the South Asian Tsunami' (January 2005).

15 Bureau of International Information Programs, US Department of State, Washington, DC, 'Exaggerated Concerns about Anti-AIDS Drug Nevarapine' (January 2005).

16 Bureau of International Information Programs, US Department of State, Washington, DC, 'Saddam's Disinformation' (January 2005).

17 Bureau of International Information Programs, US Department of State, Washington, DC, 'AIDS as a Biological Weapon' (January 2005).

18 Bureau of International Information Programs, 'About Us'.

19 Bureau of International Information Programs, US Department of State, Washington, DC, 'Al Qaeda Confirms it Carried out 9/11' (January 2005).

20 Bureau of International Information Programs, US Department of State, Washington, DC, 'Depleted Uranium' (January 2005).

21 Bureau of International Information Programs, US Department of State, Washington, DC, "Definitions" (January 2005).

22 Bureau of International Information Programs, US Department of State, Washington, DC, 'Soviet Disinformation' (January 2005).

23 Bureau of International Information Programs, 'About Us'.

24 Bureau of International Information Programs, US Department of State, Washington, DC, 'Countering Misinformation', January 2005.

25 Bureau of International Information Programs, US Department of State, Washington, DC, 'Countering Misinformation', February 2005.

26 Bureau of International Information Programs, 'About Us'.

27 Bureau of International Information Programs, US Department of State, Washington, DC, 'United States Involved in Lebanese Assassination' (April 2005).

28 Bureau of International Information Programs, US Department of State, Washington, DC, 'A Trio of Disinformers' (April 2005).

29 Bureau of International Information Programs, US Department of State, Washington, DC, 'Burned Quran not a Hate Crime' (June 2005).

30 Bureau of International Information Programs, US Department of State, Washington, DC, 'The US Take-Over of the Amazon Myth' (July 2005).

31 Bureau of International Information Programs, US Department of State, Washington, DC, 'How to Identify Misinformation' (July 2005).

32 Bureau of International Information Programs, US Department of State, Washington, DC, '9/11 Revealed' (September 2005).

33 Bureau of International Information Programs, US Department of State, Washington, DC, 'North Korea Persists in 54 Year Old Disinformation' (November 2005).

34 Bureau of International Information Programs, US Department of State, Washington, DC, 'US is *not* Harvesting Organs in Iraq' (November 2005).

35 Bureau of International Information Programs, US Department of State, Washington, DC, 'United States has no Plans for a Military Base in Paraguay' (November 2005).

36 Bureau of International Information Programs, US Department of State, Washington, DC, 'Plan 'Balboa' not a US Plan to Invade Venezuela' (January 2006).

37   Bureau of International Information Programs, US Department of State, Washington, DC, 'Misinformation about the "Gladio/Stay Behind" Networks Resurfaces' (January 2006).
38   Bureau of International Information Programs, US Department of State, Washington, DC, 'September 11 Conspiracy Theories' (January 2006).
39   Bureau of International Information Programs, US Department of State, Washington, DC, 'AIDS as a Biological Weapon' (14 January 2005), pp. 1–2.
40   *Ibid.*, p. 2.
41   *Ibid.*, pp. 1–3.
42   Bureau of International Information Programs, US Department of State, Washington, DC, 'Economics' (October 2009).
43   See, for instance, M. Taibbi, 'The Great American Bubble Machine', *Rolling Stone* (5 April 2010).
44   Bureau of International Information Programs, US Department of State, Washington, DC, 'Conspiracy Theories and Misinformation' (October 2009).
45   *Ibid.*
46   For a comprehensive survey and analysis of the key sources of Arab-Muslim resentment towards America see J. L. Esposito and D. Mogahed, ' "Battle for Muslims' Hearts and Minds": The Road Not (Yet) Taken', *Middle East Policy*, 14:1 (2007), pp. 27–41.
47   Esposito and Mogahed, 'Battle for Muslims' Hearts and Minds', pp. 27–41.
48   Claims about human rights abuses by US forces or the use of chemical weapons and depleted uranium tipped ordinance were more relevant, but they were never the central points of controversy informing Arab-Muslim animus towards the United States. Moreover, these issues were dealt with in tandem with a whole raft of borderline absurd topics that may have implied equivalence and so delegitimised them by association.
49   'Military' and 'Other', in Bureau of International Information Programs, US Department of State, 'Conspiracy Theories and Misinformation'.
50   'Health', in Bureau of International Information Programs, 'Conspiracy Theories and Misinformation'.
51   'Military', in Bureau of International Information Programs, 'Conspiracy Theories and Misinformation'.
52   'Outer Space', in Bureau of International Information Programs, 'Conspiracy Theories and Misinformation'.
53   'Economic', in Bureau of International Information Programs, 'Conspiracy Theories and Misinformation'.
54   'US Domestic', in Bureau of International Information Programs, 'Conspiracy Theories and Misinformation'.
55   'Latin America', in Bureau of International Information Programs, 'Conspiracy Theories and Misinformation'.
56   'Other', in Bureau of International Information Programs, 'Conspiracy Theories and Misinformation'.
57   Bureau of International Information Programs, 'How to Identify Misinformation', p. 1.
58   Edelman cited in G. Sussman, *Branding Democracy: US Regime Change in Post-Soviet Eastern Europe* (New York: Peter Lang Publishing, 2010), p. 41.
59   G. W. Bush, cited in R. Jackson, *Writing the War on Terrorism*, pp. 109–110. According to Bush this terrorist network was ubiquitous and omnipresent – '[the network] operates in remote jungles and deserts, and hides in the centres of large cities.'
60   G. Greenwald, 'Obama Confidant's Spine Chilling Proposal', *Salon*. Available at www.salon.com/topic/cass_sunstein (accessed 1 March 2015). Greenwald was writing in response to an article published by Sunstein that argues for government agents to

infiltrate conspiracy theorist groups and introduce alternative views, thereby under-mining their conspiracy theories. Interestingly, the problem of conspiracy theory is hitched here to a broader account of Internet culture and the echo-chamber effect, which connect directly with the DOT's attempt to introduce counter-narratives to jihad-ist propaganda disseminated online. See C. Sunstein and A. Vermeule, 'Conspiracy Theo-ries: Causes and Cures', *Journal of Political Philosophy*, 17:2 (2008), pp. 202–227.

61   See K. Goshorn, 'Strategies of Deterrence, Frames of Containment', *Theory and Event*, 4:3 (2000). Available at http://muse.jhu.edu/journals/theory_and_event/v004/4.3r_goshorn.html (accessed 1 March 2015). Anti-conspiracy discourse is at least as danger-ous to vibrant democracy as the quality of political interpretation. The possibility of ideological dissent and critical engagement with power is severely curtailed where the personal and professional costs of dissent and critique are prohibitively high.

62   *Ibid.*

63   For a comprehensive account of covert US action abroad, see W. Blum, *Killing Hope: US Military and CIA Interventions Since WWII* (London: Zed Books, 2003). Richard Jackson has drawn out the broader contradiction between the image of US foreign policy as essentially benign and the historical substance of its foreign policy practice by examin-ing the issue of state terrorism/state sponsored terrorism. See Jackson, 'The Ghosts of State Terror', pp. 360, 385–387.

64   M. Mahmood, M. O'Kane, C. Madlena and T. Smith, 'Revealed: Pentagon Link to Iraqi Torture Centers', *Guardian*. Available at www.guardian.co.uk/world/2013/mar/06/pentagon-iraqi-torture-centres-link (accessed 1 March 2015).

65   V. Gamble, 'Under the Shadows of Tuskegee: African American Health Care', *American Journal of Public Health*, 87:11 (1997), pp. 1773–1778; F. Gray, *The Tuskegee Syphilis Study* (Montgomery, AL: Newsouth Books, 1998).

66   S. E. Lederer, 'The Cold War and Beyond: Covert and Deceptive American Medical Experi-mentation', in T. E. Beam (ed.), *Military Ethics*, Vol. II (Falls Church, VA: Office of the Surgeon General, United States Army, 2003), pp. 506–528.

67   Joint Chiefs of Staff, US Department of Defence, Washington, DC, 'Justification for US military intervention in Cuba (Top Secret)' (March 1962), p. 13.

68   B. Woodward and K. Bernstein, *All the President's Men* (New York: Simon & Schuster, 1974).

69   For a good survey of the debate here see Yahya Kamalipour and Nancy Snow (eds), *War, Media, and Propaganda: A Global Perspective* (Oxford: Bowman & Littlefield, 2004).

70   D. Barstow, 'Behind Analysts, The Pentagon's Hidden Hand', *New York Times*. Available at www.nytimes.com/2008/04/20/washington/20generals.html?_r=1 (accessed 1 March 2015).

71   J. Gerth, 'Military's Information War is Vast and Often Secretive', *New York Times*. Available at www.nytimes.com/2005/12/11/politics/11propaganda.html?pagewanted =print (accessed 1 March 2015). Also, it is worth noting that domestic propaganda like the payment of generals and commentators is illegal under the Smith-Mundt Act of 1948. See A. W. Palmer and E. L. Carter, 'The Smith-Mundt Act's Ban on Domestic Propaganda: An analysis of the Cold War Statute Limiting Access to Public Diplomacy', *Communications Law and Policy*, 11:1 (2006), pp. 1–34.

72   For a survey of the debate see Kamalipour and Snow (eds), *War, Media, and Propaganda*.

73   Bureau of International Information Programs, 'How to Identify Misinformation', p. 3.

74   A sceptical interlocutor might respond that a consistent pattern of deception and lying by the Bush administration led Congress and large segments of the American public to believe that Saddam Hussein had WMDs.

75 Admittedly, some research was more comprehensive, particularly around the origins of AIDS and the baby parts myth. See Bureau of International Information Programs, US Department of State, Washington, DC, 'The Baby Parts Myth' (30 May 1996).

76 Bureau of International Information Programs, 'How to Identify Misinformation', p. 3.

77 See, for instance, C. McGreal, 'Wikileaks Reveals Video Showing US Air Crew Shooting Down Iraqi Civilians', *Guardian*. Available at www.guardian.co.uk/world/2010/apr/05/wikileaks-us-army-iraq-attack (accessed 1 March 2015).

78 A key example of this dynamic is Seymour Hersh's reporting on the My Lai massacre. See S. Hersh, 'An Atrocity Uncovered: November 1969', reproduced in M. J. Bates *et al.* (eds), *Reporting From Vietnam, Part Two: American Journalism 1969–1975* (Washington: Library of American, 1998), pp. 13–27.

79 Bureau of International Information Programs, 'A Trio of Disinformers', pp. 2–3. For a comprehensive review of the Abu Ghraib media reporting, see the 'Abu Ghraib Navigator', *New York Times*. Available at http://topics.nytimes.com/topics/news/international/countriesandterritories/iraq/abu_ghraib/index.html (accessed 1 March 2015).

80 L. Khatib, W. Dutton and M. Thelwall, 'Public Diplomacy 2.0: A Case Study of the US Digital Outreach Team', *The Middle East Journal*, 66:3 (2012), p. 453.

81 See,Bureau of International Information Programs, US Department of State, Washington, DC, 'Digital Outreach Team' (January 2009). See also F. Hanson, 'Revolution @ State: The Spread of Ediplomacy', *Lowey Institute for International Affairs: Analysis* (2012), p. 18.

82 As distinct from the Counter-misinformation Team's static debunking effort, which merely produced content for the State Department website, US embassies abroad and interested news outlets.

83 W. Nelles, 'American Public Diplomacy as Pseudo-Education: A Problematic National Security and Counter-Terrorism Instrument', *International Politics*, 41:1 (2004), p. 73.

84 *Ibid.*

85 N. J. Cull, 'The Road to Public Diplomacy 2.0: The Internet in US Public Diplomacy', *International Studies Review*, 15:1 (2003), p. 130.

86 *Ibid.*

87 N. Fielding and I. Cobain, 'Revealed: US Spy Operation that Manipulates Social Media', *Guardian*. Available at www.theguardian.com/technology/2011/mar/17/us-spy-operation-social-networks (accessed 24 February 2015).

88 *Ibid.*; A. Spillius, 'Pentagon Buys Social Networking 'Spy Software', *Telegraph*. Available at www.telegraph.co.uk/technology/social-media/8389577/Pentagon-buys-social-networking-spy-software.html (accessed 24 February 2015); A. Lee, 'US Military Launches Spy Operation Using Fake Online Identities', *Huffington Post*. Available at www.huffingtonpost.com/2011/03/17/online-persona-management_n_837153.html (accessed 24 February 2015).

89 Lee, 'US Military Launches Spy Operation Using Fake Online Identities'.

90 *Ibid.*

91 The DOT began as a small three-person operation in 2006 and expanded to a team of ten by 2009. The operation continued to grow under the Obama administration until the consolidation of strategic communication in the State Department lead Centre for Strategic Counterterrorism Communications (CSCC), which saw the DOT grow to a staff of 70. For an account of its early operation see, 'Arabic Speakers Monitor Net Chats', *Washington Times*. Available at www.washingtontimes.com/news/2007/mar/8/20070308-111426-4682r/?page=all (accessed 13 January 2015); and W.

155

Pincus, 'State Department Tries Blog Diplomacy', *Washington Post*. Available at www
.washingtonpost.com/wp-dyn/content/article/2007/11/18/AR2007111801114.
html (accessed 16 January 2015. For an account of the DOT in 2013–14, see J.
Straziuso, 'For US Counterterrorism Team, Online is the new Frontline', *Times of Israel*.
Available at www.timesofisrael.com/for-us-counterterrorism-team-online-is-the-new
-frontline/ (accessed 14 January 2015); A. Suebsaeng, 'The State Department is
Actively Trolling Terrorists on Twitter', *Mother Jones*. Available at www.motherjones
.com/politics/2014/02/state-department-cscc-troll-terrorists-twitter-think-again
-turn-away (accessed 16 January 2015); and J. Silverman, 'The State Department's
Twitter Jihad', *Politico Magazine*. Available at www.politico.com/magazine/story/2014/
07/the-state-departments-twitter-jihad-109234.html#.VLboQFoujww (accessed 16
January 2015).

92 J. C. York, 'Dangerous Social Media Games', *Al Jazeera*. Available at www.aljazeera
.com/indepth/opinion/2012/01/201211111642310699.html (accessed 24 February
2015).

93 Khatib, Dutton and Thelwall, 'Public Diplomacy 2.0', p. 547.

94 *Ibid.*, p. 466.

95 *Ibid.*

96 *Ibid.*

97 *Ibid.*, p. 459.

98 *Ibid.*

99 *Ibid.*

100 *Ibid.*

101 *Ibid.*

102 M. Lynch, 'Engaging the Muslim World Beyond Al Qaeda', conference paper, 2009.
Available at www.marclynch.com/wp-content/uploads/2011/04/Ruger09_Lynch.pdf
(accessed 21 February 2015).

103 Khatib, Dutton and Thelwall, 'Public Diplomacy 2.0', p. 462.

104 See James K. Glassman, 'How to Win the War of Ideas', *Wall Street Journal* (24 June
2008), available at www.wsj.com/articles/SB121426568607498451 (accessed 24
February 2015).

105 This consolidation was helped by a strong working relationship between Clinton and
Secretary of Defense Robert Gates, who agreed that diplomats rather than military
personnel best execute soft power strategies. See Cull, 'The Road to Public Diplomacy
2.0', p. 135.

106 See 'Executive Order 13584: Developing an Integrated Strategic Counterterrorism Ini-
tiative', White House, Office of the Press Secretary, 9 September, 2011. Available at
www.whitehouse.gov/the-press-office/2011/09/09/executive-order-13584–developing
-integrated-strategic-counterterrorism-c (accessed 24 January 2015); and also, 'Centre
for Strategic Counterterrorism Communications' (United State Department of State,
2015). Available at www.state.gov/r/cscc/ (accessed 24 February, 2015).

107 V. Wagner, 'US Cyber Team Takes on Al Qaeda', *Technews World*. Available at www
.technewsworld.com/story/75238.html (accessed 15 January 2015).

108 A. Speri, 'The US State Department Tweeted Photos of Dead Islamic State Fighters –
Then Changed its Mind', *Vice*. Available at https://news.vice.com/article/the-us-state-
department-tweeted-photos-of-dead-islamic-state-fighters-then-changed-its-mind
(accessed 15 January 2015).

109 J. Silverman, 'The State Department's Twitter Jihad' *Politico Magazine*. Available at www
.politico.com/magazine/story/2014/07/the-state-departments-twitter-jihad-109234.
html#.VLboQFoujww (accessed 16 January 2015).

110 H. Brown, 'Meet the State Department Team Trying to Troll ISIS into Oblivion', *Think Progress*. Available at http://thinkprogress.org/world/2014/09/18/3568366/think-again-turn-away/ (accessed 16 January 2015).

111 Silverman, 'The State Department's Twitter Jihad'.

112 'Arabic Speakers Monitor Net Chats', *Washington Times*. Available at www.washington-times.com/news/2007/mar/8/20070308–111426–4682r/?page=all (accessed 13 January 2015).

113 J. McLaughlin, 'Why US Government Tweeters are Finding it Tough to Fight ISIS Online', *Mother Jones*. Available at www.motherjones.com/politics/2014/09/isis-social-media-state-department (accessed 15 January 2015).

114 *Ibid.*

115 Silverman, 'The State Department's Twitter Jihad'.

116 Brown, 'Meet the State Department Team Trying to Troll ISIS into Oblivion'.

117 R. Katz, 'The State Department's Twitter War with ISIS is Embarrassing', *Time*. Available at http://time.com/3387065/isis-twitter-war-state-department/ (accessed 16 January 2015).

118 *Ibid.*

119 *Ibid.*

120 *Ibid.*

121 M. Leonard and C. Smewing, 'Propaganda will not Sway the Arab Street', *Financial Times* (27 March 2003).

122 M. Lynch, 'Engaging the Muslim World Beyond Al Qaeda', pp. 161–162.

123 *Ibid.*

124 Leonard and Smewing, 'Propaganda will not Sway the Arab Street'.

125 Mark Lynch, 'Taking Arabs Seriously', *Foreign Affairs*, 8:5 (2003), p. 81.

126 *Ibid.*, p. 209; E. Comor and H. Bean, 'America's 'Engagement' Delusion: Critiquing a Public Diplomacy Consensus', *International Communications Gazette*, 74:3 (2012), pp. 203–220.

127 See for instance, E. Said, *Orientalism* (London: Routledge, 2003), pp. xiii–xxiii; and E. Said, 'Adrift in Similarity', *Al Ahram* (11–17 October 2001).

128 *Ibid.*

129 *Ibid.* Susan Buck-Morss, *Thinking Past Terrorism: Islamism and Critical Theory on the Left* (London: Verso, 2003).

130 R. Euben, 'Mapping Modernities, "Islamic" and "Western"', in Fred Dallmayr (ed.), *Border Crossings: Towards a Comparative Political Theory* (Oxford: Lexington, 1999), pp. 11–37. For an elaborated treatment of these themes see R. Euben, *Enemy in the Mirror: Islamic Fundamentalism and the Limits of Modern Rationalism: A Work of Contemporary Political Theory* (Princeton NJ: Princeton University Press, 1999).

131 Euben, 'Mapping Modernities', pp. 11–37.

132 *Ibid.*

133 *Ibid.*

134 *Ibid.*

135 *Ibid.*

136 *Ibid.*, p. 15.

137 R. Bellah, cited in George, *Discourses of Global Politics*, p. 140.

138 George, *Discourses of Global Politics*, p. 141.

139 M. Lynch, 'Engaging the Muslim World Beyond Al Qaeda', p. 163.

Conclusion

THIS BOOK HAS TRACED the Arab-Muslim paranoia narrative from its intellectual origins in Cold War liberalism, through post-9/11 foreign policy commentary on terrorism, to the heart of the Bush administration's War of Ideas doctrine. I have shown that this narrative delegitimised criticism of American power, buttressed existing foreign policy practices, and secured an image of America as benign and misunderstood in its international political interactions. It shut down space for critical engagement with elite power and foreign policy controversy, or dissent from the ideological status quo, and foreclosed the possibility of genuine dialogue across cultural horizons.

These delegitimising dynamics had their roots in a particular liberal view of populism, which I explored via an engagement with the Richard Hofstadter's 'paranoid style' paradigm. In this paradigmatic account conspiracy theories are located on the periphery of pluralistic American democracy as the irrational pathology of angry extremists, and contrasted with a rational political centre where sensible politics occurs. I associated this concern about political paranoia with a broader post-war liberal project involved in the production of a particular political order and the management of dissent in that context. This account has been extrapolated into a pervasive understanding of conspiracy theory in the international political context – an understanding promulgated by media commentators, foreign policy experts and government officials. In this account conspiracy theories are said to emerge not just on the political fringes of liberal democracies, but also on the periphery of international power and legitimacy in a Western geopolitical world-view. Here unstable minds coincide with unstable regions. This paranoid style framework is reinforced by an orientalist narrative that situates Arab-Muslim resentment towards America as the product of a dysfunctional culture, full of bitterness, self-denial and blame. Like post-war liberal orthodoxy, secured by contrast with the irrational views of alienated extremists, the image of liberal modernity is secured by contrast with the irrational views of backwardsArab-Muslims. In this sense, the Arab-Muslim paranoia narrative entailed a powerful form of ideological reproduction. The crucial point here is that the production of Western or American identity through the Arab-Muslim paranoia narrative was inseparable from the projection of a particular Arab-Muslim identity. Thus, the 'Orient' did not exist as a pre-discursive object in the world that was simply uncovered and documented by disinterested scholars, commentators and policy makers. Rather, it was implicated in a powerful identity politics where knowledge and power went hand in hand.

It was in this context that conspiracy theories emerged as a subject of concern for American foreign policy commentators after 9/11. Yet explaining the origins the terrorist attacks necessarily required a consideration of the opaque and intertwined history of Islamic extremism and US foreign policy. For this reason the Arab-Muslim paranoia narrative needs to be understood as just one narrative in a wider debate, where blowback accounts of US foreign policy in the Middle East dwelt on covert operations and secret connections, and identitarian accounts emphasised the threat of diabolical terrorist masterminds with vast networks spanning the world's major cities. We need to consider the concerns of foreign policy commentators about Arab-Muslim conspiracy theories as part of a conspiracy discourse, which is to say the way conspiracy narratives are demarcated and their positions of authority or illegitimacy sustained, through rules and regularities that circulate in discursive regimes.

In this wider conspiracy discourse, concerns about Arab-Muslim paranoia helped disqualify criticism of American power and limit interpretations of 9/11. This narrative directed attention away from the substance of specific claims and towards the deeper pathologies of the people making them. This dynamic was buttressed by a broader modernist discourse organised around an opposition between Western modernity and an Arab-Muslim world bound by time and history. This oppositional configuration is reductive of cultures, identities and political circumstance, which exceed these narrow caricatures. The power of the Arab-Muslim paranoia narrative was that it produced certainty and stability, rational politics and coherent identity, foreign policy orthodoxy in the face of a contingent and threatening world. In this sense, the Arab-Muslim paranoia narrative in post-9/11 foreign policy commentary was involved in an ongoing process of boundary maintenance.

This boundary maintenance dynamic was carried on into the Bush administration's War of Ideas strategy, which aimed to address the root causes of terrorism by winning the hearts and minds of Arab-Muslim publics thought vulnerable to radicalisation. But in this policy context the Arab-Muslim paranoia narrative also tended to produce the conditions it sought to allay, since its underlying structure was derived from a set of power relations that situated Arab-Muslims firmly in pejorative terms. These dynamics embedded a strong countervailing force against engagement with Arab-Muslim people, who were framed here as inherently problematic. At the same time, the more controversial and unsavoury aspects of the US War on Terror undercut the task of promoting American values and countering misinformation about American foreign policy. Indeed, when genuine grievances were reduced to misperception, already cynical Arab-Muslim publics were entitled to be sceptical about the authenticity of US government information. Moreover, by propounding the ideals of liberal democracy, the War of Ideas established a contrast between these purported values and the often-ruthless pursuit of American interests. This tension had the potential to produce cynicism about American values, and the suspicion of conspiracies, double-dealing and ulterior motives. The same tension flowed through into US State Department public diplomacy efforts, undermining attempts at engagement with Arab-Muslim people. The language of paranoia and misinformation rebuffed rather than connected, while the credibility of the US government was a matter of serious contention for Arab-Muslim audiences who were attuned to hypocrisy and propaganda.

More broadly, my analysis of conspiracy discourse was designed not just to understand the narrow effects of this specific issue, but as a window into the underlying priorities and exclusions animating American foreign policy after 9/11. I have shown, for instance, that the Arab-Muslim paranoia narrative operated in tandem with, and was illustrative of a wider delegitimising discourse that congregated around issues of contention and controversy in American foreign policy. Indeed, my argument connects with a broader literature that shows how the War on Terror discourse acted to disqualify dissent, reproduce foreign policy orthodoxy, and secure a particular set of international political arrangements.[1] These strategies of deterrence and frames of containment point to the way power and authority are mobilised to secure particular interpretations and render others inconceivable. This issue is of crucial significance to foreign policy commentators and diplomats, but also everyday people trying to make sense of international politics and US foreign policy.

At the same time, the case studies also highlight the importance of creating the space in which to deliver an authoritative message: mustering the trappings of credibility, securing audience fidelity, and preventing competing narratives from gaining traction. This is especially significant in the context of an increased focus on soft power approaches to US foreign policy, which emphasise the importance of cultural capital and credibility in shaping international politics. Public diplomacy remains a central part of this soft power strategy, continuing under the Obama administration, particularly in the area of online counter-radicalisation programmes like the Digital Outreach Team. This book has shown that the way the US government communicates with global publics is often problematic – a highly charged struggle for standing and authority, where the language of paranoia and irrationality are regularly evoked. More fundamentally, the tension between the pursuit of US national interest and the image of America advanced for global public consumption seems likely to undermine that one indispensable resource crucial to successful communication: credibility. As the State Department has discovered in its online forays, there is a not unjustified presumption against official information, particularly on foreign policy, and a high sensitivity to public relations campaigns, advertising strategies and propaganda.

Overall, this book has illustrated the potent delegitimising work that takes place around sites of foreign policy controversy. I have demonstrated that foreign policy language is imbricated with power and authority that legitimises some claims and disqualifies others. I have pointed to the processes through which American foreign policy orthodoxy is secured and dissenting views managed. And I have shown decisively that our own political culture can never be separated from the kind of world we encounter. We are all, already, on the inside; our identities and possibilities for action bound up in, and shot through with, political culture in one form or another – and it is with these cultural materials that legitimacy and illegitimacy are ultimately produced.

NOTE

1   For an incisive commentary on this research see R. Jackson, 'Knowledge, Power and Politics in the Study of Political Terrorism', in R. Jackson, M. B. Smyth and J. Gunning (eds), *Critical Terrorism Studies: A New Agenda* (Hoboken: Taylor & Francis, 2009). The broader edited volume by Jackson *et al.* surveys work problematising the orthodox account of terrorism.

SELECT BIBLIOGRAPHY

See individual endnotes for details of newspaper and popular journal articles not listed here, as well as references to US government documents, speech transcripts and reports.

Ahmed, S., *The Cultural Politics of Emotion* (New York: Routledge, 2004).

Ajami, Fouad, 'The Sentry's Solitude', *Foreign Affairs*, 80:6 (2001), pp. 2–16.

Anderson, J. W., 'Conspiracy Theories, Premature Entextualization, and Popular Political Analysis', *Arab Studies Journal*, 4:1 (1996), pp. 96–102.

Ashley, Richard, 'Untying the Sovereign State: A Double Reading of the Anarchy Problematique', *Millennium: Journal of International Studies*, 17:2 (1988), pp. 227–262.

Bale, Jeffrey, 'Political Paranoia v. Political Realism: On Distinguishing Between Bogus Conspiracy Theories and Genuine Conspiratorial Politics', *Patterns of Prejudice*, 41:1 (2007), pp. 45–60.

Barkin, Michael, *A Culture of Conspiracy: Apocalyptic Visions in Contemporary America* (Berkeley: University of California Press, 2003).

Bartlett, Jamie and Carl Miller, *The Power of Unreason: Conspiracy Theories, Extremism and Counter-Terrorism* (London: Demos, 2010).

Baum, Mathew and Phillip Potter, 'The Relationship between Mass Media, Public Opinion and Foreign Policy: Towards a Theoretical Synthesis', *Annual Review of Political Science*, 11 (2008), pp. 39–65.

Beam, Thomas E. (ed.), *Military Ethics*, Vol. II (Falls Church, VA: Office of the Surgeon General, United States Army, 2003).

Beardon, Milton, 'Afghanistan, Graveyard of Empires', *Foreign Affairs*, 80:6 (2001), pp. 17–30.

Bergen, Peter L., *The Osama Bin Laden I Know: An Oral History of Al Qaeda's Leader* (New York: Free Press, 2005), p. 205.

Bergen, Peter L., 'Review: Picking up the Pieces: What We can Learn From – and About – 9/11', *Foreign Affairs*, 81:2 (2001), pp. 169–175.

Bernstein, Richard, *Beyond Relativism and Objectivism* (Philadelphia: University of Pennsylvania Press, 1983).

Birchall, Claire, *Knowledge Goes Pop: From Conspiracy Theory To Gossip* (London: Berg Publishers, 2006).

——, 'Just Because You're Paranoid, Doesn't Mean They're Not Out to Get You', *Culture Machine*, 6 (2004), pp. 1–10.

——, 'Conspiracy Theories and Academic Discourses: The Necessary Possibility of Popular (Over)Interpretation', *Continuum: Journal of Media & Cultural Studies*, 15:1 (2001), pp. 67–76.

Bleiker, Roland, 'Retracing and Redrawing the Boundaries of Events: Postmodern Interferences with International Theory', *Alternatives*, 23 (1998), pp. 471–497.

Bleiker, Roland and Emma Hutchison, 'Fear No More: Emotions and World Politics', *Review of International Studies*, 34:1 (2008), pp. 115–135.

Blum, William, *Killing Hope: U.S. Military and CIA Interventions Since WWII* (London: Zed Books, 2003).

Booth, Ken and Tim Dunne (eds), *Worlds In Collision* (London: Palgrave Macmillan, 2002).

Bratich, Jack, *Conspiracy Panics: Political Rationality and Popular Culture* (New York: State University of New York Press, 2008).

——, 'Public Secrecy and Immanent Security', *Cultural Studies*, 20:4–5 (2006), pp. 494–499.

Bratich, Jack, Mark Fenster and Hye-Jin Lee, 'When Theorists Conspire: An Inte(re)view Between Mark Fenster and Jack Bratich', *International Journal of Communications*, 3 (2009), pp. 961–972.

Brown, David S., *Richard Hofstadter: An Intellectual History* (Chicago: Chicago University Press, 2006).

——, 'Redefining American History: Ethnicity, Progressive Historiography and the Making of Richard Hofstadter', *The History Teacher*, 36:4 (2003), pp. 527–548.

Buck-Morss, Susan *Thinking Past Terrorism: Islamism and Critical Theory on the Left* (London: Verso, 2003).

Bunzel, John H., *Anti-politics in America: Reflections on the Anti-political Temper and its Distortion of the Democratic Process* (New York: Alfred A. Knopf, 1967).

Burke, Anthony, *Fear of Security: Australia's Invasion Anxiety* (Melbourne: Cambridge University Press, 2008).

——, 'Iraq: Strategy's Burnt Offerings', *Global Change, Peace and Security*, 17:2 (2005), pp. 202–209.

Burke, Anthony and Matt McDonald, *Critical Security Studies in the Asia Pacific* (Manchester: Manchester University Press, 2007).

Burke, Jason, *Al Qaeda: The True Story of Radical Islam* (London: Penguin, 2004).

Burke, John P., *Honest Broker? The National Security Advisor and Presidential Decision Making* (Texas: Texas A&M Press, 2009).

Butler, J., 'Explanation and Exoneration, Or What We Can Hear', *Social Text*, 20:3 (2002), p. 178.

Campbell, David, 'Time is Broken: The Return of the Past in Response to September 11', *Theory & Event*, 5:4 (2002). http://muse.jhu.edu/journals/theory_and_event/v005/5.4campbell.html (accessed on 28 July 2015).

——, *Writing Security: United States Foreign Policy and the Politics of Identity* (Manchester: Manchester University Press, 1998).

Chomsky, Noam, 'Middle East Terrorism and the American Ideological System', *Race and Class*, 28:1 (1986), pp. 1–28.

Coady, D. 'Introduction: Conspiracy Theories', *Episteme: A Journal of Social Epistemology*, 4:2 (2007), pp. 131–134.

——, *Conspiracy Theories: The Philosophical Debate* (Aldershot, Hampshire: Ashgate, 2006).

Cohen, Norman, *Warrant for Genocide: The Myth of the Jewish World-Conspiracy and the Protocols of the Elders of Zion* (New York: Harper & Row, 1967).

Cohen, S., *Folk Devils and Moral Panics* (St Albans: Paladin, 1973).

Coker, Christopher, *Reflections on American Foreign Policy Since 1945* (New York: St Martin's Press, 1989).

Comor, E. and H. Bean, 'America's 'Engagement' Delusion: Critiquing a Public Diplomacy Consensus', *International Communications Gazette*, 74:3 (2012).

Connolly, William, *Pluralism* (Durham: Duke University Press, 2005).

—— (ed.), *The Bias of Pluralism* (New York: Atherton Press, 1969).

Croft, Stuart, *Culture, Crisis and America's War on Terror* (Cambridge: Cambridge University Press, 2006).

Cuordileone, K. A. 'Politics in an "Age of Anxiety"': Cold War Political Culture and the Crisis in American Masculinity, 1949–60', *The Journal of American History*, 87:2 (2000), pp. 515–545.

Curry, Richard O. and Thomas M. Brown (eds), *Conspiracy: The Fear of Subversion in American History* (New York: Holt, Reinhart & Winston, 1972).

Dahl, Robert, *Democracy in the United States* (Boston: Houghton Mifflin, 1981).

Dallmayr, Fred (ed.), *Border Crossings: Towards a Comparative Political Theory* (Oxford: Lexington, 1999).

Dean, Jodi, 'Theorizing Conspiracy Theory', *Theory and Event*, 4:3 (2000). www.muse .jhu.edu/journals/theory_and_event/v004/4.3r_dean.html (accessed 28 July 2015).

—— (ed.), *Cultural Studies and Political Theory* (Ithaca: Cornell University Press, 2000).

——, 'Virtual Fears', *Signs*, 24:4 (1999), pp. 1069–1078.

——, *Aliens in America: Conspiracy Cultures from Outerspace to Cyberspace* (New York: Cornell University Press, 1998).

Debord, Guy, *Comments of the Society of the Spectacle* (London: Verso, 2002).

De Haven-Smith, Lance, *Conspiracy Theory in America* (Austin: University of Texas Press, 2013).

Der Derian, James (ed.), *Critical Practices in International Theory: Selected Essays* (New York: Routledge, 2009).

——, 'The War of Networks', *Theory & Event*, 5:4 (2002). http://muse.jhu.edu/journals/ theory_and_event/v005/5.4derderian.html (accessed 28 July 2015).

——, *Antidiplomacy: Spies, Lies, Speed and War* (Cambridge, MA: Blackwell, 1992).

Der Derian, James and Michael Shapiro (eds), *International/Intertextual Relations: Postmodern Readings of World Politics* (Lexington, MA: Lexington Books, 1989).

Devatak, Richard, 'After the Event: Don Dellilo's White Noise and September 11 Narratives', *Review of International Studies*, 35 (2009), pp. 791–198.

Dirks N. B., *Castes of Mind: Colonialism and the Making of Modern India* (Princeton, NJ: Princeton University Press, 2001).

Dolan, Chris, 'The Shape of Elite Opinion on U.S. Foreign Policy, 1992 to 2004', *Politics & Policy*, 36:4 (2008), pp. 542–584.

Doran, Michael Scott, 'Somebody Else's Civil War', *Foreign Affairs*, 81:1 (2002), pp. 22–42.

Dunne, Tim, Milja Kurki and Steve Smith (eds), *International Relations Theories: Discipline and Diversity* (Oxford: Oxford University Press).

Easthope, Anthony and Kate McGowen (eds), *A Critical Cultural Studies Reader* (Toronto: University of Toronto Press, 1997).

Esposito, John L. and Dalia Mogahed, 'Battle for Muslims' Hearts and Minds: The Road Not (Yet) Taken', *Middle East Policy Review*, 14:1 (2007), pp. 27–41.

Euben, Roxanne, *Enemy in the Mirror: Islamic Fundamentalism and the Limits of Modern Rationalism: A work of Contemporary Political Theory* (Princeton, NJ: Princeton University Press, 1999).

Fenster, Mark, *Conspiracy Theories: Secrecy and Power in American Culture* (Minneapolis: University of Minneapolis Press, 2008).

Fenster, Mark and Jack Bratich, 'Dialogues in Communication Research', *Journal of Communication Enquiry*, 33:3 (2009), pp. 279–286.

Foucault, Michel, *Madness and Civilization: A History of Insanity in the Age of Reform* (Oxford: Routledge, 2001).

Foucault, Michel, *The Archeology of Knowledge* (New York: Routledge, 2002).

Gaddis, John Lewis, 'Grand Strategy in the Second Term', *Foreign Affairs*, 84:1 (2005), pp. 2–15.

——, 'A Grand Strategy of Transformation', *Foreign Policy*, 133 (2002), pp. 50–57.

Gamble, Vanessa, 'Under the Shadows of Tuskegee: African American Health Care', *American Journal of Public Health*, 87 (1997), pp. 1773–1778.

Geary, Daniel, 'Richard Hofstadter Reconsidered', Reviews in American History, 35:3 (2007), pp. 425–431.

George, Jim, *Discourse of Global Politics: A Critical (Re)Introduction to International Relations* (Boulder, CO: Lynne Rienner, 1994).

George, John and Laird Wilcox, *American Extremism* (Amherst, NY: Prometheus Books, 1996).

Goldberg, Robert, 'Who Profited from the Crime: Intelligence Failure, Conspiracy Theory, and the Case of September 11', *Intelligence and National Security*, 19:2 (2004), pp. 249–261.

——, *Enemies Within: The Culture of Conspiracy in Modern America* (New Haven: Yale University Press, 2001).

Goshorn, Keith, 'Strategies of Deterrence and Frames of Containment: On Critical Paranoia and Anti-conspiracy Discourse', *Theory & Event*, 4:3 (2000). http://muse.jhu .edu/journals/theory_and_event/v004/4.3r_goshorn.html (accessed 28 July 2015).

Gray, Fred, *The Tuskegee Syphilis Study* (Montgomery, AL: Newsouth Books, 1998).

Gray, Matthew, *Conspiracy Theories in the Arab World: Sources and Politics* (New York: Routledge, 2010).

Griffin, D. R., *Debunking 9/11 Debunking: An Answer to Popular Mechanics and Other Defenders of the Official Conspiracy Theory* (Petaluma, CA: Olive Branch Press, 2007).

Grovogui, S., 'Postcolonialism', in Tim Dunne, Milja Kurki and Steve Smith (eds), *International Relations Theories: Discipline and Diversity* (Oxford: Oxford University Press), pp. 238–256.

Herman, A., *The Worldwide Web and Contemporary Cultural Theory: Magic, Metaphor, Power* (London: Routledge, 2000).

Hersh, S., 'An Atrocity Uncovered: November 1969', reproduced in M. J. Bates *et al.* (eds), *Reporting From Vietnam, Part Two: American Journalism 1969–1975* (Washington: Library of American, 1998), pp. 13–27.

Heywood, Andrew, *Political Ideologies: An Introduction* (New York: Palgrave Macmillan, 2007).

Higgott, Richard, *Political Development Theory: The Contemporary Debate* (London, Taylor & Francis, 2005).

Hindess, Barry, 'The Past is Another Culture', *International Political Sociology*, 1:4 (2007), pp. 325–338.

——, *Discourses of Power: From Hobbes to Foucault* (Oxford: Blackwell, 1996).

Hirsh, M., 'Bush and the World', *Foreign Affairs*, 81:5 (2002), pp. 18–43.

Hoffman, David, 'Beyond Public Diplomacy', *Foreign Affairs*, 81:2 (2002), pp. 83–95.

Hofstadter, Richard, *The Paranoid Style and other Essays* (Cambridge, MA: Harvard University Press, 1965).

——, 'The Paranoid Style in American Politics', *Harper's Magazine* (November 1964), pp. 77–86.

Howe, Daniel Walker and Peter Eliot Finn, 'Richard Hofstadter: The Ironies of an American Historian', *Pacific Historical Review*, 43:1 (1974), pp. 1–23.

Huntington, S. P, 'The Clash of Civilizations', *Foreign Affairs*, 72:3 (1993), pp. 22–59.

Hustings, Ginna and Martin Orr, 'Dangerous Machinery: "Conspiracy Theorist" as a Transpersonal Strategy of Exclusion', *Symbolic Interaction*, 30:2 (2007), pp. 127–150.

Irwin, R., 'An Orientalist Mythology of Secret Societies', in Arndt Graf, Schirin Fathi and Ludwig Paul (eds), *Orientalism and Conspiracy: Politics and Conspiracy Theory in the Islamic World* (London: I. B. Tauris, 2001), pp. 99–100.

Jackson, R., 'Culture, Identity and Hegemony: Continuity and (the Lack of) Change in US Counterterrorism Policy from Bush to Obama', *International Politics*, 48:2/3 (2011), pp. 390–411.

——, 'The Ghosts of State Terror: Knowledge, Politics and Terrorism Studies', *Critical Studies on Terrorism*, 1:3 (2009), pp. 377–392.

——, 'Constructing Enemies: 'Islamic Terrorism' in Political and Academic Discourse', *Government and Opposition*, 42:3 (2007), pp. 394–426.

——, *Writing the War on Terrorism: Language, Politics, and Counter Terrorism* (Manchester: Manchester University Press, 2005).

Jackson, Richard, Marie Breen Smyth and Gunning Jereon, *Critical Terrorism Studies: A New Agenda* (Hoboken: Taylor & Francis, 2009).

James, David Brion, *The Fear of Conspiracy: Images of Un-American from the Revolution to the Present* (Ithaca: Cornell University Press, 1971).

Jameson, Fredric, *Postmodernism, or, the Cultural Logic of Late Capitalism* (Durham, NC: Duke University Press, 1991).

Jentleson, Bruce, *With Friends Like These: Reagan, Bush and Saddam, 1982–1990* (New York: Norton, 1994).

Joffe, Joseph, 'Axis of Envy', *Foreign Policy*, 132 (2002), pp. 68–69.

Jones, Laura, 'The Common Place Geopolitics of Conspiracy', *Geography Compass*, 6:1 (2012), pp. 44–59.

——, 'How do the American People Know? Embodying Post-9/11 Conspiracy Discourse', *GeoJournal*, 75 (2010), pp. 359–371.

——, 'A Geopolitical Mapping of the Post 9/11 World: Exploring Conspiratorial Knowledge through Fahrenheit 9/11 and The Manchurian Candidate', *Journal of Media Geography*, 111 (2008), pp. 44–50.

Kamalipour, Yahya and Nancy Snow (eds), *War, Media, and Propaganda: A Global Perspective* (Oxford: Bowman & Littlefield, 2004).

Keeley, B. 'Of Conspiracy Theories', *The Journal of Philosophy*, 96:3 (1999), pp. 109–126.

Khatib, W. Dutton and M. Thelwall, 'Public Diplomacy 2.0: A Case Study of the US Digital Outreach Team', *The Middle East Journal*, 66:3 (2012), pp. 453–472.

Kennedy, Liam and Scott Lucas, 'Enduring Freedom: Public Diplomacy and US Foreign Policy', *American Quarterly*, 57:2 (2005), pp. 309–333.

Knight, Peter (ed.), *Conspiracy Nation: The Politics of Paranoia in Post-War America* (New York: New York University Press, 2002).

——, *Conspiracy Culture: From Kennedy to the X-Files* (London: Duke University Press, 2000).

——, 'Everything is Connected: Underworld's Secret History of Paranoia', *Modern Fiction Studies*, 45:3 (1999), pp. 811–836.

Krauthammer, Charles, 'The Neoconservative Convergence', *Commentary* (July–August 2005).

Lasswell, Harold, *Power and Personality* (New York: Viking Press, 1948).

——, *Psychopathology and Politics* (New York: Viking Press, 1930).

Lewis, Bernard, 'What Went Wrong', *The Atlantic* (January 2002), pp. 43–45.

——, 'The Roots of Muslim Rage', *The Atlantic* (September 1990), pp. 1–8.

Lipset, Seymour Martin and Earl Raab, *The Politics of Unreason: Right Wing Extremism in America, 1790–1970* (New York: Harper & Row, 1970).

Lynch, Mark, 'Taking Arabs Seriously', *Foreign Affairs*, 8:5 (2003), pp. 81–94.

Machiavelli, Niccolo, *The Prince and the Discourses* (New York: The Modern Library, 1950[1532]).

Malak, Abbas (ed.), *News Media and Foreign Relations: A Multifaceted Perspective* (Norwood, NJ: Abex, 1996).

Marcus, George (ed.), *Paranoia Within Reason: A Casebook on Conspiracy as Explanation* (Chicago: University of Chicago Press, 1999).

Marshal, Joshua, 'Remaking the World: Bush and the Neoconservatives', *Foreign Affairs*, 82:2 (2002), pp. 142–146.

McCarthy, Thomas A., 'From Modernism to Messianism: Liberal Developmentalism and American Exceptionalism', *Constellations*, 14:1 (2007), pp. 3–30.

Mead, Walter Russell, 'The American Foreign Policy Tradition', *Foreign Affairs*, 81 (2002), pp. 163–176.

Mearsheimer, John J. and Stephen M. Walt, 'An Unnecessary War', *Foreign Policy*, 134:1 (2003), pp. 50–59.

Melly, Timothy, *Empire of Conspiracy: The Culture of Paranoia in Post-War America* (Ithaca: Cornell University Press, 2000).

Mills, C. Wright, *The Power Elite* (Oxford: Oxford University Press, 2000).

Moten, Jonathan, 'The Roots of the Bush Doctrine: Power, Nationalism, and Democracy Promotion in US Strategy', *International Security*, 29:4 (2005), pp. 112–156.

Nelson, Cary and Lawrence Grossberg (eds), *Marxism and the Interpretation of Culture* (Chicago: University of Illinois Press, 1988).

Neumann, Iver, 'Self and Other in International Relations', *European Journal of International Relations*, 2:2 (1996), pp. 138–174.

Nietzsche, Freidrich, *The Gay Science* (Cambridge: Cambridge University Press, 2007).

Oliver, T. E. and T. J. Wood, 'Conspiracy Theories and the Paranoid Style(s) of Mass Opinion', *American Journal of Political Science*, Early release (2014).

Olmsted, Katherine, *Real Enemies: Conspiracy Theories and American Democracy, World War I to 9/11* (Oxford: Oxford University Press, 2009).

Palmer, Allen W. and Edward L. Carter, 'The Smith-Mundt Act's Ban on Domestic Propaganda: An analysis of the Cold War Statute Limiting Access to Public Diplomacy', *Communications Law and Policy*, 11:1 (2006), pp. 1–34.

Paltridge, Brian, *Discourse Analysis: An Introduction* (London: Continuum, 2006), 179–197.

Peterson, Peter G., 'Public Diplomacy and the War on Terrorism', *Foreign Affairs*, 81:5 (2002), pp. 74–94.

Pidgen, C. 'Conspiracy Theories and the Conventional Wisdom', *The Journal of Philosophy*, 96:3 (1999), pp. 219–232.

Pipes, Daniel, *The Hidden Hand: Middle East Fears of Conspiracy* (London: Macmillan Press 1998).

——, *Conspiracy! How the Paranoid Style Flourishes and Where it Comes From* (New York: Simon & Schuster, 1997).

Piscatori, James, 'Religion and Realpolitik: Islamic Responses to the Gulf War', *Bulletin of the American Academy of the Arts*, 45:1 (1991), pp. 17–39.

Post, Jerold M., *Leaders and Their Followers in a Dangerous World: The Psychology of Political Behaviour* (Ithaca: Cornell University Press, 2004).

Pratt, Ray, 'Theorising Conspiracy Theory', *Theory and Society*, 32 (2003), pp. 255–271.

Roberts, Adam, *Fredric Jameson* (London: Routledge, 2007).

Roberts, J. M., *The Mythology of Secret Societies* (London: Secker & Warburg, 1972).

Robins, Robert S. and Jerrold M. Post, *Political Paranoia: The Psychopolitics of Hatred* (New Haven, CT: Yale University Press: 1998).

Rose, Gideon and Jonathan Tepperman (eds), *The U.S. vs. Al Qaeda: A History of the War on Terror* (New York: Council on Foreign Relations, 2011).

Rostow, Walt, *The Stages of Economic Growth: A Non-Communist Manifesto* (Cambridge: Cambridge University Press, 1971).

Rouleau, E., 'Trouble in the Kingdom', *Foreign Affairs*, 81:4 (2002), pp. 75–89.

Rubin, B., 'The Real Roots of Arab Anti-Americanism', *Foreign Affairs*, 81:6 (2002), pp. 73–85.

Said, Edward, *Power, Politics and Culture: Interviews with Edward Said* (New York: Vintage Books, 2002).

Said, Edward, *Orientalism* (London: Penguin, 2003).

Sargent, Lyman (ed.), *Extremism in America: A Reader* (New York: New York University Press, 1996).

Shapiro, Michael, 'Wanted Dead or Alive', *Theory & Event*, 5:4 (2002). http://muse.jhu .edu/journals/theory_and_event/v005/5.4shapiro.html.

Silberstein, Sandra, *War of World: Language and Politics After 9/11* (London: Routledge, 2002).

Silverstein, P. A., 'An Excess of Truth: Violence, Conspiracy Theorizing and the Algerian Civil War', *Anthropological Quarterly*, 75:4 (2002), pp. 643–674.

Silverstein, P. A., 'Regimes of (Un)Truth: Conspiracy Theory and the Transnationalization of the Algerian Civil War', *Middle East Report*, 214 (2000), pp. 6–10.

Snyder, Don M., *The National Security Strategy: Documenting Strategic Vision* (Carlisle Barracks, PA: Strategic Studies Institute, 1995).

Strauss, Mark, 'Anti-Globalism's Jewish Problem', *Foreign Policy*, 130 (2003), pp. 58–67.

Sunstein, Cass and Adrian Vermeule, 'Conspiracy Theories: Causes and Cures', *Journal of Political Philosophy*, 17:2 (2009), pp. 202–227.

Sussman, G., *Branding Democracy: US Regime Change in Post-Soviet Eastern Europe* (New York: Peter Lang Publishing, 2010), p. 41.

Talbot, Strobe and Nayan Chanda (eds), *The Age of Terror: America and the World After 9/11* (New York: Basic Books, 2001).

Tarnas, Richard, *The Passion of the Western Mind* (London: Pimlico, 1991).

Todd, Paul, Jonathan Bloch and Patrick Fitzgerald, *Spies, Lies and the War on Terror* (London: Zed Books, 2009).

Van der Veer, P. *Imperial Encounters: Religion and Modernity in India* (Princeton, NJ: Princeton University Press, 2001).

Van Dijk, T. A., 'Principles of Critical Discourse Analysis', *Discourse and Society*, 4:2 (1993), pp. 249–283.

Victoroff, Jeff, 'The Mind of the Terrorist: A review and Critique of Psychological Approaches', *The Journal of Conflict Resolution*, 49:1 (2005), pp. 3–42.

Von Clausewitz, Carl (J.J. Graham, Trans.), *On War* (Radford, VA: Wilder Publications, 2008).

Weis, Carol H., 'What America's Leaders Read', *The Public Opinion Quarterly*, 38:1 (1974), pp. 1–22.

West, H. G. and T. Sanders (eds), *Transparency and Conspiracy: Ethnographies of Suspicion in the New World Order* (Durham, NC: Duke University Press, 2003).

White, Stephen K. and J. Donald Moon (eds), What is Political Theory? (London: Sage, 2004).

Woodward, Bob, *State of Denial: Bush at War, Part III* (New York: Simon & Schuster, 2006).

Woodward, Bob and Karl Bernstein, *All the President's Men* (New York: Simon & Schuster, 1974).

Wright, L., *The Looming Towers: Al Qaeda's Road to 9/11* (London: Penguin, 2006).

Zonis, Marvin and Craig M. Joseph, 'Conspiracy Thinking in the Middle East', *Political Psychology*, 15:3 (1994), pp. 433–459.

169

INDEX